A HANDBOOK FOR

PERSONALIZED
COMPETENCY-BASED
EDUCATION

Robert J.
MARZANO

Jennifer S.
NORFORD

Michelle
FINN

Douglas
FINN III

With Rebecca Mestaz & Roberta Selleck

MARZANO
Resources

555 North Morton Street
Bloomington, IN 47404
888.849.0851
FAX: 866.801.1477

email: info@MarzanoResources.com
MarzanoResources.com

Visit **MarzanoResources.com/reproducibles** to download the free reproducible in this book.

Printed in the United States of America

Library of Congress Control Number: 2017901210

ISBN: 978-1-943360-13-0

Text and Cover Designer: Abigail Bowen

Table of Contents

Reproducible page is in italics.

Chapter 2
How Will the Learning Environment Support Student Agency? . . .37

Chapter 3
How Will Instruction Support Student Learning? 69

About the Authors

Robert J. Marzano, PhD, is the cofounder and CAO of Marzano Resources in Denver, Colorado. During his fifty years in the field of education, he has worked with educators as a speaker and trainer and has authored more than forty books and three hundred articles on topics such as instruction, assessment, writing and implementing standards, cognition, effective leadership, and school intervention. His books include *The New Art and Science of Teaching, Leaders of Learning, The Classroom Strategies Series, A Handbook for High Reliability Schools, Awaken the Learner, Managing the Inner World of Teaching,* and *Collaborative Teams That Transform Schools.* His practical translations of the most current research and theory into classroom strategies are known internationally and are widely practiced by both teachers and administrators. He received a bachelor's degree from Iona College in New York, a master's degree from Seattle University, and a doctorate from the University of Washington.

Jennifer S. Norford, MA, is the chief program officer at Marzano Research in Denver, Colorado. She has more than twenty years of experience as a teacher, instructional materials developer, technical assistance provider, research and development specialist, and development director in preK–12 and postsecondary settings. She has coauthored books and journal articles, contributed to numerous product development and research projects, and developed online courses. She has extensive experience developing new lines of sponsored program work, cultivating and maintaining productive partnerships, and managing large-scale projects. At Marzano Research, she provides leadership for the portfolio of research, technical assistance, and consulting projects by setting programmatic vision and strategic direction, developing new lines of program work, and building new partnerships.

She earned three degrees from Virginia Tech: a master of arts in English, a bachelor of arts in English, and a bachelor of science in civil engineering.

To learn more about Jennifer S. Norford's work, follow @JenniferNorford on Twitter.

Michelle Finn is a professional development associate for Marzano Resources with thirteen years of experience working with competency-based educational systems as a teacher in rural Alaska and Maine and as a coach and trainer. Her passion lies in making competency-based education a reality for students as well as making implementation attainable for both teachers and leaders. Her classroom experience spans K–8, and she has been fortunate to partner with her husband, Douglas, throughout their competency-based journey. Michelle graduated summa cum laude from the University of Maine with a bachelor of science in elementary education.

Douglas Finn III is a professional development associate for Marzano Resources. He has thirteen years of experience teaching, designing, coaching, and implementing competency-based education systems throughout the United States. Prior to joining Marzano Resources, he worked as a high school science and mathematics teacher at one of the leading competency-based school districts in the United States. During that time, he was involved in curriculum development, strategic planning, and professional development within the school. He and his wife, Michelle, also co-taught grades K–8 in a one-room schoolhouse off the coast of Maine for four years. Later in his career, Douglas served as a consultant and coach for the Re-Inventing Schools Coalition developing, presenting, and providing evaluation services at the national level. He received a bachelor's degree in geology from the University of Montana.

Rebecca Mestaz, MA, is an experienced leader in the field of competency-based systems and personalized learning. Throughout her tenure as an educator she has served in a variety of roles, including classroom teacher, reading specialist, site and district leader, and coach for leaders and teachers. In her work with Lindsay Unified School District in California, she led two schools through the transition from traditional instruction to a competency-based learning system. She has also served as an embedded consultant for the Charleston County School District Personalized Learning Department in South Carolina, where she provided onsite support for leadership and schools. She provides training and coaching support to build competency-based systems throughout the United States. Rebecca earned a master of arts in administrative services from Fresno Pacific University in California and a bachelor of arts from California State University, Bakersfield.

Roberta Selleck, PhD, has served in public education for more than thirty years in numerous capacities. Her career includes teaching and serving in various leadership positions including superintendent in multiple states. She uses her expertise as a leadership consultant, an advocate for school reform, and champion for competency-based learning efforts across the United States. Her committed leadership to improve public education focuses on empowering students to take ownership of their learning through systematic transformations that personalize education based on mastery and the unique needs of each individual learner. Roberta led one of the first large-scale district transformations in the United States where student-centered learning became the norm. She has provided professional development training to support competency-based learning systems at the district, state, and national levels. Additionally, she is an active community member, having served on the Colorado Governor's Educational Council, several education associations, and community service clubs. She earned a bachelor of arts from the University of Southern Colorado, a master of arts from Western State Colorado University, and a doctor of philosophy in educational administration from the University of Colorado.

Introduction

Why Competency-Based Education and Personalized Learning?

One of the most prominent issues in a traditional classroom is the struggle to meet the learning needs and maintain the engagement of all students in a class. Often the hardest students to reach are those on the periphery of the learning continuum; for example, the quick learners who rapidly grasp the material then disengage from learning, or the struggling students who avoid asking questions or trying their best because they know they don't understand. A solution to help educators reach these students is a shift to competency-based education and personalized learning, an educational reform growing rapidly in prominence within K–12 classrooms.

The Foundation for Excellence in Education (n.d.) defined *competency-based education* as:

> A system of instruction where students advance to higher levels of learning when they demonstrate mastery of concepts and skills regardless of time, place or pace. In a traditional system, **time** is the **constant** and **learning** is the **variable**, meaning students spend a set amount of time on certain subjects and advance at predetermined intervals (course units and grade levels) regardless of whether or not they have mastered the material.

This definition highlights the basic premise of competency-based education: that students demonstrate mastery—sometimes called *proficiency* or *competency*—of required knowledge and skills. However, some definitions expand on that single factor. For example, one of the more common definitions of competency-based education is the International Association for K–12 Online Learning's (iNACOL) five-part definition:

1. Students advance upon demonstrated mastery.
2. Competencies include explicit, measurable, transferable learning objectives that empower students.
3. Assessment is meaningful and a positive learning experience for students.
4. Students receive rapid, differentiated support based on their individual learning needs.

5. Learning outcomes emphasize competencies that include application and creation of knowledge along with the development of important skills and dispositions. (Patrick, Kennedy, & Powell, 2013, p. 22)

Although similar to the definition from the Foundation for Excellence in Education, iNACOL expanded the definition to address what a *competency* is—an explicit, measurable, transferable learning objective that encompasses knowledge creation as well as skills and dispositions. The iNACOL definition also addresses assessment and differentiation.

Personalized learning, on the other hand, refers to education driven by each student's unique needs and often implies teachers tailoring their instruction, assessment, and even content to individual students. Although Susan Patrick, Kathryn Kennedy, and Allison Powell (2013) emphasized that "personalized learning is not equal to competency-based learning," they acknowledged that "they are related and terms are often (mistakenly) used interchangeably" (p. 22). For example, the U.S. Department of Education's webpage Competency-Based Learning or Personalized Learning defines competency-based learning as an approach that "allows students to progress as they demonstrate mastery of academic content, regardless of time, place, or pace of learning" and "provide[s] students with personalized learning opportunities" (U.S. Department of Education, n.d.).

As a final example, the Gates Foundation identified four essential attributes for a personalized learning model (RAND Corporation, 2014).

1. **Learner profiles:** The teacher records each student's individual skills, gaps, strengths, weaknesses, interests, and aspirations.

2. **Personal learning paths:** Each student has learning goals and objectives. Learning experiences are diverse, and teachers match them to the individual student's needs.

3. **Competency-based progression:** Students advance based on demonstrated mastery. Teachers continually assess student progress against clearly defined standards and goals.

4. **Flexible learning environments:** Teachers use multiple instructional delivery approaches that continuously optimize available resources to support student learning.

This definition encompasses mastery or competency against standards, varied and individualized instructional approaches, and reporting of data that identify individual characteristics. As evidenced by these various definitions of *personalized learning* and *competency-based education*, there is much overlap in how they are defined in the field. Definitions occasionally combine the two terms, and educators often incorporate *competency-based* into the definition of personalized learning (for example, see Charleston County School District, n.d.; KnowledgeWorks, 2016).

Next, we discuss the benefits of competency-based education in the K–12 system.

The Benefits of Competency-Based Education in the K–12 System

While the competency-based education and personalized-learning movement in higher education has focused on reducing costs and increasing access to higher education, in K–12 education, the movement also emphasizes maximizing student engagement, closing achievement gaps, and meeting the needs of all students. While these are impressive accomplishments themselves, a comprehensive competency-based system can produce results that go well beyond them. Subsequent chapters describe that competency-based education can involve basic changes in the very structure of K–12 schooling that solve inherent problems in the current system. Here are some examples.

- Students are moved on to the next grade level even though they have not adequately mastered content at their current grade level.

- Students are not allowed to move on to more advanced content because their peers are not ready to do so.

- Students have little or no say in how they are taught, how they are assessed, or the topics they would like to learn.

Competency-based education addresses all of these. While shifting to a competency-based system is not easy, its potential benefits far outweigh the complexity and hard work involved in moving to such a system. Therefore, it is easy to understand how competency-based education is increasing in prominence.

The Growing Prominence of Competency-Based Education

Competency-based education is not new. As discussed in numerous articles (see, for example, Le, Wolfe, & Steinberg, 2014; Nodine, 2016), the roots of competency-based education "reach back to the progressive education ideals of the early 1900s, and the ideas gained popularity in the form of mastery learning during the 1970s and 1980s" (Le et al., 2014, p. 1). Several factors have contributed to the growing prominence of competency-based education in both higher education and K–12 education. In the K–12 arena, these factors include the standards movement, the push for personalization, and the evolution of technological tools (Le et al., 2014). In higher education, the growth of online technologies and hybrid models, increased focus on student outcomes, use of direct assessment, and pressure to lower costs for higher education have all contributed to the rise of competency-based models (Nodine, 2016). The importance of students graduating from the K–12 system ready for postsecondary education or a career and the growing necessity for higher education credentialing and degrees in the workforce link the calls for and efforts to develop competency-based approaches across the K–16 spectrum (Le et al., 2014; Nodine, 2016).

In higher education, for example, the U.S. Department of Education announced the Experimental Sites Initiative in July 2014 (U.S. Department of Education, 2014). Also known as the competency-based education (CBE) experiment, the program offered institutions of higher education flexibility in using prior learning assessments to grant credits for content that students had previously mastered, providing federal aid to students enrolled in self-paced competency-based education programs, and allowing a mix of direct-assessment coursework and credit-hour coursework in the same program.

In 2015, the Department of Education expanded the CBE experiment to allow institutions to charge tuition on a subscription basis, a method designed to allow students to learn as much as possible in the shortest amount of time without paying for additional courses (U.S. Department of Education, 2015). The Personalized Learning program at Northern Arizona University is one example of this type of program; it offers self-paced online degrees that forego traditional fixed due dates and schedules (Northern Arizona University, n.d.). Tuition for the university's personalized learning program is a flat rate for unlimited access to the program's online lessons for six months. Some universities offer similar online competency-based programs, while others combine different approaches such as competency-based and traditional credit-hour courses.

Although opportunities such as those afforded by the Experimental Sites Initiative are providing avenues to change the traditional higher education system, many competency-based programs translate competency credits into credit hours to facilitate credit transfer and federal financial aid, and for accreditation purposes for the institutions (Ford, 2014). Many of these programs are in the early stages and despite the recent proliferation of and attention on them, many questions remain about their impacts on students and learning, as well as the ability to scale these models (Ford, 2014; Kelchen, 2015; Nodine, 2016). Still, the opportunities and possibilities that competency-based approaches present—meeting the needs of diverse students based on an assessment of each student's knowledge, skills, and gaps; lowering costs by allowing students to move at their own pace; providing more information about what students actually know and can do—continue to propel the movement in K–12 and postsecondary education.

During a visit to Indiana in the fall of 2015, Secretary of Education Arne Duncan praised Purdue University's move toward a competency-based education model and encouraged more K–12 schools to adopt the approach:

> I just think it's the right thing to do. Whether it's an advanced physics class here or engineering, or whether it's algebra as a ninth-grader—if you can demonstrate that you know algebra, why should you sit in that chair for nine months? (as cited in Schneider & Paul, 2015)

Indeed, initial results from K–12 districts that have moved to personalize the learning process have indicated enhanced student engagement and more positive attitudes, increased student persistence when confronted with challenging tasks, and increased collaboration among students (District Reform Support Network, 2016a). In one case "blended classrooms out-performed those in non-blended classrooms by as much as 45 percent in reading and 56 percent in math, and surpassed their growth targets by 18 percent in math and 36 percent in reading" and increased the number of students taking college courses during high school from 7 percent to more than 25 percent (District Reform Support Network, 2016b). Promising results such as those from the Race to the Top District sites, lessons educators learned from research on effective educational strategies (Alli, Rajan, & Ratliff, 2016; Le et al., 2014), and the logical premise that personalized learning might help all students reach their potential are all aspects contributing to the expansion of competency-based education.

CompetencyWorks, a collaborative initiative that provides information and knowledge about competency-based education in the K–12 education system, reported the following:

> Nearly 90 percent of states have created some room for competency-based innovations. The leading states of New Hampshire, Maine, Vermont, and Colorado have started down the path to redesign personalized, competency-based policies and education by re-aligning their systems, creating proficiency-based diplomas, and converting credits to recognize skills learned rather than time in class. Arizona, Connecticut, Iowa, Kentucky, Ohio, Oregon, and Rhode Island have all established enabling policies to create space for districts to innovate. Delaware, Hawaii, and North Carolina are actively studying what it means to have a personalized, competency-based system. Others have created "seat-time waivers" that allow districts and schools to offer competency-based credits. (Sturgis, 2015, pp. 5–6)

In December 2015, Congress passed the Every Student Succeeds Act (a reauthorization of the Elementary and Secondary Education Act). The Every Student Succeeds Act includes important provisions to support competency-based education and personalized learning in K–12 schools, including provisions that allow states to do the following.

- Redesign assessments for student-centered learning
- Pilot new assessment systems that align with competency-based education approaches
- Implement personalized, blended, and online learning approaches

In response, as early as January 2016, state legislatures and boards of education were moving to implement these types of provisions. In a letter to the U.S. Department of Education, the California Department of Education suggested that the state be allowed to implement a competency-based system in which schools report student performance relative to competencies rather than traditional grade levels (Torlakson & Kirst, 2016). Touted as the "future of education," lawmakers in Florida passed a bill (HB 1365) to establish a pilot program to test competency-based approaches which will allow students to move ahead after demonstrating mastery of content. In Georgia, Governor Nathan Deal recommended a similar "move on when ready" provision that would allow students to move ahead in subjects in which they demonstrate competency (Tagami, 2016). Resulting from a 2013 recommendation for the Governor's Task Force for Improving Education, the Idaho Department of Education established a mastery-based education initiative to create the Idaho Mastery Education Network starting with twenty "incubator" schools and districts in 2016–2017 (Idaho State Department of Education, 2017).

Finally, the growing prominence of competency-based education is supported by funding from not only the U.S. federal government but also private organizations and national associations, including the Council of Chief State School Officers (CCSSO, 2014), iNACOL (2015), the League for Innovation in the Community College, the Bill & Melinda Gates Foundation (Morris, 2014), the Carnegie Foundation (Carnegie Corporation of New York, 2013), and the Nellie Mae Education Foundation (2016), among others. Since 2010, the Next Generation Learning Challenges—supported by several of the organizations listed previously—has funded more than 150 grant recipients including schools, colleges and universities, and teams of innovators, educators, and technology professionals. In a separate program, the Gates Foundation has funded more than fifty public charter and district schools to implement a variety of approaches to personalized learning that includes a competency-based progression for students. In sum, the K–12 arena is primed for the increasingly prominent competency-based educational approach to be implemented in districts and classrooms.

The Birth of Personalized Competency-Based Education

Discussion in the field made clear the need to create a "cohesive understanding of how personalized learning and competency education go hand in hand" (Sturgis, 2016a) when moving away from the traditional classroom model. We thus refer to the approach described in this book as *personalized competency-based education* (PCBE). It has the following characteristics, which include elements of various definitions of competency-based education and personalized learning.

- Students move on to the next level within a subject area only after they have demonstrated proficiency at the current level.

- Students learn content at their own pace, so time is not a factor in judging their competencies.

- Students have multiple opportunities and ways to learn specific content.

- Students have multiple opportunities and ways to demonstrate proficiency with specific content.

- Students develop agency (a central focus, in addition to proficiency with academic content).

- Students have a voice in the teaching and learning process.

- Students have choices in the teaching and learning process.

The suggestions in this book represent decades of research and practice into competency-based education and personalized learning from two organizations: the Re-Inventing Schools Coalition (RISC) and Marzano Resources. Marzano Resources exists to turn research results into practical strategies for classroom teachers and school administrators. In 2014, Marzano Resources acquired RISC, a nonprofit established in 2002 with the mission of helping districts, schools, and classrooms transition from teacher-driven, time-based education systems to learner-centered, competency-based systems so that all students succeed. More detailed information on the Re-Inventing Schools Coalition and Marzano Resources's involvement follows.

Re-Inventing Schools Coalition

The Re-Inventing Schools Coalition has its roots in a 1994 reform effort in the Chugach School District in Alaska. With headquarters in Anchorage, Alaska, the district serves villages scattered throughout twenty-two thousand square miles of remote areas in south central Alaska, much of which is accessible only by plane, boat, and train. In 2016, the district had three brick-and-mortar schools (Whittier Community School, Tatitlek Community School, and Chenega Bay School), served close to three hundred homeschoolers, and operated a short-term residential school in Anchorage. In 1992–1993, the district had an enrollment of 132 students and very few graduates. Less than 25 percent of students scored proficient or better in language arts and mathematics, and the district retained approximately 55 percent of its teachers (Sturgis, 2016a). Student achievement was low, and students were not reading at grade level. The community and school board began asking the district hard questions about why it was not preparing students to be successful in school or in their lives (Sturgis, 2016a). Simply put, the district was failing its students and the communities it served.

In 1994, Superintendent Roger Sampson and Assistant Superintendent Richard A. DeLorenzo initialized a comprehensive restructuring process that began with a focus on students (Sturgis, 2016b). Sampson and DeLorenzo brought together a team of educators who worked with input from community members, parents, and students to develop a vision for the district and to restructure district policies and practices. Chugach School District organized its vision around the premise that each student should master knowledge and skills in key standard areas, moving ahead only when he or she demonstrated true proficiency. Students would move at their own pace and be held to a high academic standard, graduating only when they could prove they had mastered the required knowledge and skills. Seat time would no longer be the measure of advancement.

Not everyone thought this new approach was a good idea. Some students, parents, community members, and teachers balked at the new system, especially in the beginning. To meet these constituents' expressed concerns, Chugach School District used a shared vision process to discuss and acknowledge these concerns and issues. The open dialogue that stemmed from this process helped stakeholders in the district see that they had a voice and were able to influence the work of the district.

One of the first and most powerful steps Chugach School District took was identifying the critical content all students would be expected to master. Again, the district developed the content areas and associated standards based on what communities, parents, and students identified as important. The content areas included academic, cultural, and personal and social skills. With the essential content identified, Chugach School District addressed instruction and assessment, which focused on five primary areas generated from the shared vision process: (1) individual student needs, (2) basic skills proficiency, (3) character education, (4) school-to-life transitions, and (5) technology. Instruction and assessment were designed to incorporate student interests and provide students with multiple ways to demonstrate proficiency. Measuring student performance in a variety of ways provided feedback that teachers could use to customize student learning. Teachers created individual learning plans for every student in the district.

The district soon moved away from traditional grade levels, developed assessments and reporting systems aligned with standards, and established a much higher bar for student achievement. In tandem, the district applied for and was granted a waiver from the Alaska Department of Education and Early Development to forego traditional Carnegie units as graduation requirements and instead use students' demonstrated performance on graduation-level district assessments tied to the standards.

Within a few years of implementing this performance-based system, Chugach School District realized significant improvements in student achievement. The percentage of students participating in college entrance exams rose, teacher turnover rates fell, and test scores improved (DeLorenzo, Battino, Schreiber, & Carrio, 2009; Sturgis, 2016a). Perhaps more important, students began to take ownership of their education. Manifesting the district's purpose—*empowering student ownership of learning and success*—students led and partnered with their teachers in every phase of learning. Goal setting was a specific skill taught at every grade level, and students also tracked their own progress, rightly sharing this responsibility with their teachers.

In 2001, Chugach School District received one of the United States' most prestigious awards, the Malcolm Baldrige National Quality Award, which recognizes U.S. organizations in the business, health care, education, and nonprofit sectors for performance excellence. The president of the United States gives out this prestigious award—the only formal recognition of the quality and performance excellence of both public and private U.S. organizations the president bestows. The American Society for Quality administers the Baldrige Award and promotes sharing successful performance strategies and the benefits derived from using these strategies.

In 2002, Chugach School District Superintendent Richard A. DeLorenzo established the Re-Inventing Schools Coalition, along with colleagues Wendy J. Battino and Rick M. Schreiber. RISC began to spread the word about competency-based systems, at first working primarily with Alaska districts and gradually expanding to work with more than 250 schools and 150,000 students in thirty U.S. school districts to support the transition from a traditional, time-based model to a personalized, competency-based system.

Marzano Resources

Marzano Resources was founded in 2008 as Marzano Research Laboratory. However, cofounder Robert J. Marzano has been directly or indirectly involved in competency-based education and personalized learning since before its founding. In 1996, Marzano published his first book related to competency-based education. *A Comprehensive Guide to Designing Standards-Based Districts, Schools, and Classrooms* (Marzano & Kendall, 1996) was one of the first widely disseminated texts to lay out a variety of approaches to what was then referred to as *standards-based schooling* and is now referred to as competency-based education. Interestingly, this book helped forge a relationship between RISC's work and Marzano's work. In the book *Delivering on the Promise*, DeLorenzo and his colleagues (2009) noted that reading *A Comprehensive Guide to Designing Standards-Based Districts, Schools, and Classrooms*, which was a description of how a comprehensive personalized competency system might manifest, made them realize that they had created a system to which many others were aspiring.

The CBE movement spawned many questions, including the utility of grading practices. In 2000, Marzano wrote the book *Transforming Classroom Grading*. This publication provided one of the first explanations of how report cards could be changed to provide information about students' status and progress on specific standards. Its title alludes to the extent a traditional overall grading system and letter grades (A, B, C, D, F) were entrenched in K–12 education. In the year 2000, the mere suggestion of providing more information on a report card other than the overall grade was considered transformational in nature.

In 2006, Marzano wrote *Classroom Assessment and Grading That Work*. This book further delineated how teachers could use classroom assessment as one of the primary ways of measuring students' status and growth. By this time, the concept of standards-based grading was gathering popularity and momentum but was not well understood from the perspective of classroom assessment. This book laid out one of the first technical discussions of the nature of reliability and validity in a system designed to provide precise estimates of students' performance on standards.

In 2007, Marzano and RISC jointly sponsored a conference in Denver, Colorado, on competency-based education. The purpose of the conference was to provide schools and districts with a deeper understanding of the nature of competency-based education and a clear pathway to develop such a system. To a great extent, this conference was one of the first large-scale efforts to start a new wave of competency-based initiatives. In attendance at the conference were administrators from Adams County School District 50 (now called Westminster Public Schools) and Lindsay Unified School District, two of the more prominent systems involved in the early development of PCBE models. Both of these districts used the joint services of Marzano Resources and RISC to craft their personalized competency-based systems. The Westminster Public Schools (2011) call their system a *Competency-Based System*, and their approach to learning is based on four core beliefs: (1) learning is the constant, (2) time is the variable, (3) personalized delivery, and (4) systemic and systematic. Lindsay Unified School District (2017) refers to its system as a *Performance-Based System*, which is built on four foundational concepts: (1) commitment to personalized mastery learning, (2) competency-based rigor, (3) transparent accountability, and (4) learner ownership of their education.

Marzano Resources has continued to develop more refined tools for PCBE systems. For example, in 2010, Marzano published the book *Formative Assessment & Standards-Based Grading*, which articulated coordinated versions of competency-based education and standards-referenced reporting. Over the years since the publication of the 1996 book, Marzano Resources and its precursor organizations have worked with schools across the United States to develop competency-based and standards-referenced systems. Marzano Resources has worked with a number of districts in Maine, Lake County School District in Florida, and Charleston County School District in South Carolina (among others) to design, develop, and implement versions of PCBE systems. Each school and district creates a unique system to meet the needs of its students. Marzano Resources assists schools and districts in creating systems adapted to their local context and needs by providing a set of design questions, the answers to which provide the foundation for a cohesive and coherent system.

Next, we introduce the seven questions that teachers and administrators should answer when implementing a PCBE system.

The PCBE Model in K–12 Classrooms

The aim of this handbook is to provide a comprehensive guide to implementing a successful personalized competency-based education model in K–12 classrooms. Teachers and administrators will learn the differences between traditional and PCBE classrooms and emerge equipped to plan for, teach within, and assess a classroom in which proficiency, not time, is the guiding factor. For a PCBE system to be effective, it must be designed so that each piece works in concert with the other pieces in such a way that the whole is greater than the sum of the parts. To accomplish this, K–12 district- and school-level administrators and teachers must craft answers to seven questions. These questions are derived from our cumulative experiences working with districts and schools on PCBE design and implementation over twenty-five years. In short, we believe that answering these questions using the direction provided in the following chapters entails a step-by-step process any district or school can follow. The questions are:

1. What content will we address?

2. How will the learning environment support student agency?

3. How will instruction support student learning?

4. How will teachers measure student proficiency?

5. How will scheduling accommodate student learning?

6. How will reporting facilitate student learning?

7. How do schools and districts transition to a PCBE system?

This book devotes one chapter to each of these questions and provides specific guidance on how to answer them. We will guide administrators and teachers through the differences between traditional and PCBE classrooms and emerge with the knowledge and motivation to successfully implement a PCBE system in K–12 classrooms.

Chapter 1

What Content Will We Address?

One of the first questions a school or district seeking to create a PCBE system should consider is, What content will we address? Three general categories are commonly part of the answer to this question: (1) traditional academic content, (2) cognitive skills, and (3) metacognitive skills. The content should also be accompanied by tools that allow for easy and appropriate assessment of learning in PCBE classrooms. Hence, we will also discuss the creation of learning targets and proficiency scales, and the translation of existing progressions or rubrics into proficiency scales. While identifying content for a PCBE system, it is important to remember that all subject areas are applicable. Even though the examples in this book generally deal with mathematics, science, social studies, and English language arts, a PCBE approach can also apply to physical education, foreign languages, the arts, and high school electives. We address some of these issues in subsequent sections of this chapter.

Traditional Academic Content

Traditional academic content is knowledge historically taught in K–12 schools and includes content areas such as English language arts, world history, geography, economics, biology, chemistry, algebra, geometry, foreign languages, computer science, and so on. Identifying what students should know and be able to do regarding traditional academic content would appear to be a fairly straightforward process since the United States has had common standards since the early 1990s.

The history of the standards movement is an interesting one. The movement began in 1989 when President George H. W. Bush and the state governors held a summit on education, which resulted in a number of goals for the educational future of the United States (Kendall & Marzano, 2000). These goals focused on increasing student achievement and academic rigor and proposed assessing all students' knowledge of core subjects at the end of fourth, eighth, and twelfth grades (Kendall & Marzano, 2000). In response to these goals and with funding from the federal government, many content-area organizations developed academic standards for their subjects. By the mid-1990s, all states were required to adopt or create academic standards and assessments for English language arts and mathematics. The passage of the No Child Left Behind Act in 2002 continued to propel the standards movement and the creation of benchmarks and standardized assessments (Shepard, 2008).

While these developments were based on well-intentioned goals, problems with the standards movement soon became apparent—one was that each state developed its own benchmarks and assessments, creating a great deal of variability in the standards students had to meet. In 2009, the National Governors Association Center for Best Practices and the Council of Chief State School Officers attempted to solve this problem by leading the effort to create the Common Core State Standards (CCSS; NGA & CCSSO, 2010a, 2010d). The CCSS were intended to define a set of standards for mathematics and English language arts that all states could adopt, creating a level of national consistency that had been absent. While the CCSS initiative began with great acceptance and popularity—a group of governors, chief state school officers, and education experts from forty-eight states, two territories, and the District of Columbia developed the standards—it quickly met strong resistance. Initially, forty-five states, the Department of Defense Education Activity, Washington, D.C., Guam, the Northern Mariana Islands, and the U.S. Virgin Islands adopted the CCSS for English language arts and mathematics. Minnesota adopted English language arts standards only. Alaska, Nebraska, Texas, and Virginia never adopted the CCSS (Kane, Owens, Marinell, Thal, & Staiger, 2016).

The CCSS initiative website describes how the standards were envisioned as a way to provide clear and consistent expectations to "ensure that all students graduate from high school with the skills and knowledge necessary to succeed in college, career, and life, regardless of where they live" (CCSS Initiative, n.d.). The best existing state standards; the experience of numerous teachers, content experts, and state leaders; the expectations of higher education, workforce training programs, and businesses; and feedback from the public informed development of the CCSS. Despite being based on an extensive body of evidence, the CCSS have stirred controversy among educators and the public stemming from concerns regarding the federal role in education, poor rollout and implementation, and issues associated with testing. Indiana, Michigan, Missouri, New Jersey, Oklahoma, and South Carolina reversed their adoption of the CCSS (*Education Week*, 2016), and many states have backed out of their initial CCSS assessments (Gewertz, 2015).

In addition to the CCSS, a similar initiative in science and engineering led to the Next Generation Science Standards (NGSS), published for state adoption in 2013 (NGSS Lead States, 2013). Twenty-six lead state partners and several national groups developed the NGSS, including the National Research Council, the National Science Teachers Association, and the American Association for the Advancement of Science. The NGSS sought to provide updated content, link content and practices, emphasize depth over breadth, and focus on the application of science knowledge through inquiry and engineering design processes.

Given the level of attention that has been paid to identifying standards in various subject areas for American students, it might seem to be an easy task to articulate the traditional academic content that teachers should address when designing a PCBE system—simply use the newest versions of the standards in a given subject area. While straightforward, this process does still require special attention to three areas, including (1) choosing from traditional content, (2) prioritizing and unpacking standards, and (3) using the Critical Concepts.

Choosing From Traditional Content

When districts and schools examine how to articulate standards, it is easy to recognize the problems of using current versions of standards. To illustrate, consider this Common Core standard for eighth-grade reading: "Determine the meaning of words and phrases as they are used in a text, including figurative, connotative, and technical meanings; analyze the impact of specific word choices on meaning and tone, including analogies or allusions to other texts" (RI.8.4; NGA & CCSSO, 2010a, p. 36). While this standard provides some direction, it contains a great deal of content. Specifically, this standard includes the following information and skills.

- Students will understand what figurative, connotative, and technical meanings are.

- Students will be able to identify specific word choices made by an author.

- Students will be able to analyze the impact of specific word choices.

- Students will understand what tone is.

- Students will understand what an analogy is.

- Students will understand what an allusion is.

- Students will be able to analyze analogies and allusions.

Clearly, this single standard contains a good many discrete pieces of content. If one extends this concept across the standards for a specific grade level, the problem of too much content becomes obvious. To illustrate, in their analysis of the CCSS, Robert J. Marzano, David C. Yanoski, Jan K. Hoegh, and Julia A. Simms (2013) identified seventy-three standard statements like this one for eighth-grade English language arts. If one makes a conservative assumption that each of those statements contains about five component skills like those listed previously, this estimate would mean that for eighth grade, there are 365 specific pieces of content students are expected to master—an impossibility in a 180-day school year. This situation is even more extreme when one considers that the seventy-three standards statements do not include the college and career readiness anchor standards for English language arts.

The situation is a little better for mathematics. To illustrate, consider the following seventh-grade mathematics standard, "Use measures of center and measures of variability for numerical data from random samples to draw informal comparative inferences about two populations" (7.SP.B.4; NGA & CCSSO, 2010d, p. 50). This standard includes the following elements.

- Students will understand what different measures of center and measures of variability are.

- Students will be able to calculate different measures of center and measures of variability.

- Students will understand what populations are.

- Students will understand what a random sample is.

- Students will understand what comparative inferences are and will be able to draw comparative inferences from data.

- Students will be able to make inferences based on measures of center and variability.

In their review of the CCSS for mathematics at the seventh-grade level, Marzano and his colleagues (2013) found twenty-nine such statements. Again, assuming about five component elements per standard statement, seventh-grade mathematics would involve 145 component elements—much more realistic given a 180-day school year. But again, the 145 component elements estimated for seventh-grade mathematics do not include the mathematical practice standards.

One can observe the same pattern in many state standards documents. Consider the Texas Essential Knowledge and Skills at the fifth-grade level in English language arts: there are approximately thirty standards statements, and many include subcomponents. If we again use the conservative estimate of five elements per standard, we arrive at about 150 elements of knowledge and skill that fifth graders are expected to learn in English class. To illustrate, consider the following standard:

> Students understand, make inferences and draw conclusions about the structure and elements of poetry and provide evidence from text to support their understanding. Students are expected to analyze how poets use sound effects (e.g., alliteration, internal rhyme, onomatopoeia, rhyme scheme) to reinforce meaning in poems. (Tex. Educ. Code §110.16[b][4], 2008)

This standard contains the following elements.

- Students will understand the structure and elements of poetry.

- Students will be able to make inferences and draw conclusions about the structure and elements of poetry.

- Students will be able to find and present textual evidence to support their conclusions.

- Students will understand alliteration.

- Students will understand internal rhyme and rhyme scheme.

- Students will understand onomatopoeia.

- Students will understand the relationship between sound and meaning in poetry.

- Students will be able to analyze poems for sound and meaning and explain how sound supports meaning.

Even from the perspective of this brief discussion, it is clear that attempting to teach and assess all standards is an exercise in futility. A first step, then, in becoming a PCBE school or district is to prioritize and reduce the number of standards teachers will teach and assess.

Prioritizing and Unpacking Standards

Tammy Heflebower, Jan K. Hoegh, and Phil Warrick (2014) detailed a process for solving the problem of too much content in standards. It involves four steps that teams of content-expert teachers and curriculum directors carry out: (1) analyze standards documents, (2) select preliminary prioritized standards, (3) categorize prioritized standards, and (4) review the final selection. The term *content expert* might be operationally defined as teachers who have a great deal of experience teaching a subject area and a thorough understanding of their local standards for that subject area. It is important to note that Heflebower and colleagues (2014) recommend that administrators are also involved in this process, not necessarily for the purpose of making content decisions but to provide a schoolwide or districtwide perspective on the viability of the process or resource constraints within which the process must operate.

It is also important to note that with elective courses at the high school level, educators might not have easy access to documents describing their subject areas. Usually, though, even a modicum of investigation will yield some useful resources. For example, in 2000, Kendall and Marzano published the third edition of *Content Knowledge: A Compendium of Standards and Benchmarks for K–12 Education*. It reviewed and synthesized multiple standards documents for fourteen subject areas: (1) mathematics, (2) science, (3) history, (4) English language arts, (5) the arts, (6) civics, (7) economics, (8) foreign languages, (9) geography, (10) health, (11) physical education, (12) technology, (13) behavioral studies, and (14) life skills. That compendium was updated in 2014 in a free online version (McREL International, 2014). In the worst-case scenario where teachers can't find any standards and only a few teachers (or even a single teacher) offer the content, educators with knowledge of the subject should make the best decisions they can at that time and then continually revise their standards over time while seeking authoritative resources.

First, the teachers who will take part in the prioritization process must review the standards documents, even if they feel they are familiar with them. This step is as simple as the teachers reading through the standards that apply to their content area and grade level. Teachers should do this individually before meeting with their teams to complete the rest of the process.

Second, teachers should create a preliminary ranking of standards by importance. Each teacher should code each standard in one of these three ways: (1) important for students to know, (2) helpful for students to know, or (3) supplementary material for students. Once teachers have individually rated the standards, grade-level and course teams can compare their ratings and come to a consensus about which standards are essential. Teams should also conduct an informal time audit during this step by estimating how much time it will take to teach the prioritized standards and comparing that number to the available instructional time. While there is no fixed way to conduct a time audit, a typical approach is to start with the traditional Carnegie unit approach. Since this approach is more than one hundred years old, adaptations are commonly necessary to meet the structure of modern school schedules. However, the overall logic behind the approach is still sound and serves as a reference point for related approaches.

The original *Carnegie unit* consisted of 120 hours of contact time with a teacher over the course of a school year. From one perspective, this can be interpreted as 120 days, each involving one hour of academic content instruction at a specific grade level. However, many classes at the high school level are about fifty minutes, which means that it would require about 145 days or about twenty-nine weeks. Since most schools have about a 180-day (that is, thirty-six week) school year, enough margin is available for holidays and days lost to state testing and other noninstructional activities.

At the elementary level, school districts compute time requirements for instruction somewhat differently. First of all, the school districts use guidelines from their local state departments of education to establish time requirements at the elementary level. Elementary schools often do not employ class periods like those used in high school, and individual teachers frequently schedule the blocks of time spent on specific subject areas. Many states and local education agencies, however, provide recommendations for how much instructional time should be allotted to various subject areas on a daily or weekly basis. For example, Missouri and Arizona each recommend that students in grades 1–3 receive sixty minutes of English language arts, sixty minutes of mathematics, and thirty minutes of science instruction each day (Arizona Department of Education, n.d.; Missouri School Improvement Program, n.d.). New York City recommends that students in grades 3–5 receive seventy-five minutes of English language arts and seventy-five minutes of mathematics instruction each day, along with 180 minutes of science instruction per week (NYC Department of Education, n.d.). Teachers can use their local recommendations to estimate yearly instructional time and conduct a time audit.

Third, teams should categorize their prioritized standards into strands or themes. This allows teachers to easily see the main topics they have selected and how the standards relate to each other. This step is important because it is easier to conceptualize several groups of standards than it is to keep track of many individual standards. To illustrate, consider the following topics in fifth-grade English language arts.

- Analyzing text organization and structure
- Analyzing ideas and themes
- Analyzing claims, evidence, and reasoning
- Analyzing narratives
- Analyzing point of view
- Comparing texts
- Analyzing language
- Generating text organization and structure
- Generating claims, evidence, and reasoning

- Finding sources and research
- Generating narratives
- Considering audience, purpose, and task
- Dealing with revision
- Considering parts of speech
- Editing

These might be organized into the following strands.

- Reading
  - Analyzing text organization and structure
  - Analyzing ideas and themes
  - Analyzing claims, evidence, and reasoning
  - Analyzing narratives
  - Analyzing point of view
  - Comparing texts
- Writing
  - Generating text organization and structure
  - Generating claims, evidence, and reasoning
  - Finding sources and research
  - Generating narratives
  - Considering audience, purpose, and task
  - Revising text
  - Editing
- Language
  - Analyzing language
  - Considering parts of speech

Fourth and finally, teams should review the prioritized standards and categories. All the grade-level and course teams display their own prioritized standards and review those of other teams, especially those of the grade levels or courses immediately preceding and following their own. For example, the third-grade team would focus primarily on reviewing the standards prioritized by the second- and fourth-grade teams. Typically, one team member should stay with the team's set of prioritized standards to answer questions and record feedback, while the rest of the teachers provide feedback to other teams. Once the review is complete, teams should adjust their prioritized standards in response to the feedback from adjacent grade levels or courses.

Teacher teams having difficulty prioritizing and unpacking standards may find it helpful to use a set of Marzano Resources–developed unpacked standards. The process of identifying these topics will be discussed in the following section.

Using the Critical Concepts

While districts and schools can engage in prioritizing and unpacking standards on their own, they might use a set of Marzano Resources–developed unpacked standards. As described by Simms (2016), the purpose of the Critical Concepts project was to create a focused set of topics derived from a rigorous analysis of standards documents. See MarzanoResources.com/educational-services/critical-concepts to find topics themselves (referred to as essential topics). To illustrate, the following are the essential science topics for fourth grade.

- Energy
- Motion
- Light and vision
- Waves
- Information transfer
- Geographic features
- Earth changes
- Earth's history
- Natural hazards
- Natural resources
- Plant needs
- Animal needs

Essential K–12 topics are available free of charge for mathematics, English language arts, and science. These topics can provide important guidance to districts or schools as they prioritize their standards.

In addition to the essential topics themselves, each topic encompasses one or more learning targets. For example, the following is the learning target associated with the topic of light and vision: The student will explain how vision is a product of light reflecting off objects and entering the eye. Finally, each learning target is embedded in a progression of knowledge referred to as a proficiency scale. These are described in a subsequent section of this chapter (page 25).

Schools or districts use the essential topics identified in the Critical Concepts to help them create their own systems (Simms, 2016). That is, a school or district can adopt or adapt these topics. They might also add other topics. However, our caution is that increasing the number of topics might strain the system and make assessment and recordkeeping difficult. Additionally, keeping the number of topics for traditional content relatively small allows for the addition of other topics that we refer to as cognitive and metacognitive skills.

Cognitive Skills

Students use *cognitive skills* to "effectively process information and complete tasks. Cognitive skills are required for tasks involving retrieval, comprehension, analysis, and utilization of knowledge" (Marzano et al., 2013, p. 24). With the advent of the focus on college and career readiness, there has been a resurgence in the interest in such skills. Table 1.1 provides our recommended list of cognitive skills.

Table 1.1: Recommended Cognitive Skills

COGNITIVE SKILL	DEFINITION
Generating conclusions	Combining information to create new ideas
Identifying common logical errors	Analyzing conclusions or arguments for validity or truth
Presenting and supporting claims	Using reasons and evidence to support new ideas
Navigating digital sources	Finding relevant information online or in electronic resources and assessing its credibility
Using problem solving	Navigating obstacles and limiting conditions to achieve a goal
Using decision making	Selecting the best option from among several good alternatives
Experimenting	Generating explanations for events or phenomena and testing the accuracy of those explanations
Investigating	Identifying questions about a topic, event, or idea and discovering answers, solutions, or predictions
Identifying basic relationships between ideas	Understanding and recognizing how two ideas are connected by time, cause, addition, or contrast
Generating and manipulating mental images	Creating images, symbols, or imagined situations in one's mind and using them to test ideas and solutions

Teachers would address cognitive skills somewhat differently from traditional academic content. Teachers would not explicitly teach all the skills depicted in table 1.1 at each grade level. Rather, they would teach certain skills at certain times and within the context of specific subject areas. Examples of scope and sequence are depicted in tables 1.2 and 1.3 (pages 20–21) for grades K–8 and high school, respectively. As shown, cognitive skills can be reasonably and adequately dispersed throughout the curriculum. In grades K–3, the curriculum heavily emphasizes identifying basic relationships between ideas and generating and manipulating mental images because they are so basic to the analysis and processing of information. The K–8 curriculum emphasizes some skills throughout (like generating conclusions). The upper-grade-level curriculum emphasizes other skills, like navigating digital sources.

Table 1.2: Scope and Sequence of Cognitive Skills for Grades K–8

COGNITIVE SKILL	K	1	2	3	4	5	6	7	8
Generating conclusions		X		X		X		X	
Identifying common logical errors			X		X		X		X
Presenting and supporting claims			X		X		X		X
Navigating digital sources						X		X	X
Using problem solving		X		X		X	X	X	
Using decision making			X		X		X		X
Experimenting		X			X	X		X	
Investigating				X	X		X		X
Identifying basic relationships between ideas	X	X	X	X					
Generating and manipulating mental images	X	X	X	X					

Table 1.3: Scope and Sequence of Cognitive Skills for High School

COGNITIVE SKILL	GRADE 9 ENGLISH LANGUAGE ARTS	GRADE 9 MATHEMATICS	GRADE 9 SOCIAL STUDIES	GRADE 9 SCIENCE	GRADE 10 ENGLISH LANGUAGE ARTS	GRADE 10 MATHEMATICS	GRADE 10 SOCIAL STUDIES	GRADE 10 SCIENCE
Generating conclusions	X				X			
Identifying common logical errors	X				X			
Presenting and supporting claims	X		X	X				X
Navigating digital sources								
Using problem solving		X				X		
Using decision making			X				X	

Experimenting				X				X
Investigating	X		X		X		X	
Identifying basic relationships between ideas								
Generating and manipulating mental images								

At the secondary level, some cognitive skills naturally fit with certain subject areas. For example, presenting and supporting claims fits with English language arts and science. Problem solving fits with mathematics, experimenting fits with science, and investigating fits with English language arts and social studies. Also note that in table 1.3, cognitive skills are not explicitly taught above grade 10. At these levels, the cognitive skills should be a well-formed set of tools students can use in a variety of ways.

It is important to note that teaching cognitive skills requires direct instruction (just like traditional content). To illustrate, consider the cognitive skill of presenting and supporting claims. To execute this skill effectively, a student needs to understand the basic structure of a well-designed and well-supported assertion, which involves the following four components.

1. **Claim:** This component presents an opinion or suggests that a certain action is needed—for example, "We should increase the amount of recess time at our school."

2. **Grounds:** This provides an initial reason for the claim—for example, "Physical activity is good for students' minds and bodies."

3. **Backing:** This component presents evidence or facts to back up the grounds—for example, "Research shows that movement increases blood flow to the brain, bringing more oxygen and sugars that help the brain perform better."

4. **Qualifiers:** This notes exceptions to the claim—for example, "However, extra recess can be hard to schedule because students are required to spend a certain amount of time in class each day."

Direct instruction on presenting and supporting claims would also involve information about specific types of evidence, such as the following.

- **Expert opinions:** Statements that experts in the field make
- **Research results:** Data or conclusions that scientists gathered through experiments or investigations
- **Factual information:** Statements that are generally acknowledged or proven to be true

Equally important to cognitive skills are metacognitive skills—another set of skills that might be the focus of PCBE.

Metacognitive Skills

Metacognitive skills are those someone uses to provide executive control over one's actions. They help people perform mental and physical actions more effectively and efficiently. Literature has mentioned metacognitive skills for decades, although by different names. In the late 1980s and early 1990s, some referred to them as *meditational tools* (Costa, 1991). Others referred to them as *mental habits* or *habits of mind* (Costa & Kallick, 2009; Ennis, 1985, 1987, 1989; Paul, 1990). The Common Core State Standards refer to them as *practice skills* (NGA & CCSSO, 2010a, 2010b, 2010c, 2010d, 2010e). Cognitive psychology literature refers to them as *conative skills* (Kolbe, 1990; McCombs & Whisler, 1989; Snow, 1989). Throughout all of these various perspectives, the term *metacognitive* is a foundational component. Hence, we refer to these skills as metacognitive skills. Table 1.4 lists our recommended metacognitive skills.

Table 1.4: Recommended Metacognitive Skills

METACOGNITIVE SKILL	DEFINITION
Planning for goals and making adjustments	Setting long- or short-term goals, making plans to accomplish those goals, and making adjustments to plans as needed
Staying focused when answers and solutions are not immediately apparent	When engaged in trying to solve a complex problem, recognizing frustration and re-engaging in the task
Pushing the limits of one's knowledge and skills	Setting or adjusting goals so that they require acquiring new knowledge or skills, rather than staying within one's comfort zone
Generating and pursuing one's own standards of excellence	When working toward creating a product, determining what the end result should look like and how success will be judged
Seeking incremental steps	Acquiring knowledge or skills in manageable chunks to avoid becoming overwhelmed, and examining each part's relationship to the whole
Seeking accuracy	Analyzing sources of information for reliability and verifying information by consulting multiple sources
Seeking clarity	When taking in new information, noticing one's own confusion and seeking to alleviate it
Resisting impulsivity	Noticing the desire to react or form a conclusion and pausing to revise that response or collect more information
Seeking cohesion and coherence	Monitoring the relationships between individual parts of a system and the relationships between the parts and the whole and making adjustments if they are unstable or not producing the desired results

Metacognitive skills might be treated like cognitive skills in that teachers can introduce them at specific grade levels and within specific content areas. Tables 1.5 and 1.6 (pages 23–24) provide a scope and sequence for such skills in grades K–8 and high school, respectively. Table 1.5 indicates that K–8 teachers can address some metacognitive skills—like planning for goals and making adjustments—evenly across the grade levels. Others, like generating and pursuing one's own standards of excellence, are more appropriate at higher grade levels. Table 1.6 indicates that certain metacognitive skills seem to fit more naturally with specific subject areas. For example, staying focused when answers and solutions are not immediately apparent fits well with mathematics, whereas seeking cohesion and coherence seems to fit well with English language arts, particularly writing.

Table 1.5: Scope and Sequence of Metacognitive Skills for Grades K–8

METACOGNITIVE SKILL	K	1	2	3	4	5	6	7	8
Planning for goals and making adjustments		X	X		X		X		X
Staying focused when answers and solutions are not immediately apparent		X		X		X		X	
Pushing the limits of one's knowledge and skills						X		X	
Generating and pursuing one's own standards of excellence					X				X
Seeking incremental steps			X		X		X		X
Seeking accuracy		X		X		X		X	
Seeking clarity	X		X		X				
Resisting impulsivity	X			X				X	
Seeking cohesion and coherence			X		X		X		X

Table 1.6: Scope and Sequence of Metacognitive Skills for High School

METACOGNITIVE SKILL	GRADE 9 ENGLISH LANGUAGE ARTS	GRADE 9 MATHEMATICS	GRADE 9 SOCIAL STUDIES	GRADE 9 SCIENCE	GRADE 10 ENGLISH LANGUAGE ARTS	GRADE 10 MATHEMATICS	GRADE 10 SOCIAL STUDIES	GRADE 10 SCIENCE
Planning for goals and making adjustments			X				X	
Staying focused when answers and solutions are not immediately apparent		X				X		
Pushing the limits of one's knowledge and skills	X				X			

continued →

METACOGNITIVE SKILL	GRADE 9 ENGLISH LANGUAGE ARTS	GRADE 9 MATHEMATICS	GRADE 9 SOCIAL STUDIES	GRADE 9 SCIENCE	GRADE 10 ENGLISH LANGUAGE ARTS	GRADE 10 MATHEMATICS	GRADE 10 SOCIAL STUDIES	GRADE 10 SCIENCE
Generating and pursuing one's own standards of excellence	X				X			
Seeking incremental steps								
Seeking accuracy				X				X
Seeking clarity				X				X
Resisting impulsivity		X				X		
Seeking cohesion and coherence	X				X			

It is important to note that like cognitive skills, teaching metacognitive skills requires direct instruction. To illustrate, consider the metacognitive skill of planning for goals and making adjustments. The first part of the skill involves identifying a goal—a student might set a goal such as "I want to score proficient or above on the assessment this week." The next step in this skill involves identifying the actions the student must execute to accomplish the goal. In this example, the student might plan to do the following.

- Do practice exercises early in the week
- Meet with the teacher about any questions or confusions
- Use increased understanding to complete more practice exercises
- Make sure to get enough sleep before the assessment

While students are executing these actions, they must continuously monitor whether they must make any changes. In this example, while doing practice exercises early in the week, the student might realize that he has not yet consistently mastered basic information, such as related vocabulary words, so he adjusts by reviewing and practicing that content before practicing the more complex content.

As with the cognitive skills, metacognitive skills can be taught at a rudimentary level in primary grades and progress to relatively complete versions by high school.

Once stakeholders have selected the content—traditional academic content, cognitive skills, and metacognitive skills—they plan to teach in a PCBE classroom, they must create tools with which to measure students' proficiency progressions. To do this, we recommend embedding learning targets within proficiency scales.

Learning Targets and Proficiency Scales

After step 4 of the prioritization process described by Heflebower and colleagues (2014), educators should have a viable list of essential topics with their associated learning targets. They should then organize this information into proficiency scales. As we describe in chapter 4 (page 97), proficiency scales form the basis for measuring students' progress and providing them with feedback. Every essential topic should be accompanied by a proficiency scale. In fact, we prefer to call essential topics *measurement topics* to emphasize their function within a PCBE system.

Now we will delve into creating proficiency scales, as well as translating existing learning progressions or rubrics into proficiency scales.

Creating Proficiency Scales

The prioritization process lays the groundwork for creating proficiency scales. Table 1.7 contains sample measurement topics that might be established after phase 4 for eighth-grade mathematics, sixth-grade English language arts, and fifth-grade science.

Table 1.7: Sample Measurement Topic Sets

EIGHTH-GRADE MATHEMATICS	SIXTH-GRADE ENGLISH LANGUAGE ARTS	FIFTH-GRADE SCIENCE
Exponents	Analyzing Text Organization and Structure	Gravity
Cube and Square Roots	Analyzing Ideas and Themes	Matter
Scientific Notation	Analyzing Claims, Evidence, and Reasoning	Properties of Matter
Rational and Irrational Numbers	Analyzing Narratives	Celestial Motion
Linear Equations	Analyzing Point of View	Celestial Objects
Systems of Linear Equations	Comparing Texts	Earth Systems
Quadratic Equations	Analyzing Language	Ecosystem Interactions
Concept of Functions	Generating Text Organization and Structure	Engineering Design Problems
Linear Functions	Generating Claims, Evidence, and Reasoning	Solutions for Engineering Design Problems
Volume	Considering Sources and Research	Scientific Method
Transformations, Similarity, and Congruence	Generating Narratives	
Angles of Two-Dimensional Figures	Considering the Audience, Purpose, and Task	
Line and Angle Constructions	Dealing With Revision	
Pythagorean Theorem	Considering Parts of Speech	
Bivariate Categorical Data	Editing	
Bivariate Measurement Data		

As described previously, it is important that each measurement topic listed in table 1.7 is accompanied by one or more *learning targets*—explicit statements that articulate the specific knowledge and skills that students must exhibit to demonstrate mastery of a measurement topic. If teachers have not generated learning targets as a result of prioritizing standards, it is important that they do so before attempting to create proficiency scales. A single measurement topic might have more than one learning target associated with it. To illustrate, consider the eighth-grade mathematics measurement topic bivariate measurement data. This measurement topic includes three learning targets.

1. Describe patterns of association in a set of bivariate measurement data represented with a scatterplot.

2. Write the equation of a line of best fit to model a linear association in a set of bivariate measurement data represented with a scatterplot.

3. Use the equation of a linear model of bivariate measurement data to solve problems.

To be considered proficient in the topic bivariate measurement data, a student would have to demonstrate the knowledge and skills detailed in these statements.

Various measurement topics have differing numbers of learning targets. As another example, consider the sixth-grade English language arts measurement topic analyzing text organization and structure. This measurement topic contains the following two learning targets.

1. Explain how each major section of a text contributes to the overall organizational structure of the text.

2. Explain how each line or stanza of a poem contributes to the overall organizational structure of the text.

Finally, the fifth-grade science measurement topic of matter is composed of the following three learning targets.

1. Explain that all matter is composed of small, invisible particles.

2. Explain that the weight of matter is conserved when substances change temperature.

3. Explain that the weight of matter is conserved when substances are mixed.

Table 1.8 provides examples of measurement topics from mathematics, English language arts, science, and social studies.

Table 1.8: Sample Measurement Topics and Learning Targets

SUBJECT AREA	MEASUREMENT TOPIC	LEARNING TARGETS
Mathematics (Grade 8)	Slope and Intercept	Students will derive the equation $y = mx + b$ from a line on the coordinate plane.
		Students will demonstrate that the slope is the same between any two points on a nonvertical line using similar triangles.

English Language Arts (Grade 7)	Using Appropriate Citations and Sources	Students will use print and digital sources to answer a research question.
		Students will assess the credibility and accuracy of sources.
		Students will cite sources when quoting or paraphrasing the data or conclusions of others.
Science (High School)	Energy Conversion	Students will explain how to convert energy from one form to another.
Social Studies (Grade 6)	Native Latin American Cultures	Students will describe the expansion and decline of the Mayan, Incan, and Aztecan civilizations.
		Students will compare the social, religious, and technological aspects of the Maya, Inca, and Aztec civilizations.

Table 1.8 demonstrates that measurement topics often contain more than one learning target. Educators must decide whether measurement topics that have two or more learning targets should be split into more than one measurement topic. There are at least two criteria that would lead one to conclude that multiple learning targets should remain under one measurement topic: (1) they can be taught together, and (2) they can and should be measured together.

To be taught together, learning targets should have a great deal of overlapping information. To illustrate, consider the following two learning targets for the sixth-grade English language arts measurement topic analyzing ideas and themes.

1. Students will explain how a writer introduces and conveys the main idea of a text using its key details.

2. Students will explain how a writer conveys a theme through specific details in a text.

These two learning targets contain quite a bit of overlapping information. The concepts of *main idea* and *theme* are closely related, and both learning targets involve identifying how details contribute to a larger element.

The second criterion for keeping multiple learning targets within a measurement topic is that they covary. If two or more learning targets *covary*, an increase in a student's ability relative to one target predicts an increase in his or her ability relative to the others. For example, if a student increased her skill at using key details to identify the main idea of a text, we would likely expect that her ability to use details to identify a theme would also increase.

Another option when using learning targets to define a measurement topic is to construct a proficiency scale. Proficiency scales have their grounding in learning progressions. Marzano (2010) described *learning progressions* as "a series of related learning goals [learning targets] that culminate in the attainment of a more complex learning goal" (p. 11). In this way, learning progressions describe the steps that students and teachers need to take to eventually reach a learning target or master a topic.

In its simplest form, a proficiency scale (see figure 1.1) is a statement of progressively more complex expectations regarding the knowledge and skills within a measurement topic.

Score 4.0	Advanced content
Score 3.0	Target content
Score 2.0	Simpler content necessary for proficiency
Score 1.0	With help, partial success with score 2.0 content and score 3.0 content
Score 0.0	Even with help, no success

Figure 1.1: Generic form of a proficiency scale.

The best way to understand a proficiency scale is to start with score 3.0. It is the target content (that is, the fulcrum) of every scale. The statement of expectations for each measurement topic is recorded here. For example, consider this statement of expectations for fifth-grade science measurement topic: Classify materials based on their properties (magnetism, conductivity, density, solubility, boiling point, melting point). This target would become the score 3.0 content of a proficiency scale. Score 4.0 content involves going above and beyond the expectations listed at the score 3.0 level. This often requires students to make inferences and applications not addressed in class.

The score 2.0 content is the simpler, directly taught content that students must learn to demonstrate competence. This last point is critical. Score 2.0 should not contain all the information and skill necessary to accomplish the score 3.0 expectations, but it should contain the content the teacher feels must be directly taught to students. For the score 3.0 science content displayed in figure 1.2, the score 2.0 content might be as follows.

- Students will recognize and recall basic vocabulary, such as *magnetism, conductivity, density, solubility, boiling point, melting point*
- Students will perform basic processes, such as:
  - Making observations to identify the properties of a material
  - Taking measurements to identify the properties of a material

Score 2.0 content typically includes key vocabulary, basic processes, and basic details. Score 1.0 does not involve specific content. Rather, it indicates that a student can demonstrate partial understanding of or skill at the score 2.0 and 3.0 levels, but only with help. Finally, score 0.0 indicates that, even with help, a student cannot demonstrate knowledge of or skill at any of the content. See figure 1.2 for the complete scale for this science measurement topic.

Score 4.0	The student will: • Solve an engineering problem involving decisions about which material, based on its properties, will best satisfy a set of requirements and constraints
Score 3.5	In addition to score 3.0 performance, partial success at score 4.0 content
Score 3.0	The student will: Classify materials based on their properties (magnetism, conductivity, density, solubility, boiling point, melting point)
Score 2.5	No major errors or omissions regarding score 2.0 content, and partial success at score 3.0 content
Score 2.0	The student will: Recognize and recall basic vocabulary, such as *magnetism, conductivity, density, solubility, boiling point, melting point* The student will perform basic processes, such as: • Making observations to identify the properties of a material • Taking measurements to identify the properties of a material
Score 1.5	Partial success at score 2.0 content, and major errors or omissions regarding score 3.0 content
Score 1.0	With help, partial success at score 2.0 content and score 3.0 content
Score 0.5	With help, partial success at score 2.0 content but not at score 3.0 content
Score 0.0	Even with help, no success

Figure 1.2: Complete proficiency scale for a fifth-grade science learning target.

Notice that the scale in figure 1.2 has half-point scores. This greatly enhances the scale's use as a measurement device. Score 0.5 means that a student can demonstrate partial knowledge of the score 2.0 content with help (but no knowledge of score 3.0 content). Score 1.5 indicates that the student independently demonstrates partial knowledge of the score 2.0 content. Score 2.5 means that a student demonstrates knowledge of the score 2.0 content and has partial success with the score 3.0 content. Score 3.5 means that a student is proficient with the score 3.0 content and demonstrates partial knowledge of or skill at the score 4.0 level.

As mentioned previously, in some cases a proficiency scale will contain more than one learning target at the score 3.0 level. To illustrate, consider figure 1.3 (pages 30–31). Note that each of the two elements at the score 3.0 level has its own list of score 2.0 knowledge. For example, the first score 3.0 learning target addresses the topic of evaluating algebraic expressions. Its score 2.0 content includes knowledge about variables, operators, expressions, and the order of operations. Also note that even though there are two elements for score 3.0 and two lists of simple content at the 2.0 level, there is only one statement at the 4.0 level. This is because the score 4.0 expectation requires a student to integrate and apply the score 3.0 and 2.0 content for both learning targets.

Score 4.0	The student will: • Compute the value of the variable in a single-variable algebraic equation that includes multiple types of operators (for example, find the value of x in the equation $5(x + 7) / 3 - 5 = 10$.
Score 3.5	In addition to score 3.0 performance, partial success at score 4.0 content
Score 3.0	The student will: 1. **Evaluate algebraic expressions when given integer values for variables** (for example, calculate the value of the expression $5(x + 7) / 3 - 5$ when given an integer value for x). 2. **Identify the additive identity, multiplicative identity, additive inverse, and multiplicative inverse of an algebraic expression** (for example, calculate the additive identity, multiplicative identity, additive inverse, and multiplicative inverse of $5x = +7$).
Score 2.5	No major errors or omissions regarding score 2.0 content, and partial success at score 3.0 content
Score 2.0	1. The student will recognize or recall specific vocabulary (for example, *algebraic expression, expression, integer, operation, operator, order of operations, symbol, value, variable*) and perform basic processes such as: • State that a variable is a symbol that represents an unknown value. • State that an operator is a symbol that represents a mathematical operation. • Explain that the order of operations is the universally agreed-upon order in which operators are to be applied. • State that an expression is a group of numbers, symbols, and operations that represents a value. • State that an algebraic expression is an expression that contains numbers, operators, and at least one variable. • Explain that the order of operations dictates that parentheses are to be applied first, then exponents, then multiplication and division (from left to right), and then addition and subtraction (from left to right). 2. The student will recognize or recall specific vocabulary (for example, *additive identity property, additive inverse property, expression, multiplicative identity property, multiplicative inverse property, operation, reciprocal, symbol, value*) and perform basic processes such as: • State that the additive identity is the value that, when added to an expression, does not change the value of that expression, and is equal to 0. • State that the multiplicative identity is the value that, when multiplied with an expression, does not change the value of that expression, and is equal to 1. • Explain that the additive inverse is the value that, when added to an expression, results in a value of 0. • Explain that the multiplicative inverse is the value that, when multiplied with an expression, results in a value of 1. • Explain that an expression's multiplicative inverse is also known as its reciprocal. • Explain that the multiplicative inverse of an expression is equal to 1 divided by the expression. For example, the multiplicative inverse of $5x$ is $\frac{1}{5}x$.
Score 1.5	Partial success at score 2.0 content, and major errors or omissions regarding score 3.0 content

Score 1.0	With help, partial success at score 2.0 content and score 3.0 content
Score 0.5	With help, partial success at score 2.0 content but not at score 3.0 content
Score 0.0	Even with help, no success

Figure 1.3: Proficiency scale with two elements at score 3.0.

Proficiency scales for cognitive skills would follow the same format as proficiency scales for traditional content. However, the cognitive skills can't be differentiated from grade level to grade level like traditional content. For example, it is difficult to describe how the cognitive skill of decision making would be different from grade 4 to grade 5. Debra Pickering (2010), however, noted that cognitive skills should be articulated at four levels: K–2, 3–5, 6–8, and 9–12. Table 1.9 contains an example of score 3.0 content for the cognitive process of decision making.

Table 1.9: Score 3.0 Content for Decision Making

LEVEL	SCORE 3.0 CONTENT
Grades K–2	• The student identifies decisions that people make daily. • The student understands that a decision is made when you select from among alternatives.
Grades 3–5	• The student utilizes a basic process for decision making. • The student understands the interactions between alternatives and criteria.
Grades 6–8	• The student utilizes a process for decision making that includes alternatives, criteria, and priority weights.
Grades 9–12	• The student frames important decision-making tasks and establishes relevant and useful alternatives, criteria, and priority weights. • The student analyzes important historical, current, and future decisions from the perspective of the adequacy of the alternatives, criteria, and priority weights.

This sequence represents a logical K–12 progression of understanding and skill regarding decision making. To delineate the progression of knowledge and skill within each grade range, proficiency scales would be designed for each of the four levels. To illustrate, figure 1.4 (pages 31–32) depicts a decision-making proficiency scale for grades 3–5.

Score 4.0	The student is able to explain how changing or adding criteria or alternatives would have changed the decision.
Score 3.5	In addition to score 3.0 performance, partial success at score 4.0 content
Score 3.0	The student executes the five-step decision-making process and describes the logic behind his or her final decision.
Score 2.5	No major errors or omissions regarding score 2.0 content, and partial success at score 3.0 content

continued →

Score 2.0	The student recognizes and recalls basic vocabulary such as *alternative*, *criteria*, *decision matrix*, and so on. The student is able to explain and exemplify the following steps: (1) state the decision you are making; (2) identify and describe the alternatives; (3) identify and describe the criteria; (4) identify which alternatives meet which criteria; and (5) identify which alternative meets the most criteria.
Score 1.5	Partial success at score 2.0 content, and major errors or omissions regarding score 3.0 content
Score 1.0	With help, partial success at score 2.0 content and score 3.0 content
Score 0.5	With help, partial success at score 2.0 content but not at score 3.0 content
Score 0.0	Even with help, no success

Figure 1.4: Proficiency scale for decision making for grades 3–5.

Proficiency scales for the metacognitive skills have a slightly different logic from the proficiency scales for traditional content or cognitive skills. Robert J. Marzano and Jana S. Marzano (2015) noted that metacognitive skills require some amount of learner will or volition in the context of social-emotional learning. For example, a student may understand that it is important to push the limit of one's knowledge and skill but rarely makes the decision to do so. Consequently, a proficiency scale for such a metacognitive skill would have to incorporate this volitional component. Figure 1.5 depicts such a proficiency scale.

Score 4.0	The student makes conscious decisions to push the limit of his or her knowledge and skills in appropriate situations and executes an effective strategy to do so.
Score 3.5	In addition to score 3.0 performance, partial success at score 4.0 content
Score 3.0	• The student can execute an effective strategy to push the limit of his or her knowledge and skill. • The student can articulate those situations in which it would be beneficial to push the limit of his or her knowledge and skill.
Score 2.5	No major errors or omissions regarding score 2.0 content, and partial success at score 3.0 content
Score 2.0	• The student recognizes and recalls basic vocabulary such as *pushing oneself*, *limits of knowledge*, *limits of skill*, *managing oneself*, and so on. • The student is able to explain and exemplify the following process: (1) identify if you would benefit from pushing the limit of your knowledge and skill in the current task; (2) identify the knowledge or skill on which you wish to push yourself; (3) identify questions you would like to answer about the knowledge or skill you've identified; (4) keep asking yourself if you've answered the questions you've posed; and (5) when the task is complete, summarize what you've learned.
Score 1.5	Partial success at score 2.0 content, and major errors or omissions regarding score 3.0 content

Score 1.0	With help, partial success at score 2.0 content and score 3.0 content
Score 0.5	With help, partial success at score 2.0 content but not at score 3.0 content
Score 0.0	Even with help, no success

Figure 1.5: Proficiency scale for pushing the limits of one's knowledge and skill.

The proficiency scale for the metacognitive skill of pushing the limits of one's knowledge and skill has the voluntary use of this skill, once learned, as the 4.0 level of execution. This distinction is because metacognitive skills, while teachable and therefore learnable, cannot and should not be imposed on students. Ultimately, students must individually determine the manner in and extent to which they will habitually push the limits of their knowledge and skill, generate and pursue their own standards of excellence, and so on. While it is the job of public education to ensure that all students graduate with important metacognitive skills, it is most probably not its job to ensure that all students utilize those skills in their lives outside of school.

Translating Existing Learning Progressions or Rubrics Into Proficiency Scales

Many schools have already created learning progressions or rubrics that they wish to continue using. To illustrate, consider the progression for the concept of buoyancy (Herman & Choi, 2008). The ultimate learning goal is for students to understand that an object will float, or be buoyant, in a medium if the object is less dense than that medium. As they work toward attaining this goal, students might demonstrate the following levels of understanding (from lowest to highest).

- Students think that floating depends on being flat, hollow, filled with air, or having holes.
- Students think that floating depends on having a small size, heft, or amount, or that it depends on being made out of a particular material.
- Students know that floating depends on having a small mass, or that floating depends on having a large volume.
- Students know that floating depends on having a small mass and a large volume.
- Students know that floating depends on having a small density.
- Students know that floating depends on having less density than the medium.

Clearly, defining the learning progression as exemplified here will help teachers and students identify current levels of knowledge and provide feedback for reaching higher levels of understanding.

To use this progression as a proficiency scale, one could map each level of understanding onto an appropriate level of the scale, as shown in figure 1.6 (page 34).

Score 4.0	Students know that floating depends on having less density than the medium.
Score 3.5	Students know that floating depends on having a small density.
Score 3.0	Students know that floating depends on having a small mass and a large volume.
Score 2.5	Students know that floating depends on having a small mass, or that floating depends on having a large volume.
Score 2.0	Students think that floating depends on having a small size, heft, or amount, or that it depends on being made out of a particular material.
Score 1.5	Students think that floating depends on being flat, hollow, filled with air, or having holes.
Score 1.0	With help, partial success with accurate score 2.0 and 3.0 content
Score 0.5	With help, partial success with accurate score 2.0 content, but not with score 3.0 content
Score 0.0	Even with help, no success

Source: Herman & Choi, 2008.

Figure 1.6: Proficiency scale created from a pre-existing learning progression.

Teachers could use a similar process with a pre-existing rubric; they would look at the levels described on the rubric and map each one to a level of the proficiency scale. For example, if an English language arts teacher has a rubric that assesses elements of students' writing using levels such as emerging, developing, competent, experienced, and exceeds expectations, that teacher might translate these levels into a proficiency scale as shown in table 1.10.

Table 1.10: Translating Rubric Levels to Proficiency Scale Levels

RUBRIC LEVEL	PROFICIENCY SCALE LEVEL
Exceeds Expectations	Score 4.0
Experienced	Score 3.5
Competent	Score 3.0
Developing	Score 2.5
Emerging	Score 2.0

While it is certainly possible to adapt existing learning progressions and rubrics to a proficiency scale format, there are important differences. Probably the most important difference is that many learning progressions and rubrics are designed for assessment purposes only and offer little guidance for instructional purposes or even assessment design. To illustrate, reconsider the proficiency scale in figure 1.6 based on the work of Joan L. Herman and Kilchan Choi (2008). The levels certainly describe a progression of competence but do not describe viable targets for learning. This is most obvious at the lower levels. For example, consider the lowest levels in the learning progression (Herman & Choi, 2008).

- Students think floating depends on having a small size, heft, or amount, or that it depends on being made out of a particular material.

- Students think that floating depends on being flat, hollow, filled with air, or having holes.

These statements both represent misconceptions in students' thinking. While these levels provide very useful information, they are not easily translated into instructional or assessment activities. This issue is a growing problem in PCBE.

An approach that is becoming quite popular is what we refer to as a *scoring rubric*. With such an approach, students often receive very general feedback (such as *superior* on grammar and mechanics and *poor* on persuasiveness), or they are rated according to a frequency or consistency metric (such as *occasionally* on "applying properties of operations as strategies to add and subtract rational numbers" and *rarely* on "applying properties of operations as strategies to multiply and divide rational numbers"). These methods, although they provide some specificity for scoring purposes, do not delineate what a student knows regarding the target content. Another potential problem with scoring scales is depicted in figure 1.7.

Performance Indicator	Develop and use a model to describe the function of a cell as a whole and ways parts of cells contribute to the function (MS-LS1-2; NGSS Lead States, 2013).		
EMERGING	**PROGRESSING**	**COMPETENT**	**EXEMPLARY**
The student can state the function of each organelle in a cell.	Using an illustration of a cell, the student can identify each cell structure and describe its functions.	The student can develop and use a model to describe the function of a cell as a whole and ways parts of cells contribute to the function.	The student can create real-world analogies for the function of a cell as a whole and ways parts of cells contribute to the function.

Figure 1.7: Scoring criteria for a performance indicator.

Although these scoring criteria provide some information about the content students should know (for example, the function of a cell and the ways parts of cells contribute to the function), the levels of the scale narrow the assessment options available to teachers. This is because the levels of the scale are stated as activities or assessments. For example, to demonstrate the *emerging* level, a student must "state the function of each organelle in a cell," whereas to demonstrate the *progressing* level, the student must use an illustration to identify the cell structures and then describe its functions. These activities do not define distinct knowledge or skill and, in fact, one might argue that using an illustration to identify cell structures might be an easier task than stating the function of cell structures without using an illustration.

The use of proficiency scales sets the foundation for this book's approach to teaching, learning, assessing, and measuring. As illustrated previously, a proficiency scale differs from a learning progression or a rubric: a scale explicitly defines and organizes the content knowledge and skills that a student must master at each level, whereas a scoring rubric communicates expectations of quality around a given task.

The proficiency scale creates a progression teachers can use to determine the current level of a student's knowledge and skill.

A proficiency scale also serves as an aid for planning instruction—students at different points along the learning progression (the scale) will engage in different instructional or learning activities. Using a series of frequent assessments (discussed in detail in chapter 4, page 97), teachers and individual students know at any given time where each student is on the scale and what content each student needs to learn in order to progress. In this way, the proficiency scale provides transparency of the learning targets, the student's current status, and next steps in the form of a learning continuum. There is no mystery as to what a student's current knowledge and skills are and what must be learned.

Summary

In this chapter, we discussed issues associated with the content that we will address in the PCBE system. We recommend that a PCBE system include traditional academic content (for example, English language arts, mathematics, and science), cognitive skills (skills we use to process information), and metacognitive skills (skills that help us perform mental and physical actions more effectively and efficiently). Schools that wish to implement a PCBE system must address the issue of too much academic content by prioritizing standards and creating a reasonable number of measurement topics for each grade or performance level. We suggest treating cognitive and metacognitive skills differently from academic content. Rather than teaching individual cognitive or metacognitive skills explicitly at each grade or performance level, we recommend dispersing these skills across the K–12 range within the context of specific subject areas. However, it is important to note that, just as with academic content, both cognitive and metacognitive skills require direct instruction. Finally, in this chapter we discussed learning targets (which articulate the specific knowledge and skills students must exhibit to demonstrate mastery of a measurement topic) and proficiency scales (which define a progression of knowledge and skills within a measurement topic). We recommend the use of proficiency scales as the foundation for teaching, learning, assessing, and measurement in a PCBE system. The next chapter addresses the learning environment in a PCBE classroom.

Chapter 2

How Will the Learning Environment Support Student Agency?

Transitioning to a PCBE system not only requires a shift in how teachers view content but also a shift in the way they view learning. For example, classroom management strategies common in a traditional system are often less effective in a PCBE system because they are based on the assumption that the teacher is responsible for and in charge of all teaching, learning, and assessment activities. In a PCBE system, students not only have the invitation but also the right to share in these responsibilities. We use the phrase "students have the right" to emphasize an important point about PCBE. Traditional K–12 education has placed students in a passive role within the classroom. They have virtually no say in what happens relative to teaching, learning, and assessment activities. It seems intuitively obvious that inviting students to provide input into these activities should enhance their engagement and teach valuable skills. The research and theory cited in the following discussion attest to this. However, we go one step further and assert that learners of all ages have the basic right to such input within an education system that is designed to maximize the potential of its constituents. A PCBE system, as described in this handbook, would ensure that right is honored.

One way of framing this necessary shift required for a competency-based system is through the lens of self-efficacy. At its core, *self-efficacy* involves the belief that one is ultimately in control of one's own life and the development of the accompanying skills to actualize this belief. This perspective might be the most important outcome that a formal education can provide to students. The importance of self-efficacy has been recognized for years. For example, reporting on studies they conducted in the 1990s, Dale H. Schunk and Frank Pajares (2005) noted that "despite the influence of mental ability, self-efficacy beliefs made a powerful and independent contribution to the prediction of performance" (p. 93). The construct of self-efficacy is closely related to many terms associated with PCBE systems, including *student agency*, which can be defined as "the capacity and propensity to take purposeful initiative—the opposite of helplessness" (Ferguson, 2015, p. 1). Reporting on "the influence of teaching on emotions, motivations, mindsets, and behaviors that we associate with agency," Ronald F. Ferguson (2015) similarly posited,

"The development of agency may be as important an outcome of schooling as the skills we measure with standardized testing" (p. 1).

The model presented in this book is founded on the assumption that PCBE must begin with student agency as a primary goal. PCBE systems that do not make student agency a primary focus run the risk of creating a process in which students progress through content levels in a rigid manner, rather than the intended flexible and personalized process. Learning the mindsets, behaviors, and skills associated with agency are both individual and group responsibilities. Strategies that can assist students in developing agency, as we'll discuss in this chapter, include establishing a system for setting and monitoring classroom goals; creating and using standard operating procedures; integrating student voice and choice into the teaching and learning process; and creating a more flexible physical environment.

Setting and Monitoring Classroom Goals

Establishing a system for setting and monitoring goals creates and sustains a classroom where students are more independent and less reliant on the teacher. This process can also help students connect to the school's shared vision and develop a sense of ownership for achieving the vision. Regardless of the PCBE system's schedule (see chapter 5, page 133 for a discussion), each student will have a primary association with one student reference group. This group might be the students who typically share the most common levels of performance. If this is not the case, the reference group might be akin to a traditional homeroom structure. Reference groups should employ the joint tasks described in this section, such as a homeroom in an elementary school or an advisory period in middle or high school. For example, in many traditional elementary schools, students stay in the same classroom all day. In a PCBE elementary school, students may have a homeroom and move to different classrooms for particular subjects. In this case, the processes described here might be carried out with the homeroom group. It is important to unpack the school's shared vision, set goals aligned with the shared vision, identify behavioral traits necessary to meet the classroom goals, create tools for measuring progress, and establish processes for setting goals, monitoring progress, and reflecting. In general, these activities send the strong message that students will have significant input into what occurs in the class. This is foundational to developing a sense of agency.

Unpack the School's Shared Vision

The reference group's first joint task is to unpack the school's shared vision. The term *unpack* in this context means working with students to more fully understand the meaning of the school's shared vision. Although students should have been engaged in the process of setting the shared vision (see chapter 7, page 171 for a discussion), exploring and connecting the language of the shared vision to classroom-level goals assist students in developing ownership of the vision. This process helps students define for themselves what their school experience should be like and provides them a voice in how the vision is enacted on a daily basis, as well as choice in how they will contribute to the vision. Teachers can facilitate the examining of the shared vision by reviewing the language of the vision and posing questions.

For example, an elementary school's shared vision might be worded as follows: Students will become lifelong learners in a supportive and inviting environment that promotes individualized learning and teamwork. Question prompts specific to this shared vision include the following.

- What does it mean to be a lifelong learner?

- Why should we be lifelong learners?

- How can my school support me as a learner?

- How can my teacher support me as a learner?

- How can we support each other as learners?

- What does good teamwork look like?

- How do I like to learn?

At the high school level, a school vision might be worded as follows: Students will engage in work they are passionate about to develop the knowledge, skills, and habits of mind necessary to succeed in college and careers, overcome obstacles to their well-being, and contribute positively to their communities. Questions specific to this vision include the following.

- What knowledge and skills are necessary to succeed in college?

- What knowledge and skills are necessary to succeed in careers?

- What are habits of mind, and how do they help us?

- What habits of mind do we want to develop in school?

- How can we contribute positively to our community?

Set Goals Aligned With the Shared Vision

The reference group answers the questions specific to the vision and generates ideas to craft a goal statement that is customized for the school's vision, their group, and the students' developmental level. For instance, the list of responses to questions about the purpose of school would be different for kindergarteners (for example, to learn, to make friends) than it would be for high school students (for example, to be prepared for college or the work force). Goal statements at various levels would therefore reflect the language and understanding that the students possess, such as the following.

- "In Ms. Smith's kindergarten class we will make friends, have fun, and learn together as a family."

- "Our class will be supportive learners and team players so we can master all the knowledge and skills of fourth grade so that we can succeed in fifth grade and beyond."

- "In biology we will strive to do our best, to collaborate with our peers, and to learn the knowledge, skills, and habits of mind to be successful in our daily lives, in college, and in our future jobs."

Identify Behavioral Traits Necessary to Meet the Classroom Goals

Once the students set classroom goals, the next step in implementing a goal-setting and monitoring system is to identify and prioritize the behavioral traits the class will monitor. This set of traits will become the *code of cooperation* (Langford, 2015), which defines how students will work together to achieve the classroom goals. Instead of instituting the common practice of dictating a set of rules that students must follow, teachers work with students to develop a list of traits or behaviors that, when consistently embraced, will help each student and the class as a whole achieve their goals. An *affinity diagram* can be useful in facilitating the list development. Using an affinity diagram involves asking guiding questions to gather input, brainstorming responses, clustering the responses into groups, and prioritizing each cluster.

Related to the previous elementary school example, teachers might ask questions like the following.

- "What words describe the qualities that would best help us reach our goals this year?"

- "How do supportive students act, think, and feel?"

- "How do team players act, think, and feel?"

- "What qualities do lifelong learners have?"

Related to the previous high school example, teachers might ask questions like the following.

- "What habits of mind do we need to develop so we can do our best?"

- "What are the qualities of good collaborators?"

- "What habits do we need to develop to be successful beyond high school?"

Next, students brainstorm qualities, traits, and behaviors in response to the questions. Sticky notes are useful tools for this step. It is important that every trait has its own sticky note and that students brainstorm individually so every student has an equal opportunity to generate ideas.

Student responses are processed using a chalkboard, whiteboard, SMART Board, or a large piece of chart paper. Students read and post their notes one by one. As each note is added, students who wrote down the same or similar ideas post their sticky notes near the first. Students continue in this manner until they have shared all notes.

Next, related ideas are clustered into a small number of groups or categories. Note that younger students may need assistance with this part of the process. When categories are established, students generate a heading that captures the essence of each cluster. The heading may or may not be one of the traits listed in the cluster. For example, if a cluster consisted of *dependable*, *honest*, and *dedicated*, students might choose a new heading of *reliable* or use one of the traits within the group such as *dependable*. An example of creating an affinity diagram is illustrated in figure 2.1.

Figure 2.1: Example of clusters within an affinity diagram.

Based on the way the students have clustered the information on the sticky notes in figure 2.1, they would create headings related to the groupings. For example, the cluster on the left might be labeled *active listening*. The middle cluster has a range of behaviors, and could be categorized as *respect*, while the rightmost cluster might have a heading of *perseverance*, *grit*, or *being a lifelong learner*. There are no wrong answers, as the goal is to capture terms and behaviors that are meaningful to the students. As such, the process should be student led, though the teacher may help students with new terminology or support them in their shared decision making if they need assistance.

With the clusters narrowed and titled, the teacher helps students to prioritize the most important three to five categories (if there are more than five). These traits become the code of cooperation for the class. Any more than five traits can become cumbersome for students to effectively monitor. Figure 2.2 (page 42) is an example of an elementary school's classroom code of cooperation. Figure 2.3 depicts a high school example.

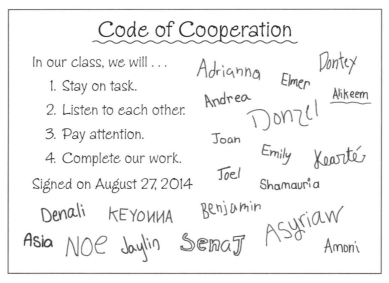

Figure 2.2: Elementary school code of cooperation.

SECOND BLOCK B DAY	WE WILL ACCOMPLISH OUR SHARED VISION BY:
In our English class, we strive to be the best versions of ourselves, and we will work together to prepare ourselves for the world so that we can accomplish anything.	Encouraging each other Having a growth mindset Trusting in ourselves Being honest Respecting each other

THIRD BLOCK B DAY	WE WILL ACCOMPLISH OUR GOALS BY:
In our English class, we strive for perfection, and we will work together to accomplish our goals so we can be successful.	Encouraging each other Having a growth mindset Being consistent Being willing to try Being resourceful

FIRST BLOCK	CODES OF COOPERATION	
We will graduate and move on.	Maturity	Positivity
Practice growth mindset.	Teamwork	Honesty
Apply the skills we learn here in our future.	Respect	Patience

Figure 2.3: High school classroom goals and codes of cooperation.

Create Tools for Measuring Progress

The next step in setting and monitoring classroom goals involves clarifying the proficiency criteria of each behavioral trait with students. Due to the complexity of behavioral norms, this process generally involves creating rubrics aligned with each trait. It is important to note that we are using the term *rubric* in reference to behaviors, whereas the term *proficiency scale* is applied to academic content as well as cognitive and metacognitive skills. As described in chapter 1 (page 11), rubrics have a much looser structure that allows teachers and students wider latitude with behaviors. More specifically, while we strongly recommend proficiency scales for content, rubrics are fine for behavioral areas.

Asking the following two questions can be helpful when developing rubrics for or with students.

1. Is this a tool the student can use to develop clarity of expectations, self-reflect, and accurately self-assess?

2. Does the wording articulate the student's growth in stages across a predetermined continuum?

Consider the example in figure 2.4 regarding self-control.

	SELF-CONTROL
4	I am on task and help my peers to get on task. I keep my hands, feet, and other items to myself. I listen to others instead of talking or doing other activities. I am a great role model.
3	I am on task 90 percent of the time. I keep my hands, feet, and other items to myself most of the time—90 percent or better. I listen most of the time.
2	I am sometimes on task—75 percent or better. I try to keep my hands, feet, and other items to myself—75 percent or better. I try to listen.
1	I need to work harder at being on task. I am not keeping my hands, feet, and other items to myself. I do not have good listening skills.

Figure 2.4: Sample behavior rubric.

The wording in figure 2.4 articulates the expectations and growth across the continuum and is written for student use, but it is not very useful for student self-assessment. The rubric uses percentages and describes behavior throughout an entire day, rather than providing students with concrete examples of what they should be doing at a particular moment in time. A better option is depicted in figure 2.5 (page 44).

Self-Control	4	3	2	1
	I am a role model for others.	I can do this myself, without reminders.	I have some success, with reminders.	My teacher is helping me on this goal.
On task	I can be a role model by: • Helping others • Predicting how we might use these skills later • Using my skills in new situations	I stay on task and stay focused on my work and class activities, including keeping my discussions on topic. I understand how being on task positively affects my learning and can give examples.	I know what being on task means. I still need reminders from my teacher.	I am learning what being on task means. I can practice this skill when my teacher helps me.
Keep to self	I can be a role model by: • Helping others • Predicting how we might use these skills later • Using my skills in new situations	I keep all my items, hands, and feet to myself and am respectful of the personal space of others. I understand how keeping to myself creates a better learning environment for everyone.	I know what keeping my items, hands, and feet to myself means. I still need reminders from my teacher.	I am learning what keeping my items, hands, and feet to myself means. I can practice this skill when my teacher helps me.
Active listening	I can be a role model by: • Helping others • Predicting how we might use these skills later • Using my skills in new situations	I keep my eyes on the speaker and my body calm while listening. I can repeat what a speaker has said. I understand how active listening helps me learn and makes others feel good.	I know what active listening is. I still need reminders from my teacher.	I am learning what active listening means. I can practice this skill when my teacher helps me.

Figure 2.5: Sample behavior rubric with concrete behavioral examples.

In figure 2.5, the individual components of self-control have been fleshed out in student-friendly language to add clarity. The continuum is focused on students developing the capacity to independently accomplish the behavioral expectations without any redirection or guidance from the teacher. It is easier for students to understand where they are on the rubric if it is tied to something tangible. At the score 1 level, there is active teacher facilitation and support. As the student moves along the continuum of the rubric, there is a shift from teacher regulation to student self-regulation. Figure 2.6 depicts another example of a behavior rubric that clarifies a class's code of cooperation for students.

Code of Cooperation Rubric	4	3	2	1
	I am a role model for others.	I can do this myself, without reminders.	I have some success, with reminders.	My teacher is helping me on this goal.
Have a growth mindset.	I use strengths to overcome weaknesses. I discuss with others how a growth mindset can help them approach challenges.	I apply a growth mindset to academic and social challenges.	I know what a growth mindset is. I need reminders to use a growth mindset to tackle obstacles.	I am learning about a growth mindset. I am working with others to use a growth mindset to approach obstacles.
Manage emotions.	I categorize emotions as frequent or infrequent and discuss reasons for emotions and strategies for dealing with them. I remind others to be aware of emotions in a nonconfrontational manner.	I know what type of reaction I am likely to have to various emotions. I recognize and cope with reactions in a variety of situations.	I understand and recognize different types of emotions and reactions. I need reminders to deal with reactions.	I am learning about different types of emotions and reactions. I am working with others to recognize emotions and reactions.
Be a team player.	I step up to be a leader. I take responsibility for actions. I model expectations for others.	I work hard to meet commitments. I follow through on assignments. I communicate with team members clearly and with respect. I help others.	I know what a team player needs to do. I need reminders to be an active participant and follow through on assignments. I need reminders to communicate with team members.	I am learning the roles and responsibilities of a team player. I am working with others to become a team player.

Figure 2.6: Sample behavior rubric that clarifies a class's code of cooperation.

Establish Processes for Using Monitoring Systems, Setting Goals, and Reflecting

Next, the teacher works with students to create a goal-setting and monitoring system that students use to record their progress, analyze their data, reflect and set goals targeting areas of improvement, and celebrate when their goals are reached. Goal setting and monitoring should occur at both the group and individual levels. That is, students should set and monitor goals as a class (for example, "Our class goal is to be at a score 3 for being on task by the end of the month"). Students should also set and monitor goals at the individual level (for example, "My goal is to be a score 4 for active listening this month"). Key questions that should drive this step include the following.

- What tools will students be capable of using to record scores on the behavioral traits?

- How will they track data longitudinally?

- How will they address goal setting?

- How will we include celebrations?

- Where and how will instruction take place?

Using Monitoring Systems

Monitoring systems should be simple enough for students to use independently, yet still contain the necessary information for self-reflection and growth. Consider the example in figure 2.7.

How did I do today? Be truthful. Be thoughtful.	October 19	October 20	October 21	October 22	October 23	October 26	October 27	October 28	October 29	October 30
Self-Control	2	2	2	3	2	2	3	3	2	3
Organization	1	1	1	2	1	2	2	1	2	2
Accountability	3	2	2	2	3	2	3	3	3	3
Respect	3	4	3	3	4	3	3	3	3	3
What have I mastered? I am doing well on respect.										
Where can I improve? I can do better on organization.										
What is my goal for the next two weeks? My goal is to be a 3 in organization.										

Figure 2.7: Sample behavioral data tracking system.

The third-grade student depicted in figure 2.7 has been tracking his scores on each area of the school-wide behavior norms, which would be defined in a behavior rubric (similar to that in figure 2.5 on page 44). Notice that the tracking form facilitates student reflection with two questions: (1) What have I mastered? and (2) Where can I improve? It also supports goal setting based on this reflection through the question, What is my goal for the next two weeks? Teachers and students should also analyze data over time to adjust when needed and celebrate improvements.

Setting Goals

Seeing longitudinal data like the example in figure 2.7 is extremely helpful for developing student agency. Notice the student sets a goal at the bottom of his tracking sheet to focus on an area (organization) in which his scores have been low. His teacher would meet with him about his goal and offer strategies for better organization. In this model, behavior becomes like any other area of learning—teachers help students build proficiency over time using clear objectives, strategies, modeling, and direct instruction when needed.

It is important to work with students to set classroom-level goals and individual goals. The classroom-level goals assist students in working together to accomplish specific objectives, while the individual goals assist students in developing self-efficacy and agency. That is, setting, working toward, and achieving individual goals assist students in developing confidence in their abilities to exert control over specific areas in their lives, such as motivations, behaviors, and the classroom environment.

As a secondary example, consider the student monitoring and goal-setting sheet in figure 2.8, which would accompany a behavior rubric such as the one in figure 2.6 (page 45). While referencing the code of cooperation rubric, students use the monitoring and goal-setting form to self-assess their progress each day. A similar goal-monitoring sheet can be used for tracking adherence to classroom goals or leadership goals (see figure 2.9, page 48).

Code of Cooperation Goal:	
How does your goal connect to the school's shared vision?	
Why do you need to work on this?	
What steps are you going to take to reach this goal?	

How are you doing? (Rate yourself daily using the code rubric.)						
Code	Monday	Tuesday	Wednesday	Thursday	Friday	Average
Have a growth mindset.						
Manage emotions.						
Be a team player.						

Evidence: Provide evidence for each day to support your self-rating.	
Monday	
Tuesday	

Figure 2.8: Sample monitoring and goal-setting sheet. continued →

Wednesday	
Thursday	
Friday	
Reflection: How did you do this week? What will you do next?	

Leadership Goal: During the month of January, we will reach a level 3 for *stay on task* on our code of cooperation.

At the end of each day, write the date in the box that shows how we performed on our leadership goal.

ADVANCED LEVEL 4	PROFICIENT LEVEL 3	DEVELOPING LEVEL 2	EMERGING LEVEL 1
1/22 1/28 1/30	1/15 1/29 1/16 1/27 1/20 1/23 1/21 1/26	1/13 1/26 1/14 1/22 1/19	1/12 1/18

Figure 2.9: Chart for monitoring adherence to a class leadership goal.

Reflecting

To monitor how the class as a whole is doing, at the end of each day, the teacher can ask students to fill out exit slips with their self-assessment scores. The teacher then collects their exit slips and examines student responses. Each day, the teacher places the average of the students' self-assessments in a tracking sheet next to the date (figure 2.10). The teacher can use the longitudinal data to celebrate successes or refocus the class's attention. If just a few students are causing issues, then the teacher establishes individual goals for those students.

Weekly monitoring for code of cooperation—Week of June 6						
CODE	**MONDAY**	**TUESDAY**	**WEDNESDAY**	**THURSDAY**	**FRIDAY**	**AVERAGE**
Have a growth mindset.	2.7	3.1	2.9	3.3		
Manage emotions.	2.5	2.6	2.4	2.3		
Be a team player.	2.8	2.6	3.0	3.2		

Figure 2.10: Weekly tracking chart for code of cooperation.

Notice that in figure 2.10, the class is tracking all three elements of the code of cooperation: (1) have a growth mindset, (2) manage emotions, and (3) be a team player. Alternatively, the class could select one of these behaviors to focus on, monitor, and track. As the school year progresses, the class may feel confident that they have mastered one or more elements in the code of cooperation and daily tracking may no longer be necessary. At this point, the teacher and students informally watch for issues—perhaps students have difficulty managing emotions around spring break, for example—and resume daily monitoring if any arise.

Again, to facilitate whole-class monitoring, students could submit their scores as exit slips. Another simple way to collect these data is to have students indicate their ratings each day by posting sticky notes or dots on chart paper or by using a marker on a whiteboard or laminated chart. This approach can be anonymous at first (to encourage sharing) and over time can lead to greater transparency and openness about progress toward goals. After students transfer their individual ratings from their monitoring and goal-setting sheets to the exit slips or the class chart, the teacher can compute and record class averages and lead discussions about each trait.

Creating and Using Standard Operating Procedures

Standard operating procedures (SOPs) are critical to establishing a classroom that promotes self-efficacy. SOPs are sets of step-by-step instructions that support students in independently achieving desired results for routines and procedures on a consistent basis. Since the teacher will not be the one controlling the pace in a PCBE classroom, students use SOPs to move through the content instead of relying heavily on whole-group instruction. This means students must bear a great deal of the responsibility for behaviors and actions traditionally managed solely by the teacher. For example, in a PCBE classroom, students must be aware of their performance levels on specific proficiency scales and plan their next steps to improve their performance. Developed SOPs give students explicit guidance and directions to assume these responsibilities, which, in turn, helps students develop a heightened sense of independence and agency, even in the primary grades.

Creating an SOP involves the following four steps.

1. Identify common inefficiencies that frequently require redirection, reminder, or more time than necessary.

2. Prioritize these based on need.

3. Determine the complexity and type of procedure. Does it require a procedural list or a flowchart?

4. Develop schoolwide and classroom procedures with student input.

There are a few critical SOPs that teachers should create for any PCBE system, including variations that address what to do if students are having difficulty on a particular topic or task. The purpose of this SOP is to gradually build student self-efficacy and to teach students to be more independent in their learning. At the beginning, a teacher might start with a procedure that has just a few steps. Figure 2.11 shows such an SOP, in which the student is required to ask a peer helper before asking the teacher during learning center time.

LEARNING CENTER SOP

Figure 2.11: Sample SOP for when a student is having difficulty.

Over time, the teacher would increase the SOP complexity, as depicted in figures 2.12 and 2.13 (pages 51–52). With these examples, the students are required to accomplish many more steps prior to seeking help from the teacher. These examples increase the complexity of the expectations by giving students more than one way to solve a problem prior to seeking support from the teacher. Like all procedures, they would have to be taught and practiced.

When a teacher introduces a new procedure, the teacher should observe students for a couple of days to see how they handle it. If the students are managing well on their own then the teacher can continue its use, but if a majority of the class is struggling with the procedure, the teacher can make necessary adjustments. In some cases, a teacher might take individual students over to the SOP explanation and walk them through it, using guided instruction to help students figure out which steps they skipped. Finally, teachers might also employ peer-to-peer instruction or peer helpers (the teacher would identify students who are meeting or exceeding the procedural expectations and ask those students to help struggling students).

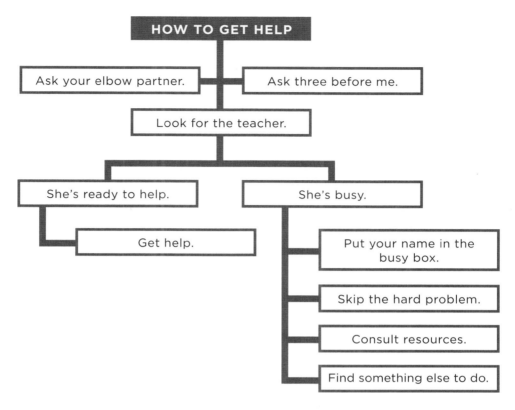

Figure 2.12: Sample advanced SOP for when a student is having difficulty.

MATHEMATICS MASTERY SOP	
STEPS	**DETAILS AND OPTIONS**
Get materials.	Data notebook, iPad, pencil
What am I trying to master today?	Check the SMART Board for my standard and level.
Practice!	Play a game from the Standard Bin.
	Work with Ms. M in a small group.
	Watch video from class website or Khan Academy.
How can I show what I know?	Completed work
	My mathematics pages
	Pictures of my dry-erase board work
	PicCollage (https://pic-collage.com)
	Educreations (www.educreations.com)
	Videos
I think I'm ready to master this!	Sign up for a conference with Ms. M.
	Take a post-test.

Figure 2.13: Mathematics mastery SOP. continued →

I thought I was ready, but I need more time.	Small-group instruction
	More practice
	Gather evidence.
Woo-hoo! I mastered the standard!	Mark proficient level on your learning plan.
	Go to Celebration Station!
	Fill out goal medal.
	Move your name on the SMART Board to "Mastered."
	Take a pretest on the next standard.

Eventually, SOPs that promote learning independence morph into related topics such as what students should do when they finish early. Figure 2.14 depicts such an SOP. Notice that the word *teacher* is not even mentioned in this SOP, as more responsibility is placed on the students themselves.

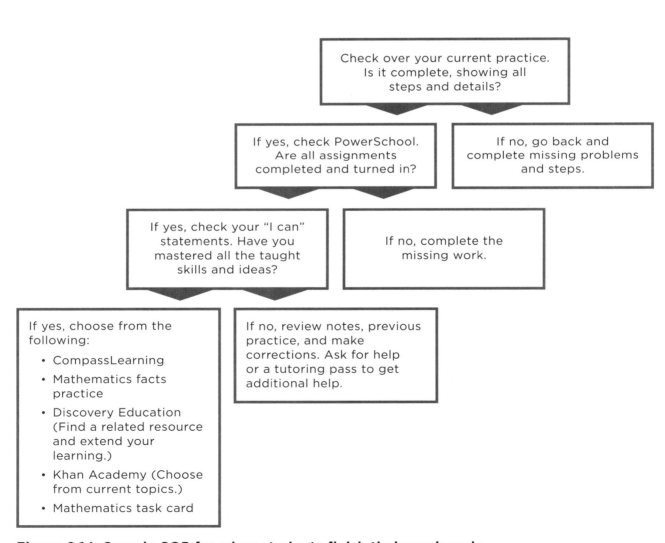

Figure 2.14: Sample SOP for when students finish their work early.

PCBE schools and classrooms should be continually updating or adding to their SOPs. The following list includes examples of commonly used SOPs.

- How to properly check out books
- What to do when done
- What to do when stuck
- When to include peer or teacher conferencing
- How to properly ask to get a drink
- How to properly sign out for bathroom breaks
- Learning center activities
- Attend a writing, reading, or mathematics workshop
- Define hallway expectations
- Communicate expectations for group work
- Get ready for and leave class

- Learn to use computers or other devices
- Troubleshoot common computer issues
- Establish bus routines
- Work in common areas
- Eat in the cafeteria
- Use equipment for special activities (physical education, science, music, art, and so on)
- Access websites or digital resources
- Log into the computer
- Deliver a sincere apology
- Use strategies for calming down
- Develop routines for the playground or recess
- Set goals

There are two basic formats for SOPs: (1) procedural lists and (2) flowcharts. Within each format, a classroom might have behavioral SOPs that address behaviors and classroom processes (for example, lining up for recess or resolving conflicts respectfully) and academic SOPs for completing content-specific activities and assignments (for example, how to pick a book or how to determine slope). The following sections will discuss these SOP formats in more detail.

Procedural Lists

A procedural list articulates simple sequential steps. Teachers often design these SOPs for situations when safety or compliance are essential (for example, in non-negotiable areas, like bus routines), when multiple solutions are not necessary (for example, hand washing), when students need a list of actionable items (for example, what to bring to class), or when there is a need for reminders (for example, how to dock the computers before leaving class). The purpose of the SOP should be to clarify expectations, increase independence and self-monitoring, solve existing problems or inefficiencies, or prevent potential problems or inefficiencies.

Use the following steps to design a procedural list: (1) determine a sequence of steps, (2) create a visual representation in an easy-to-understand format (using pictures or symbols if necessary for prereaders), and (3) ensure comprehension and compliance with regular practice and monitoring. Students will have greater levels of ownership and understanding if they are active participants in creating SOPs. The following scenario illustrates building an SOP with primary students.

A kindergarten teacher learns that he will be receiving a set of iPads for his class. Knowing the high potential for damage, misuse, or misunderstanding, he gathers the students for a meeting to brainstorm potential pitfalls and identify steps to avoid these issues. The students identify that damaging the iPads could be a serious problem. Instead of telling the students what they will do and how they will handle them, the teacher asks questions like, "When might the iPads get broken? What activities might you be doing that would be dangerous for iPads?" The students realize that moving with the iPads could potentially lead to dropping them or hitting them on something. They devise a four-step procedural list for safely carrying the iPad.

1. Grip the iPad on either end with two hands.

2. Position your hands so that your thumbs grip the side of the iPad that is facing your body and your fingers grip the side facing away from your body.

3. Hold the iPad in front of you, chest high.

4. Always walk and pay attention.

The teacher jots down their steps and illustrates with simple cartoons as they talk. They devise a second five-step procedural list for general iPad use based on the other potential problems.

1. Make sure your hands are clean.

2. Touch the screen gently.

3. Use only approved apps.

4. Follow the iPad Carrying SOP when moving.

5. Store and charge the iPad correctly.

Once teachers and students have developed and agreed on an SOP, the students can then practice until they approach or achieve mastery. In the case of the iPads, note that before the students used the devices, they helped create SOPs, so that when they received their devices, they clearly understood how to handle them responsibly. Once the students received the iPads, pictures of them correctly following the procedures could be displayed on an SOP chart to illustrate correct application. The next step in this kindergarten class might be to set goals and monitor the iPad SOPs. As students perfect the skills, goal achievement celebrations might take place, as well as taking down the SOP chart from the wall when students no longer need to refer to it. Teachers might store mastered SOPs in a binder in case new students arrive, so their classmates can show them the procedures.

A strong SOP can add learning time to the schedule. Consider the following high school example.

A high school science teacher notices in the first week of school that she has to repeatedly remind students what to bring to class and what to do when they first arrive. She notes that they frequently lose time because students leave critical items at home, forget to turn in work, and chat with others instead of getting ready for learning. Keeping a stopwatch in her pocket, she clocks the time it takes her students to prepare for instruction with minimal reminders from her. She keeps track for four days and on the fifth day, she calls attention and projects a graph of the data on the board. She explains the graph and has students figure out the average time it takes for them to get prepared for learning. The students determine that it takes nine minutes on average. The teacher then asks them to calculate how much time would be lost over the course of the remaining 167 days of school. The students are awed by the fact that they would spend more than twenty-five hours just getting ready for class if they continued their current behavior. They agree that their current habits waste time and are open to a problem-solving session on efficiency.

The teacher divides the students into teams and has each team create an arrival SOP that outlines everything students need to do when they first arrive: what they will need for class, how to turn in work, where to store their materials, and so on. Each group shares its SOP and displays it on the wall. The teacher then numbers each SOP and has every student vote on his or her favorite by writing down its number on a sticky note.

After the teacher posts the chosen SOP, the teacher asks the class to set a reasonable goal for the next week based on the data she shared. The students choose to decrease the time it takes to get ready for class each day to five minutes or less. If they are successful, the teacher tells them that as a celebration, they will receive five of the minutes back on Friday at the end of class to do what they want, within reason—perhaps chat, surf the web, explore an interest, or play a quick game.

In this example, even with the time reward, the teacher will gain back significant instructional time each week. Another noteworthy factor from this example is that the teacher worked to achieve student buy-in from the beginning. Rather than setting rules and punishing students for not following them, the teacher worked to help the students understand the problem by showing them real data and then asking them to create the procedures, set the goals, and celebrate their achievements. This process creates a classroom culture in which the students are an integral part of the decision-making process.

Teachers and students can also create procedural lists related to content. For example, a high school art teacher might work with her students to develop an SOP for reviewing a drawing when it doesn't look like they want it to. As figure 2.15 (page 56) shows, the SOP takes students through a series of steps to analyze their drawings before asking the teacher for help. Students might use the SOP to review on their own or work with a partner to go through the steps. This SOP supports student self-reflection and can help them plan next steps to improve their work.

SOMETHING'S WRONG WITH MY DRAWING!
☐ Check contours. Are your outside edges accurate?
☐ Check the negative space (the shape of the space between objects).
☐ Check proportions. Are your objects the right size relative to one another?
☐ Check the tones. Squint at your reference (still life, photo, and so on) and then at your drawing. Do you see the same amount of contrast between your tones? Are the shapes of your shadows the same?

Figure 2.15: Sample SOP for problem solving in art class.

Flowcharts

Teachers can use flowcharts when there are multiple solutions to a problem (for example, common classroom computer issues), when there are multiple choices that do not have to progress in a certain order (for example, during learning center activities), when you can apply if-then statements (for example, *if* you are finished, *then* read a book), or when you can use yes-no questions (for example, Are you stuck?). (Learning centers are discussed in chapter 3. Briefly though, they are locations where students work independently or in small groups on activities that help them better understand the content in a specific measurement topic.) It is important to note that procedural lists can have pictures and graphics to illustrate them, but this does not make them flowcharts. Rather, flowcharts depict a sequence of decision making or information processing.

Use the following five steps to design a flowchart.

1. Begin with a title or question that guides the reader to the next steps.

2. Use yes-no prompts to create multiple pathways and outcomes.

3. Develop internal loops cued by questions to define accountability steps (for example, Do you have evidence of mastery? Did you get your teacher to sign off?).

4. Create closure or a repetitive "begin again" step.

5. Ensure comprehension and compliance with regular practice and monitoring.

As with procedural lists, flowcharts might address behaviors or content. To illustrate the process of creating a flowchart with students, consider the following example.

A second-grade teacher is spending time monitoring her students' book choices during silent reading time. She wants them to be able to independently make appropriate choices, so she gathers them together and they devise a flowchart to help.

The teacher asks them what the title of the flowchart should be, and the students propose "Choosing a Good Book," which the teacher writes at the top of the whiteboard. She asks the students what strategies they should use when choosing a book, and they list different ideas. The teacher jots these down on the whiteboard. The students come up with three main ideas: (1) interest, (2) Lexile level, and (3) readability. The teacher asks, "Which one of these would be the most helpful to us when we're choosing a good book for ourselves?" The students vote on the appropriate Lexile level. The teacher writes "Do I know my Lexile level?" underneath the title. She draws two arrows downward, one indicating "Yes" and one indicating "No." As she continues questioning the students, the teacher elicits the strategies they have learned for choosing a book that is both interesting and appropriately challenging until their flowchart resembles that in figure 2.16.

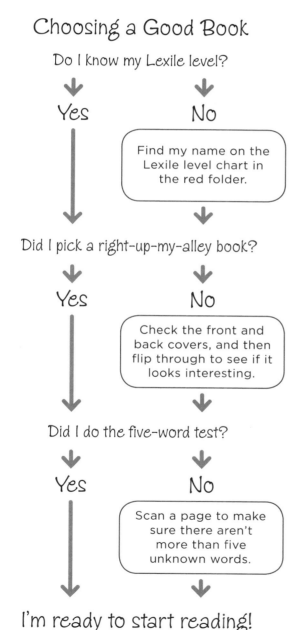

Figure 2.16: Elementary school flowchart.

Flowcharts can serve a wide variety of processes. To illustrate, consider the secondary flowchart in figure 2.17 (page 58) that helps students determine what they missed during an absence. Note that the example in figure 2.17 doesn't follow the traditional rules of flowcharts whereby specific shapes mean different things. Of course, teachers could follow those guidelines if they so desire or if it serves a real-world purpose (such as to mimic a technical manual), but it is also legitimate to be less rigid. Flowcharts can serve a wide variety of purposes, from emotional well-being (for example, how to use anger management strategies) to independently navigating learning (for example, what to do when you encounter common mathematics obstacles).

Using SOPs allows students to exercise their agency within basic classroom processes. We will now discuss how teachers can help students make decisions and provide feedback about their learning.

Integrating Student Voice and Choice Into the Teaching and Learning Process

Exercising voice and choice gives students control within the teaching and learning environment. Educators frequently mention voice and choice, two vitally important aspects of the

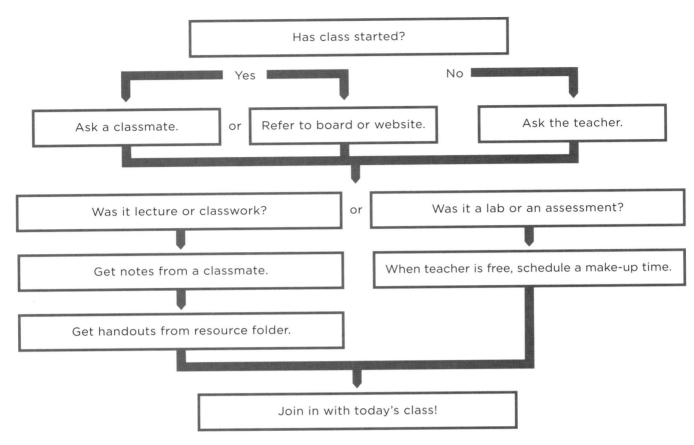

Figure 2.17: Sample secondary flowchart to determine missed work.

PCBE classroom, but there are often many problems with their implementation. Teachers often lump the terms *voice* and *choice* together in conversations about student agency. Though connected, each offers distinct opportunities and has unique effects on students. *Voice* means that adults in the school are providing all students with authentic opportunities for input and feedback regarding cultural and academic issues. *Choice* means that students make decisions or select alternatives during the learning process. Teachers can use the following guidelines to determine whether they are addressing student voice and choice adequately.

- **Follow through:** Act on student suggestions. Soliciting ideas only to ignore or do nothing with the input will break trust with students and might make them feel their teachers do not value their input.

- **Choose wisely:** Given that teachers should act on student suggestions, teachers should only select areas for student input that they are willing to change.

- **Be transparent:** Inevitably, there will be situations in which a teacher tries to implement student suggestions but then finds that they are simply not viable. In such cases, teachers should simply explain to students that the changes are not viable anymore and must be dropped or amended. Such candor allows students to admit their mistakes or make changes in their perspectives.

- **Start small:** Even small amounts of voice and choice can be significant and impactful to students. Teachers should stay within their comfort zone but work to gradually increase the limits of that zone.

Voice

Voice is an important aspect of a PCBE classroom because it helps students recognize that they are integral members of the learning environment—that teachers value their ideas and opinions. Teachers can incorporate student voice by providing students with opportunities to give feedback on academic and cultural issues in the classroom.

For example, academic issues frequently relate to class content and instruction. Students can provide feedback on a range of areas, including assessment, teacher instruction style, assignment types, unit organization, and learning topics. One way to demonstrate the impact of student voice is for teachers to keep track of student feedback over a quarter or semester. Teachers and students then might review this feedback, noting significant changes in response to it.

Cultural issues are the aspects of the classroom that relate to student behavior and environment. In particular, the classroom culture often reflects the values of the students and teachers, the class's approaches to learning and growth, and both the students' and teachers' treatment of one another. Students can provide feedback on how they perceive the classroom culture as a whole, such as what they think they do well as a class and things they can improve. For example, a teacher could provide voice by challenging students to consider which behaviors reflect an ideal culture of learning and ways that students can alter their behavior so that the culture is safe and productive for all.

There are a number of tools that provide voice, including the following.

- **Affinity diagram:** The affinity diagram is an input-gathering and processing tool to collect ideas and group them according to categories, with the final step being prioritizing by vote to narrow the list (see figure 2.1, page 41).

- **Digital platforms:** There are a variety of digital platforms (Padlet, Edmodo, and so on) available for teachers and students to gather and share input from different members.

- **Parking lot:** As the example in figure 2.18 (page 60) shows, the parking lot (Langford, 2015) is an input tool typically divided into four categories: (1) things that are going well (symbolized by a plus sign), (2) opportunities for improvement (symbolized by a delta or triangle), (3) questions (symbolized by a question mark), and (4) ideas (symbolized by a light bulb or lightning bolt). Teachers can use this tool in general terms (the overall class environment and content) or with a focused question or purpose (for example, behavior during recess this morning).

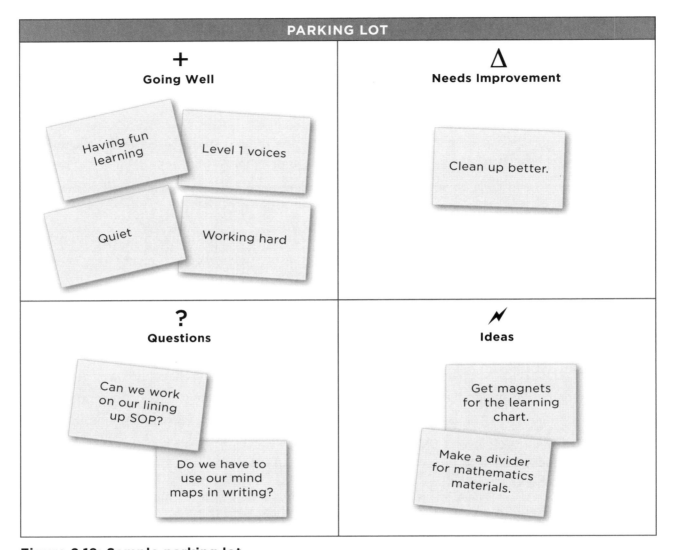

Figure 2.18: Sample parking lot.

- **Plus or delta:** This tool is a modified version of the parking lot tool. Students simply focus on pluses (what's going well) and deltas (what needs to be improved) regarding a current activity.

- **Exit slips:** Offered in a variety of formats, exit slips or tickets are a chance to get individual feedback from all students on a topic. They can be used as a quick formative assessment of learning, a way to get input about the classroom culture, a self-reflection on the day, and so on. Figure 2.19 depicts an exit slip that includes a plus column and a delta column. Students write comments in the plus (what's going well), delta (what needs to be improved), or both sections of the exit slip. For example, in the plus section a student might write, "The vocabulary game we played was really fun, and it helped me review some things." In the delta section, that same student might write, "I think we need better rules to help us get along better when we are working in teams."

Class Meeting Exit Slip	
Vision: We want to learn, have fun, and make friends.	
Code of Cooperation: Respect, Responsibility, and Safety	

Topics:	
Activities Completed:	

PLUS	DELTA

Exit slips are due each Friday.	

Figure 2.19: Sample class meeting exit slip.

- **Interactive notebooks:** Designed in a variety of formats and for a variety of purposes, the interactive notebook can be used for dialogue between students and teachers or parents and teachers with the goal to share information. As depicted in figure 2.20, interactive notebooks contain places for teacher comments and parent or student comments.

DATE	TEACHER COMMENTS	PARENT SIGNATURE	PARENT COMMENTS
November 10	Hannah is showing great determination in her writing.	John Doe	She thought she was not a strong writer, but is changing her thinking now.
December 9	Hannah has great scores this week!	Jane Doe	Yes, she does. We are very proud!
December 16	Hannah has been working especially hard on the editing process.	Jane Doe	
January 6	Reviewed Hannah's writing with her. We are hoping to check the work daily to see where she can make improvements.	John Doe	Hannah says she enjoys the time you are giving her to work on her writing. Thank you.

Figure 2.20: Sample interactive notebook entries.

- **Brainstorming:** Brainstorming is a tool to gather input from a group verbally or in writing. People generally brainstorm to get as many ideas as possible on a given subject or topic. When using brainstorming processes, teachers should provide opportunities and a safe space for all students to contribute.

- **Class meetings:** This tool can involve an organized approach structured by SOPs, or it can be an informal affair; in either case, meetings can serve as a chance for groups to gather and discuss their problems, successes, and needs on a regular basis.

Choice

There are obvious connections between voice and choice, but there are also important distinctions. Whereas voice involves authentic opportunities for input and feedback in cultural and academic areas, choice involves authentic opportunities to select alternatives within the social, environmental, and learning domains.

The *social domain* is any situation where there is interaction with other people. For example, a teacher may provide choice in a service learning project by allowing students to group themselves based on their interests or the community concerns they wish to address. In the digital age, this area has exploded in terms of opportunities, as the traditional brick-and-mortar school is no longer the sole source of interaction students may have with others. With digital tools, students can now network with people all over the globe.

The *environmental domain* is any space where students are situated and may be physical, virtual, or contrived. The physical space may be the classroom itself or any area within or around the school, but it may also be other physical environments involved during any step of the learning process (for example, a local business, the home, or a museum). Virtual spaces are any nonphysical areas students and teachers access through technology where students can share information or ideas (such as social media platforms or virtual worlds). Contrived environments may involve either physical or virtual aspects, but are created for specific purposes, usually on a more temporary basis. For example, if a debate is taking place in class, the physical arrangement of the classroom might change to better reflect a real debate, or a digital forum might be created that mimics a newsfeed where students post current events during a social studies unit. Teachers can incorporate choice by allowing students to vote or give input on the arrangement of the physical space of the classroom.

The *learning domain* is any situation in which students may access, practice, or prove mastery of any knowledge or skill in the curriculum. Students may access information through their classroom teacher either physically or virtually, through other students or teachers either physically or virtually, or from physical or digital support materials and resources. Students may prove mastery through innumerable physical or virtual acts serving as forms of assessment. One way that a teacher could incorporate choice into the learning domain is by allowing students to select which topic in a unit they would like to study first.

As with voice, there are a number of tools that teachers can use to provide choice.

- **Power voting:** This tool can come in different formats, such as Hot Dots or Spend a Dollar. The purpose is to allow students to prioritize their vote by offering multiple votes to be used in whatever way indicates their highest preferences. For example, in Spend a Dollar, students are given four votes, each worth twenty-five cents. They might choose to spend their four votes all on one item of particular importance or spread their votes out among several items. The example in figure 2.21 shows the results of a class power voting on specific animals they want to learn about in science.

Marsupials (kangaroo, koala, Tasmanian devil, wombat, opossum)	
Rodents (squirrel, marmot, prairie dog, rat, mouse)	
Primates (gorilla, ape, orangutan, baboon)	
Carnivores (wolf, fox, coyote, raccoon, wolverine)	

Figure 2.21: Power voting.

- **Choice boards:** Typically with nine squares like a tic-tac-toe board, students can pick from choices offered in each square. Boards can be customized to meet a variety of needs, such as homework options, standards or learning goals, and so on.

- **Choice menus:** Similar to choice boards, menus are set up according to different offerings. For example, *appetizers* might be introductory content and *main course* offerings might be for proficiency-level content, with *dessert* offering extra activities or extensions.

- **Preference surveys:** Teachers can gather information about student interests and preferences for how they like to learn through a variety of survey formats and utilize that information in grouping or content.

- **Interactive activity charts:** Students interact with a chart that offers multiple options and move their names, icons, or numbers to their choices.

- **Digital platforms:** Students utilize platforms such as TeacherTube (www.teachertube.com), SAFARI Montage (www.safarimontage.com), or Khan Academy (www.khanacademy.org) to access instruction or activities aligned with their target of study.

- **Must-do and may-do lists:** Students are given a set of choices, with the must-do list covering the expectations all students must complete and the may-do list offering a variety of choices for after the must-do list is finished. You can see an example of this tool in figure 2.22 (page 64).

Standard: Determine a central idea of a text and how it is conveyed through particular details; provide a summary of the text distinct from personal opinions or judgments. (RI.6.2)	
Student-Friendly Standard: I can find the main idea for my book, find important details and tell how they support the main idea, and write a summary of the book whether I liked it or not.	
Must Do You MUST complete all of these.	**May Do** You MAY CHOOSE to complete two of these.
Unpack the standard. Read a nonfiction informational book (make sure it's on your "just right" reading level). Create a main idea and details graphic organizer. Write a summary. Take the Accelerated Reader (AR) test for your book.	Watch a BrainPOP video on main idea and take the quizzes. Choose a nonfiction comprehension task card to read and complete. Read a nonfiction article in a magazine or newspaper and identify the main idea and important details.

Source for standard: NGA & CCSSO, 2010a.

Figure 2.22: Middle school English language arts choice example.

- **Task cards:** A task card is simply a card that lists a task or learning activity for students to complete. We recommend that each activity on a task card be associated with a score 2.0, 3.0, or 4.0 learning target from a specific proficiency scale. Depending on the type of task or activity, the task card may provide simple short-answer or multiple-choice questions that help students practice a skill, or it may include instructions for a longer activity. A teacher can provide a set of task cards for proficiency scales that students are currently working on. When they finish early or when they have independent working time, students can select a task card for a skill they need practice on, or for a proficiency scale they need to review for an upcoming assessment. Task cards may be self-contained activities, or they may direct students to another resource, such as the learning management system or Google Docs. Teachers can use task cards with individual students, with small groups, or in large-group activities (for example, as a quick formative assessment to get a snapshot of where students are on a particular topic). Some task cards might be labeled *challenge* cards for students who want ideas and activities to push themselves to achieve score 4.0 targets.

Authentic voice and choice create an atmosphere that sends direct messages to students regarding the invitation and the need for them to take some responsibility for their own learning.

Creating a More Flexible Physical Environment

As in every other aspect of the PCBE classroom, the traditional one-size-fits-all approach shifts to a more individualized approach. In the environmental area, this shift involves offering a variety of seating options, changing the structure of the environment as a whole, utilizing technology to expand the learning environment beyond the classroom, and offering alternative environments in which to learn.

The physical environment of the classroom can facilitate or hamper the development of student agency. For this reason, it deserves special emphasis. However, before making significant changes to the physical environment of a classroom, teachers may want to survey their students to see which aspects of the environment could be improved. For instance, a teacher might want to change the seating in her classroom to improve students' motivation and focus in class. She would provide a survey that asks students what kinds of seating they prefer, if they each want their own desk and chair, and if they would like a variety of seating options in the classroom. If the survey results indicate that the students are very excited about having a variety of seating choices, the teacher might reorganize the classroom to eliminate assigned individual desks. Changes like these often positively impact students' levels of excitement for and mindsets about learning. The decision-making process also empowers students, and they may feel a more personal connection to the classroom environment. Figures 2.23 and 2.24 (page 66) illustrate examples of traditional and reorganized classrooms.

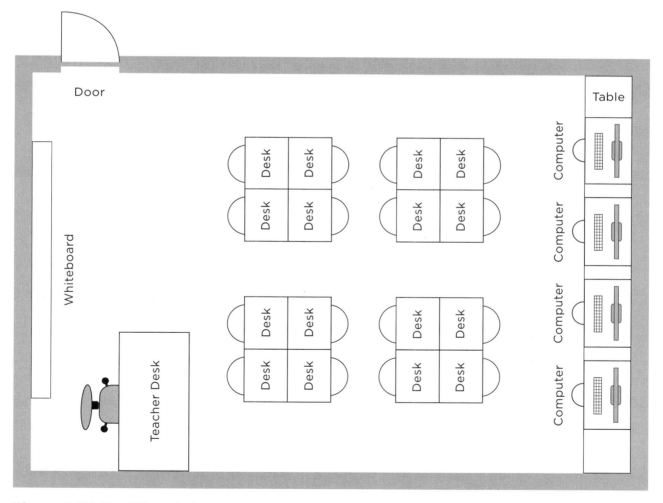

Figure 2.23: Traditional classroom setup.

Note that in figure 2.24, desks are removed, a much larger space is available in the center of the classroom, and students have a variety of places to work. Hard-seated traditional chairs have been replaced with comfortable couches, yoga balls, and various soft-seated chair options, with many easy to shift to an area of choice or need. Students using clipboards and iPads can sit on the plush rugs and couches and in nooks around the room. With more room to gather, students are able to circle up, collaborate, and exercise if need be. This classroom is one example of a possible shift in learning environment; teachers and students can be as creative as they wish with an innumerable variety of options.

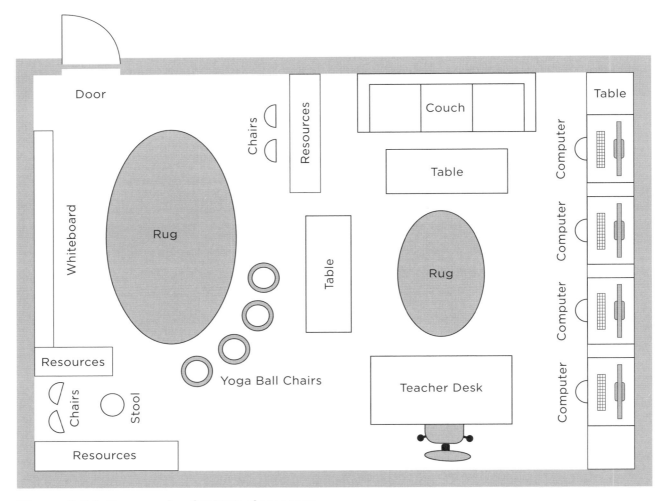

Figure 2.24: Reorganized PCBE classroom.

When developing a flexible classroom environment, teachers should use SOPs to maximize its effectiveness. In figure 2.25, students follow a furniture SOP to respectfully utilize the different options. If students are afforded other areas outside the classroom to work or collaborate, developing SOPs and support tools is also helpful. Figure 2.26 depicts an example of an independent work contract that high school students complete to work in areas outside the regular classroom. The students are offered various areas within the school environment to work, indicated in the upper right-hand corner. They fill out the measurement topics they are working on and what they will be doing, with areas for the teacher to assign times for students to return.

Furniture SOP

When you are done, put it back where you found it.

Only iPads, data binders, clipboards, and books on the seats.

Use and sit in seats and on furniture correctly.

Only touch things that are furniture (no decorations)!

Figure 2.25: Furniture SOP.

Student:	Location:
Assigning Teacher (Signature):	• Commons • Copy Area • Cubicle
Advisor:	• Meeting Room • Media Room
Measurement Topics:	
Timeline: Start: _____ Due Date: _____ If outside of classroom, time due back: _____	
Activities or Tasks:	

Figure 2.26: Independent work contract.

When designing the physical environment in a PCBE classroom, teachers should consider the following questions.

- What resources are available to create a flexible environment?

- How will I gather and utilize student input?

- What issues might arise when implementing a flexible environment, and how might teachers address them prior to deployment?

- What other areas might be available within the school for students, and what supports will students need to ensure success?

- Where and when will choice be afforded to students, and how will teachers handle infringements?

- How might technology support a flexible environment?

- How can teachers meet various learning styles and needs within the environment to create the most equity?

- How can the physical layout support student collaboration, individual learning spaces, and teacher-student interaction?

As with offering voice and choice in any area, it is important to keep in mind that every teacher has a different level of comfort and desire in terms of implementation. Not every classroom needs to include personalized learning furniture or a large variety of seating choice options to have an impact. The focus should be on discussing with students what options would be meaningful to them and seeking solutions as a class to best meet the needs of the group within the parameters that the teacher or school has set.

Summary

This chapter discussed ways the learning environment can promote student agency—that is, the learning environment should support students' having an active and meaningful role in their learning. We assert that a primary goal of a PCBE system should be to promote student agency, and we provided numerous practical strategies for creating this type of learning environment. These strategies included setting and monitoring goals, using standard operating procedures that support student independence, providing voice and choice to students, and creating a physical environment conducive to independent learning. The next chapter addresses how instruction in a PCBE system supports student learning.

Chapter 3

How Will Instruction Support Student Learning?

Perhaps the best way to understand instruction in a PCBE system is to contrast it with instruction in a traditional system. To illustrate the traditional system, consider a fifth-grade science teacher. She organizes her instruction in units. At the beginning of each unit, she communicates the intended outcomes as learning targets and posts them on the whiteboard. She then introduces new knowledge to students through direct instruction. As students start to develop content grounding, the teacher inserts other lessons designed to deepen students' understanding of concepts or allow them to practice their fluency with skills and processes. Near the end of the unit, the teacher presents students with more challenging tasks that require them to apply their knowledge in novel situations. Along the way, she administers quizzes and tests, and records scores in the gradebook along with points for homework. When the unit ends, a new one begins and the same processes are repeated. As this example illustrates, in a traditional classroom almost all instruction is geared toward the class as a whole. At any point in time, every student is probably working on the same activity and the same topic, and those who have difficulty or are working at a slower pace are given a lower grade to acknowledge the missed content. The whole class then moves on to the next scheduled topic.

In a PCBE classroom, the instructional dynamic is quite different. First and foremost, students will be working on different topics at any one point in time. To illustrate, consider a fourth-grade classroom that has twenty measurement topics with associated proficiency scales that constitute the content for that level. As described in chapter 1 (page 11), teachers generate these topics by unpacking standards and identifying the critical content. Some students might be working on topic 7, while others are working on topic 8, and still others are working on topic 12. Additionally, students will continually be looping back to those topics for which they have not yet demonstrated proficiency (that is, reached score 3.0 status). In effect, in a PCBE system, the whole class is not treated as a homogeneous group.

To make things even more complex, student grouping is intimately tied to scheduling, which we address in chapter 5 (page 133). Depending on grouping practices, there can be a wide variation in the number of topics teachers address in a given classroom. To illustrate, consider the following two scenarios.

One scenario involves a traditional system in which a school groups students in classes based on their age. For example, a mathematics teacher might be working with a class of sixth graders; however, there are students at the fifth-, sixth-, and seventh-grade levels in the topics on which they need instruction, even though they are all at the sixth-grade level chronologically. This situation imposes a heavy workload on PCBE teachers, because they would have to tailor their teaching toward three different proficiency levels, instead of just one.

In a second scenario, a school places students in classes based on their individual needs according to measurement topics. For example, based on diagnostic information obtained from classroom assessments, teachers identify students who need to finish the measurement topics for the end of fifth-grade mathematics and start working on sixth grade-mathematics in the upcoming school year. Teachers place them in a mathematics class that addresses that material, regardless of their age. With this method of grouping, the range of topics the teacher covers is dramatically reduced. As mentioned previously, there are many variations to grouping and scheduling students. Find more details and examples around scheduling in chapter 5 (page 133). The critical point here is that the structure of a PCBE system requires rethinking instruction.

Although it may seem daunting at first to move away from the traditional model, after the initial preparation is complete, a PCBE system can reduce the difficulty of in-classroom work for teachers and enhance the learning experience of students. In fact, in our experience, many teachers report that once they get used to the PCBE approach, they find the teaching process much more rewarding. This chapter aims to guide teachers through the process of preparing for a PCBE classroom. It will firstly introduce instructional strategies teachers can use in a PCBE classroom, including techniques for foundational, weekly, and daily planning to assist first-time PCBE teachers in implementing this system in their classroom. It will then discuss designing personal tracking matrices, working with students to unpack learning targets and proficiency scales, and planning instruction in a PCBE system.

Instructional Strategies

Instruction in a PCBE classroom employs many traditional classroom strategies, but executes them in different ways. There are nine dimensions of the PCBE classroom that compare with the traditional classroom: (1) whole-class instruction, (2) small-group instruction, (3) individual instruction, (4) peer-to-peer instruction, (5) external instructional resources, (6) engagement strategies, (7) relationship strategies, (8) high expectations strategies, and (9) classroom management strategies. These nine dimensions interact with traditional instructional strategies. Stated differently, if you examine traditional instruction through these nine dimensions and compare it with how they are used in a PCBE classroom, a fairly clear picture of PCBE teachers will emerge. Of course, you need a model of traditional instruction to perform the comparison. Here, we use the model described in *The New Art and Science of Teaching* (Marzano, 2017). A description of that model is presented in appendix A (page 191).

Whole-Class Instruction

In a traditional classroom, whole-class instruction is the dominant activity. The teacher leads the entire class through activities focused on specific content. Following are four categories of strategies teachers can use during whole-class instruction. The first three represent distinct types of lessons.

1. **Conducting direct instruction lessons:** Strategies in this category introduce new information or skills. Students acquire new knowledge and gain a basic understanding that is further leveraged in subsequent lessons. Specific types of strategies used during direct instruction lessons include chunking content, processing content, and recording and representing content (see appendix A, table A.5, page 195).

2. **Conducting practicing and deepening lessons:** Strategies in this category focus on helping students develop and perform a skill or process effectively and efficiently. Strategies in this category also help deepen students' understanding of information to which they have recently been exposed. Specific types of strategies used during practicing and deepening lessons include using structured practice sessions, examining similarities and differences, and examining errors in reasoning (see appendix A, table A.6, page 196).

3. **Conducting knowledge-application lessons:** Strategies in this category are designed to help students apply knowledge (that is, information, skills, and processes) in ways that are new to them. Specific types of knowledge utilization strategies include engaging students in cognitively complex tasks, providing resources and guidance, and generating and defending claims (see appendix A, table A.7, page 197).

4. **Using strategies that appear in all types of lessons:** Teachers commonly use general strategies in conjunction with any of the other three types of lessons (direct instruction, practicing and deepening, and knowledge application). General strategies include previewing strategies, highlighting critical information, reviewing content, revising knowledge, reflecting on learning, assigning purposeful homework, elaborating on information, and organizing students to interact (see appendix A, table A.8, pages 198–199).

It is important to understand the changing role of whole-class instruction in a PCBE classroom. While it is the predominant structure in a traditional classroom, it has a greatly diminished role in the PCBE classroom. As stated previously, theoretically, each student in class could be working on a different measurement topic during any given class period. Whole-class instruction, however, does have its place in the PCBE classroom.

In a PCBE classroom, whole-class instruction occurs when a teacher notices a common problem with a majority of students. For example, a mathematics teacher might notice that virtually all students are having difficulty understanding how to find the common denominator across a set of fractions. This discovery might lead the teacher to create a whole-class direct instruction lesson. Even if some students are proficient relative to this topic, they might help their peers understand the content using student-friendly examples.

In addition to focusing on common problems for the majority of students, whole-class instruction can address the cognitive and metacognitive skills described in chapter 1 (page 11). Recall that these skills and processes span multiple grade bands or grade levels. Also, recall that there are not twelve levels (corresponding to twelve grade levels) for decision making, problem solving, or the other cognitive skills. Rather, there is one version of decision making for the primary levels, one version for upper elementary, one for middle school, and one for high school. Also, recall that the skill of decision making (for example) would be assigned to a teacher responsible for a particular band of levels or grade levels. For example, a social studies teacher responsible for grades 7, 8, and 9 measurement topics might be assigned the task of teaching and reinforcing the decision-making process. This teacher would most likely approach decision making from a whole-class-instruction perspective and would plan and deliver lessons that adhere to the three types described previously: (1) direct instruction, (2) practicing and deepening, and (3) knowledge application. Again, even those students who have already demonstrated proficiency on the decision-making content would participate in these lessons, providing examples and translations of content into student-friendly terms.

Small-Group Instruction

In a traditional classroom, small-group instruction occurs when a teacher differentiates instruction based on the needs of a small group of students relative to a specific measurement topic. Small-group instruction might take the form of any of the three basic types of lessons: (1) direct instruction, (2) practicing and deepening, and (3) knowledge application (see appendix A, tables A.5–A.7, pages 195–197). For example, if the teacher in a traditional classroom notices that a small group of students is having difficulty with the concept of least common denominator, he or she might plan a brief knowledge-deepening lesson for that group. If the teacher has also noticed another small group of students having difficulty with the process of converting fractions to decimals, the teacher might organize a practicing lesson for those students. In effect, in a traditional classroom, small-group instruction is a vehicle for grouping and regrouping students.

In a PCBE classroom, the dynamic surrounding small-group instruction is similar to that in a traditional classroom. The teacher notices a need in a small group of students and then organizes a brief direct instruction, practicing and deepening, or knowledge application lesson for those students. The major difference between a PCBE classroom and a traditional classroom is that small-group instruction occurs every day. A major aspect of teacher planning in a PCBE system is identifying the small groups that must be formed on specific topics and the types of instruction that must occur with those groups.

Using alternating start times helps purposefully design small-group instruction. For instance, consider a scenario in which a teacher has identified three distinct groups in his class based on informal and formal assessments of the measurement topics. At the beginning of class, the teacher works with group one directly while groups two and three work at their own pace on either independent or peer-to-peer work. A common trap teachers fall into is providing busy work for the groups who are working independently. The idea should not be to merely occupy them until the teacher can give instruction, but rather to engage them in critical practice aligned with the targets they are currently learning. If SOPs are in place, students working independently or in peer-to-peer formats should be able to function well on their own.

After about ten or fifteen minutes, the groups rotate so that group one is now working either independently or peer to peer, group two is working with the teacher, and group three is continuing its independent work. This rotation continues based on the needs of each group. Some group times may be longer or shorter depending on the group's needs. On certain days, a particular group may not need time with the teacher while other groups may need more. Since the groups are generally working in a learning progression, other groups can use the materials created for more advanced groups when they are ready to address the same content later on, minimizing later teacher preparation.

Individual Instruction

In a traditional classroom, individual instruction occurs when a teacher works with an individual student. Again, instruction might focus on direct instruction of new knowledge, practicing and deepening knowledge, or knowledge application. However, such instruction occurs on a one-to-one basis. Individual instruction is relatively rare in a traditional classroom. In contrast, individual instruction is one of the staples of a PCBE classroom. During most PCBE class periods, the teacher has time to move around and work one-to-one with students.

One of the more powerful aspects of PCBE is the manner in which students experience one-to-one instruction. Since the stated purpose of a PCBE system is to allow students to move at their own pace, it stands to reason that there would be a great deal of one-to-one instruction. As a by-product of the increased use of individualized instruction, students are less likely to feel singled out when the teacher works with them individually. Indeed, this has been an implicit and explicit goal of the PCBE movement since its inception (DeLorenzo et al., 2009; Lindsay Unified School District, 2017; Marzano & Kendall, 1996; Reigeluth & Karnopp, 2013). Each day, students know whether they are scheduled for individualized instruction and the topics on which such instruction will focus. Armed with a student's current scores on the proficiency scale for a specific measurement topic, teacher and student celebrate the student's current level of progress and plan the best course of action to improve even more. Sometimes the teacher might use the individualized session to clarify misconceptions, to collect new assessment data, or to present new content. Teacher and student work as a team with the shared goal of enhancing the student's knowledge of the measurement topic as articulated on the proficiency scale.

Peer-to-Peer Instruction

Peer-to-peer instruction takes many forms. It is commonly associated with the work of Eric Mazur (1997), who developed his model for instruction at the college level. It relies heavily on students preparing themselves to interact with their peers by engaging in extensive prereading of the content to be the focus of instruction. This approach is sometimes referred to as "flipped" instruction and is most common at the high school and college levels. Peer-to-peer instruction is also associated with peer tutoring, cooperative learning, and peer collaboration. Peer tutoring, as its name implies, involves one student who is knowledgeable about a topic tutoring another student who is not. Cooperative learning involves a variety of structures in which students take on specific roles (for example, recorder, summarizer, or reporter) as they investigate a specific topic or issue in the context of a group. Peer collaboration is probably the least formulaic of the three, and it involves a small group of students (two or three) sharing their understandings about a topic. Shared understandings help provide confidence about specific information. Students pose shared questions to the teacher or other students in class. Of these three, peer collaboration might have the most positive effects on student motivation and learning (Damon & Phelps, 1989).

Within a PCBE classroom, peer-to-peer instruction is most closely related to peer collaboration. Students who have demonstrated proficiency on a specific measurement topic (that is, received a score of 3.0 on the proficiency scale) act as resources for students who have not. Thus, those students who have demonstrated proficiency are invited by students who have not to answer questions and provide guidance.

In our experience, in the PCBE classroom, this type of peer-to-peer instruction is quite common, whereas in a traditional classroom, it is relatively rare. There can be great power and benefit to students' learning collaboratively if there are structures in place—such as SOPs and behavioral norms—that are monitored to make peer-to-peer instruction meaningful and functional. For peer-to-peer instruction to work, students must know their own learning needs as well as the learning needs of their peers. We refer to this shared knowledge as *transparency*. This issue is commonly misunderstood and sometimes challenged from a traditional perspective. There are two types of transparency: (1) teacher-directed transparency and (2) student-directed transparency.

With teacher-directed transparency, the PCBE teacher is the holder of all information about students. If students wish to engage in peer-to-peer instruction, they come to the teacher for pairing opportunities. There may be a variety of reasons to use this approach, including the following.

- Students are just beginning the peer-to-peer instruction process, and the PCBE teacher decides to start with more guidance and control to ensure students are successful.

- There are interpersonal or maturity concerns that require a tight system with less student choice.

- The PCBE teacher wishes to keep student pacing more private.

With student-directed transparency, the students are the holders of information regarding each other's status. Rather than students coming to the teacher for information about which students they can pair or group with, the information about what other students have already completed is available to them. Students can use that information to work collaboratively with peers. To create this type of transparency, PCBE teachers develop a system in which students can see where they and their peers are in their learning progressions. Often this takes the form of a data wall with proficiency scales, where students can mark what they have completed or move their names, numbers, or icons to whatever targets they are currently working on. This approach enables the class to see who might be available to give peer-to-peer instruction on a topic or skill, or who might be working on the same content. Figure 3.1 shows all of the measurement topics for algebra 1 and the movement of a whole class. Notice that the teacher pace is indicated, as well as individual students' paces. *Teacher pace* refers to the pacing involved in covering the course material in a single academic year.

ALGEBRA 1	
MEASUREMENT TOPIC	**CLASSMATES WHO ARE WORKING ON THIS TOPIC**
Components of an Expression	
Context of an Expression	
Adding and Subtracting Polynomial Expressions	
Multiplying and Dividing Polynomial Expressions	Evan Colleen Ricky
Evaluating Polynomials	Chinyere
Linear Equations and Inequalities	Sara David Fatima Jose
Generating Equations and Inequalities	Daniella Rita Chris Marquis Rhonda Toby
Teacher Pace	
Systems of Equations and Inequalities	Anna Christina Ryan Tomas Graham Molly Katya Jacob
Quadratic Equations and Functions	Nena Janae Amin
Graphing Functions	Jacqueline
Generating Functions	
Comparing Functions	
Combining Functions	

Figure 3.1: Students' progression on algebra 1 standards.

One concern about building student-directed learning transparency is that information about each student's pace and progress should be private. This concern is a valid one, so it is important to note that student-directed transparency is not the same as, say, sharing individual test score data within a traditional system. Since all students within a PCBE system are expected to master all learning targets, the concepts of passing and failing are replaced by a learning continuum, and time is variable. As students understand that learning is the constant and that pacing varies from student to student, they naturally become more focused on their own progress and plan for it rather than furtively looking at their peers' scores.

Student-directed learning transparency, as defined here, is supported by the research of John Hattie (2009, 2012). In 2009, he published a synthesis of findings from over eight hundred meta-analyses related to student achievement. He updated his study in 2012. Of the 150 variables (that is, instructional practices) he found in the literature, the one that had the strongest relationship with student achievement was self-reported grades/student expectations. In fact, this practice is associated with a 40 percentile gain in student achievement; this is larger than the gains associated with any other variable. While self-reported grades/student expectations involves a number of components, its centerpiece is students knowing where they stand on a continuum of knowledge and then setting challenging but attainable goals: "Educating students to have high, challenging, appropriate expectations is among the most powerful influence on enhancing student achievement" (Hattie, 2012, p. 60). We believe that student-directed learning transparency lays the foundation for students determining their current status, setting challenging goals for themselves, and finding available help from their peers to accomplish these goals. The following example depicts how student-directed learning transparency might manifest.

Before her school transitioned to a competency-based system, Ms. Abbott, a fifth-grade teacher, noticed that a number of her students were struggling with the pacing of her lessons. Some students found the pace of instruction to be too fast; others found it to be too slow. As her school transitioned to the new system, she decided to implement new processes to help her students identify their pace and the pace of other members of the class. At the beginning of units, Ms. Abbott began using pretests to measure her students' competencies and to determine which learning targets they needed to work on. She then posted the learning targets for the whole unit in the classroom and allowed students to track their progress by writing their names next to the learning targets they completed. Ms. Abbott reminded her students that it didn't matter if they were ahead of or behind their classmates; everyone would learn the same content at their own pace. After implementing this transparent method of tracking progress, students often told her how much they enjoyed working at their own pace. Many noted that they no longer felt like they had to rush or wait for others to catch up. Additionally, Ms. Abbott encouraged her students to use the posted learning targets to identify peers who worked at a faster pace and could help them if they ever felt stuck. Students who were afraid to seek out help in the past commented that they felt more comfortable asking for help in this system and more motivated to learn when they could partner with their classmates.

Another challenge to peer-to-peer instruction is that students are not the teachers and should not be made to instruct other students. This issue is important to address directly with students. As noted previously, in a PCBE classroom, students are afforded more voice and choice in their learning. Peer-to-peer instruction should be one of their choices. Teachers should develop procedures that outline how students can choose to be a peer content instructor. Here are some examples.

- Students sign up for different measurement topics that they feel confident with and are willing to support others in learning.

- Students choose to act as a technology support person, perhaps for general technology use or for the use of certain applications (some refer to these students as *appsperts*).

- Students group together with at least one expert to answer questions or instruct as needed.

- Students create instructional tutorials that others can use as digital resources for peer-to-peer instruction and are linked to specific targets.

This last example involving instructional tutorials is especially useful when students do not want to slow their own pace to assist others, but still wish to help. Students can create instructional tutorials for specific targets on proficiency scales. These can serve as student proficiency demonstrations. The added benefit is that a virtual warehouse of student-created tutorials can span across years, grades, schools, and content areas. The teacher uses the tutorials to ensure students have achieved mastery, which in turn ensures the quality of the support resources for other students wishing to receive peer instruction.

External Instructional Resources

In the traditional classroom, the teacher is the primary if not the sole source of instruction. Whether instruction involves direct instruction, practicing and deepening, or knowledge application, the teacher is the source. In a PCBE classroom, it is not possible or even advisable for the teacher to be the sole source of instruction. The PCBE classroom teacher must identify alternative ways for students to receive instruction. One traditional way to provide external instruction is through learning centers. Another approach is to use Internet-based resources in a blended fashion. Specifically, as part of designing instruction, the teacher can identify resources from sites like the Khan Academy (www.khanacademy.org) for each content level in a proficiency scale. Better yet, teachers can customize video content by creating instructional tutorials on websites such as TeacherTube (www.teachertube.com) or Educreations (www.educreations .com), or with platforms such as Edmodo (www.edmodo.com) or Google Docs (www.google.com /docs/about) to create virtual warehouses of resources and videos with the capacity to share information and feedback. As discussed previously, students can also create tutorials. SOPs regarding the use of external resources should be in place so students can navigate these resources independently to improve their learning experiences.

Engagement Strategies

Engagement in a traditional classroom is operationally defined as students paying attention to what the teacher is doing or directing them to do. Common teacher engagement strategies include noticing and reacting when students are not engaged, increasing response rates, using physical movement, maintaining a lively pace, demonstrating intensity and enthusiasm, presenting unusual information, using friendly controversy, using academic games, providing opportunities for students to talk about themselves, and motivating and inspiring students (see appendix A, table A.9, pages 200–201).

In a PCBE classroom, *engagement* is defined as each student attending to the activities that will help him or her reach the next level of proficiency on a specific topic. Thus, in the PCBE classroom, the focus of engagement might be different from student to student. Consequently, teachers use some of the traditional engagement strategies sparingly in a PCBE classroom except in instances in which the teacher is employing whole-class instruction.

Quite commonly, teachers adapt a whole-class strategy for use with one student or a small group of students. For example, friendly controversy is an engagement strategy typically employed in a whole-class setting and involves organizing students into groups to take different positions on a topic. In a PCBE classroom, a teacher might employ this same engagement technique with an individual student by simply presenting another point of view to the student relative to a particular topic. In a whole-class setting, a teacher might employ the engagement strategy of providing opportunities for students to talk about themselves by organizing them into groups to discuss how the topic of a lesson relates to something in their lives. In a PCBE classroom, the teacher might simply ask individual students how they see their current work on a proficiency scale relating to their personal interests.

Relationship Strategies

In a traditional classroom, the teacher must seek out and sometimes create opportunities to interact with individual students since most interactions are with the whole class. Yet, one-to-one encounters are the very vehicles that allow the teacher to communicate to a student that he or she is supported and welcomed in the class. Thus, the traditional classroom is not organized well to facilitate relationship development.

Where the teacher in a traditional classroom must seek out opportunities for personal interactions with students, such opportunities are readily available in a PCBE classroom since the teacher is frequently working with students individually. Although the same strategies for forging relationships apply to both a traditional classroom and a PCBE classroom, these strategies are more easily deployed in a PCBE classroom. Strategies for building relationships typically include using verbal and nonverbal behaviors that indicate affection for students, understanding students' backgrounds and interests, and displaying objectivity and control (see appendix A, table A.11, pages 203–204). For example, simply smiling at a student while talking to him or her helps build relationships, as does appropriately patting a student on the shoulder to acknowledge a job well done.

High Expectations Strategies

Strategies that communicate high expectations for all students are similar to strategies for establishing relationships with students. Teachers execute both types of strategies during one-to-one interactions with students. As described before, in a traditional classroom the teacher must seek out opportunities for one-to-one interaction; in a PCBE classroom one-to-one interactions occur much more frequently. Again, strategies that communicate high expectations for students are more easily executed in a PCBE classroom and typically include demonstrating value and respect for reluctant learners, asking in-depth questions of reluctant learners, and probing incorrect answers with reluctant learners (see appendix A, table A.12, pages 204–205). For example, asking equally difficult questions of all students, regardless of a teacher's belief about differences in students' knowledge or ability, communicates high expectations for all. Of course, teachers must do this with a keen awareness of students' sense of self-esteem and status among their peers. Since teachers in PCBE classrooms commonly ask questions of students in a one-on-one setting, it is much easier to challenge a student's thinking without embarrassing him or her.

Classroom Management Strategies

In a traditional classroom, classroom management is handled by rules and procedures that relate to behavior within the whole group. Many rules and procedures focus on whole-group instruction. In general, teachers design strategies to ensure that all students are doing the same thing. Commonly, whole-class management strategies include establishing rules and procedures, organizing the physical layout of the classroom, demonstrating withitness, acknowledging adherence to rules and procedures, and acknowledging lack of adherence to rules and procedures (see appendix A, table A.10, pages 202–203). As described in chapter 1 (page 11), in a PCBE classroom, students address management through a code of cooperation they use to monitor their behaviors and standard operating procedures they are responsible for knowing and appropriately executing. To a great extent then, management in a PCBE classroom is student centered, whereas management in a traditional classroom is teacher centered.

As the preceding discussion indicates, instruction in a PCBE classroom shares some characteristics with instruction in a traditional classroom, but the two are probably more different than similar. Table 3.1 compares and contrasts the two types of instruction.

Table 3.1: Comparison of Traditional Instruction and PCBE Instruction

INSTRUCTIONAL STRATEGY	TRADITIONAL INSTRUCTION	PCBE INSTRUCTION
Whole-Class Instruction	• Is the predominant form or source for all content • Can involve direct instruction of new content, practicing and deepening knowledge, knowledge application, and general instructional strategies	Done only in specific situations, such as teaching cognitive and metacognitive skills, when the majority of students have a common problem, or for a specific measurement topic

continued →

INSTRUCTIONAL STRATEGY	TRADITIONAL INSTRUCTION	PCBE INSTRUCTION
Small-Group Instruction	Done when groups of students have common problems	• Dominant mode of grouping • Teachers explicitly plan on a daily basis.
Individual Instruction	Done to meet the needs of individual students as needed	Done to meet the needs of individual students as needed
Peer-to-Peer Instruction	Rarely used	• Is the dominant form of instruction • Requires transparency
External Instructional Resources	Rarely used	• Are the dominant form of instruction • Require virtual instructional tutorials
Engagement Strategies	Teacher executes whole-class strategies to ensure all students are attending to the same stimulus.	• Involve each student attending to his or her own specific topics • Use whole-class strategies sparingly
Relationship Strategies	• Teachers need to seek out opportunities to interact one-to-one with students. • Difficult because of teachers' predominant use of whole-class instruction	Easier for teachers to interact one-to-one with students since whole-class instruction is not predominant
High Expectations Strategies	• Teachers need to seek out opportunities to interact one-to-one with students. • Difficult because of teachers' predominant use of whole-class instruction	Easier for teachers to interact one-to-one with students since whole-class instruction is not predominant
Classroom Management Strategies	Teachers design and monitor rules and procedures.	Students and the teacher design and monitor SOPs.

Personal Tracking Matrices

An important aspect of instruction in a PCBE system is providing students with the tools they need to chart and monitor their individual learning progress. Personal tracking matrices are not necessary for PCBE but can be powerful aids to both instruction and assessment. Personal tracking matrices are akin to capacity matrices, a tool David P. Langford (2015) developed that identifies tasks or concepts and related knowledge levels to support individuals in charting their own learning toward a specific result. Here, we consider two situations in which a teacher may design a personal tracking matrix for students: (1) when standards have been unpacked as self-contained learning targets and (2) when standards have been unpacked and organized as proficiency scales.

Standards Unpacked as Self-Contained Learning Targets

In chapter 1 (page 11), we demonstrated that teachers should unpack standards as learning targets. To illustrate the nature of a learning target, consider the following two examples.

1. Explain how to evaluate a base raised to an integer exponent.

2. Explain how to evaluate exponential expressions involving the same base raised to integer exponents.

By definition, a learning target provides specific direction for what is expected of students as opposed to the more general phrasing in a standard.

As mentioned previously, we recommend that schools and districts assemble teachers and administrators to unpack standards into learning targets and then organize these into proficiency scales. However, some schools and districts treat their learning targets as self-contained content packets. This means that a given learning target is not thought of in the context of one or more other learning targets. When learning targets are treated as self-contained, it is important that they are further unpacked and stated as a personal tracking matrix. To illustrate, consider this learning target: Students will apply their knowledge of phonics (such as letter-sound relationships, consonant sounds, and vowel sounds) to decode unknown words. Figure 3.2 depicts how teachers might further unpack this learning target and embed it in a personal tracking matrix.

Name:		Date Started:		Date Completed:		
Learning Target: I can use my letter sounds and strategies to figure out words.						
Indicator	I'm just starting.	I know some but need help.	I got this!	I know even more than expected!	How I learned it (circle what you did).	Teacher sign-off
I can tell the difference between words that look alike by finding the letters that are different and sounding out the words.					Online learning Sounds and letters learning center Worked with a friend Worked with my teacher	
I can read some sight words that can't be sounded out like most words (*the, do, of, my, you*).					Online learning Sounds and letters learning center Worked with a friend Worked with my teacher	

Figure 3.2: Personal tracking matrix for a phonics learning target. continued →

I know both sounds each vowel can make.				Online learning Sounds and letters learning center Worked with a friend Worked with my teacher	
I can show which letter makes which sound in words.				Online learning Sounds and letters learning center Worked with a friend Worked with my teacher	
I know my consonant letter sounds.				Online learning Sounds and letters learning center Worked with a friend Worked with my teacher	

Notice that in figure 3.2, the learning target has been restated in student-friendly language: "I can use my letter sounds and strategies to figure out words." Personal tracking matrices typically articulate the indicators in statements that begin with "I can" or "I know." In this personal tracking matrix, indicators are listed with the more complex ones at the top and the simpler ones at the bottom. Some teachers prefer the simpler indicators at the top and the more complex at the bottom. In effect, the teacher has unpacked the learning target into specific statements of information and skills they can organize into a progression.

The personal tracking matrix also contains a scale students can use to rate their current level of performance or understanding regarding each indicator. The scale uses language students can easily relate to, ranging from "I'm just starting" to "I know even more than expected." Another variation on the four levels of the scale is as follows.

1. I can show what I learned with help.

2. I learned the simple parts.

3. I learned the simple parts and complex parts and can show what I know.

4. I can use what I learned in a new way (for example, explain or go beyond).

Notice that for the simple indicators in this personal tracking matrix (see figure 3.2)—"I know both sounds each vowel can make," "I can show which letter makes which sound in words," and "I know my consonant letter sounds"—the rating square for "I know even more than expected!" is shaded. This shading indicates that for these simple indicators, students cannot know more than expected because these indicators are basic details. For key vocabulary, basic processes, and basic details—simpler content that would be placed at score 2.0 in a proficiency scale—the rating square that indicates going beyond what was taught should be shaded to indicate that it does not apply.

The next section of the personal tracking matrix is for students to provide evidence for their rating. In this case, the teacher provided various options that students could have used to practice and demonstrate their proficiency. These resources might help students practice skills pertinent to an indicator, provide information that helps students better understand an indicator, or offer students ways to determine their level of competence relative to a specific indicator. Note that the list of ways a student can provide evidence for a specific level of competence on an indicator includes use of a teacher-created learning center, use of collaborative learning, or informal interactions with the teacher.

The personal tracking matrix has a space for the teacher to sign off and date for mastery achievement. There may also be a spot for students to note conferencing times, informal assessment dates, and other checks for understanding. Again, teachers should develop protocols around the use of personal tracking matrices. Putting some monitoring responsibility in the hands of the students not only builds deeper understanding of learning targets but also develops important cognitive and metacognitive skills.

As the personal tracking matrix fills up with representations of learning, it is easy to build in celebrations as students see what they have achieved. It is also a perfect jumping-off point for student-led conferences. There is nothing more powerful to parents than hearing from their own children exactly what they have been learning and how they worked toward mastery of their goals.

Standards Unpacked and Organized as Proficiency Scales

The second scenario in which teachers might design a personal tracking matrix is when standards have been unpacked and organized as proficiency scales. Of course, this is the approach we encourage educators to use. We described this process in chapter 1 (page 11) and highly recommend it. One of the many advantages of proficiency scales is that multiple learning targets are often combined into a single scale. This situation occurs when one learning target represents prerequisite knowledge for another learning target. In effect, if teachers developed proficiency scales, then they have already unpacked and organized standards into a progression of learning targets. To illustrate, consider the proficiency scale for high school mathematics in figure 3.3.

Score 4.0	The student will:
	Test the idea that solving linear equations by graphing is the best solution method for particular situations (for example, list situations in which solving by graphing is the most efficient solution method and situations in which solving algebraically is the most efficient solution method).
Score 3.5	In addition to score 3.0 performance, partial success at score 4.0 content

Figure 3.3: Proficiency scale for solving linear equations through graphing. continued →

Score 3.0	The student will: Solve linear equations by graphing (for example, find the point that will satisfy two linear equations by graphing both equations).
Score 2.5	No major errors or omissions regarding score 2.0 content, and partial success at score 3.0 content
Score 2.0	The student will recognize or recall specific vocabulary (for example, *linear equation, slope-intercept form, coordinate plane, intersection point*) and perform basic processes such as: • Convert a linear equation into slope-intercept form. • Graph a linear equation on a coordinate plane. • Determine the intersection point for the graphs of two linear equations. • Verify the point of intersection by inserting the coordinates into each linear equation.
Score 1.5	Partial success at score 2.0 content, and major errors or omissions regarding score 3.0 content
Score 1.0	With help, partial success at score 2.0 content and score 3.0 content
Score 0.5	With help, partial success at score 2.0 content but not at score 3.0 content
Score 0.0	Even with help, no success

A proficiency scale certainly resembles a personal tracking matrix in that the content is organized from simple to complex (with complex content at the top and simple content at the bottom), but it is not developed for ease of understanding by students. Consequently, it may be useful to translate proficiency scales into personal tracking matrices. One simple way to translate a proficiency scale into a personal tracking matrix is to restate its learning targets in less technical terms. See figure 3.4.

LEVEL	INDICATOR	MY RATING			MY EVIDENCE
		I'm still confused about this topic.	I've learned some but not all of the topic.	I've got this now.	
4.0	I can show situations in which solving a linear equation is best done through graphing versus situations in which it is best done algebraically.				
3.0	I can find the point that will satisfy two linear equations by graphing both equations.				
2.0	I can verify the point of intersection by inserting the coordinates into each linear equation.				

2.0	I can determine the intersection point of the graphs of two linear equations.				
2.0	I can graph a linear equation on a coordinate plane.				
2.0	I can convert a linear equation into its slope-intercept form.				
2.0	I can provide an explanation of the term *intersection point*.				
2.0	I can provide an explanation of the term *coordinate plane*.				
2.0	I can provide an explanation of the term *slope-intercept form*.				
2.0	I can provide an explanation of the term *linear equation*.				

Figure 3.4: Personal tracking matrix for solving linear equations through graphing.

The personal tracking matrix in figure 3.4 was created by simply rewriting each learning target in an "I can" statement format. Additionally, some elements were broken out into more detail. For example, each vocabulary term has its own line for rating. The personal tracking matrix lists content in a sequence from complex to simple. It is important to note that the personal tracking matrix in figure 3.4 lists the proficiency scale level of each indicator ranging from score 4.0 to 2.0. This labeling lets the teacher and students know which proficiency scale level is addressed by each indicator. Finally, as before, the personal tracking matrix has sections for students to rate themselves and list evidence for their ratings. It is important to note that students use a slightly different self-rating scale when a proficiency scale is the basis for a personal tracking matrix. That scale has three levels only, as follows.

1. I'm still confused about this topic.

2. I've learned some but not all of the topic.

3. I've got this now.

Student Assistance With Understanding Learning Targets and Proficiency Scales

Students' understanding of learning targets is essential to the PCBE process. If they are not clear about the expectations that are explicit and implicit in learning targets, students will not have a good sense of their current status on a proficiency scale or what they must do to improve. In some situations, it is useful to engage students in the process of examining learning targets in depth, regardless of whether they are self-contained or embedded in a proficiency scale. The following tips are helpful to keep in mind when working with students.

- Underline the important or unknown words.
  - Important words are content related. The learning target calls for the student to be able to know and define these terms. For example, a biology learning target might include the important content-related term *mitosis*.
  - Unknown words are clarity related. The student needs to know them to understand what the standard means. For example, a learning target might use the word *various*, which is not a content-related term, but students may need clarification to understand what the standard is expecting.
  - Sometimes important or unknown terms will be phrases made up of more than one word—for example, *text features* or *digital menus*.
- Determine which words signify what a student should know and which words determine what they need to be able to do.
- Circle the *dos*—the actions the student will have to take to prove mastery (see figure 3.5)—and include them as indicators. Often verbs are indicators, but not exclusively. For example, *contributes* isn't one of the indicators circled because it isn't an action the student will take to show proficiency, but rather what the structure of the text itself is contributing.

Compare and contrast the structure of two or more texts and analyze how the differing structure of each text contributes to its meaning and style.

Figure 3.5: Circling actions within a learning target or standard statement.

When first beginning to understand learning targets, it is a good idea to adjust some of the language complexity to make it more student friendly, then work with students to unpack the simpler version. This process is particularly helpful with noncontent words. If the students don't need to know the definition of *various* (as mentioned previously), then adjust that word prior to the unpacking process to create greater ease of understanding and lessen the unpacking workload. Keep in mind that most learning targets contain academic vocabulary terms that may be new to students. These terms should not be simplified in the personal tracking matrix; rather, students need to understand that learning new vocabulary is part of the process of learning the simpler content related to a learning target. When introducing learning targets, find a way for students to interact with the standard or target (for example, by asking them to underline on the SMART Board, put a sticky note on a paper template, explain to a partner what they think a word might mean, and so on).

Instructional Planning in a PCBE System

It is difficult for instruction to support student learning if teachers do it in a haphazard fashion. Planning is just as essential to effective instruction in a PCBE system as it is in a traditional system. Planning instruction in a PCBE system has some significant differences from planning in a traditional system, however. Perhaps first and foremost is that it requires much more preparation prior to the beginning of school. We refer to this as *foundational planning*. One negative feature of foundational planning is that it is labor intensive. One positive feature is that once it is done, it dramatically decreases the amount of planning that must occur from then on. In effect, foundational planning represents a one-time effort that makes teachers' ongoing planning much easier. The following sections will discuss foundational planning in more detail, as well as weekly and daily planning. (Detailed information on scheduling class time will be discussed later in chapter 5, page 133.)

Foundational Planning

The primary purpose of foundational planning is to increase learning transparency. At any moment, each student should know the answer to the question, What am I supposed to be learning right now? This means that a district or school must ensure that every teacher is aware of the measurement topics and proficiency scales the teachers must address at each level. Consequently, articulating measurement topics is the first order of business when designing a PCBE system.

Once teachers create proficiency scales for each grade or content level, then foundational planning encompasses four other important topics: (1) planning for external instructional resources, (2) planning for personal tracking matrices, (3) planning for assessments, and (4) planning for the flow of content.

Planning for External Instructional Resources

The creation, management, and organization of quality resources is a major component in planning for a PCBE classroom. The ultimate goal is to have a structured system for students to utilize tools and strategies that allow the proper balance of teacher instruction and student autonomy.

As described previously, in a PCBE system, it is impossible for teachers to provide all instruction for every level of every measurement topic to every student. This situation is the natural consequence of students moving at their own pace through the content. Consequently, teachers must provide external instructional resources for scores 2.0, 3.0, and 4.0 content in each proficiency scale. These web-based or hard-copy resources allow students to address the content at a particular scale level independently. Figure 3.6 (page 88) provides an example of specific resources teachers might use for a specific proficiency scale. As shown, external instructional resources might include hard-copy directions for specific activities, examples of work from students, Khan Academy videos, teacher-created screencasts, specific pages in a textbook, practice sheets, and short formative assessments.

4	Describe and defend what might occur to climatic patterns in a specific location given a dramatic change in one specific process of the water cycle.	• Hard-copy directions for specific requirements regarding what must be addressed • Examples from previous students
3	Have an understanding of: • How the water cycle processes (condensation, precipitation, surface runoff, percolation, evaporation) impact climate changes • The effects of temperature and pressure in different layers of Earth's atmosphere	• Khan Academy video • Teacher-created screencasts • Pages in a book • Practice sheets • Short formative assessments
2	Recognize and recall basic terms such as: *climatic patterns, atmospheric layers, stratosphere,* and *troposphere.* Recognize or recall isolated details such as: • Precipitation is one of the processes of the water cycle. • The troposphere is one of the lowest portions of the Earth's atmosphere.	• Khan Academy video • Teacher-created screencasts • Pages in a book • Practice sheets • Short formative assessments

Figure 3.6: Resources based on a proficiency scale for the measurement topic atmospheric processes and the water cycle.

When identifying resources, it is useful to think in terms of the three types of lessons described previously: (1) direct instruction, (2) practicing and deepening, and (3) knowledge application lessons. For each level of content, strategies pertaining to one or more of these types of lessons might be appropriate. For example, consider the score 2.0 content in figure 3.6. Recognizing and recalling specific vocabulary terms and details might require direct instruction strategies like ensuring that content is chunked into digestible bites and including activities or worksheets that ensure students record and represent their understanding. The score 3.0 content (understanding how the water cycle processes impact climate changes and the effects of temperature and pressure on the atmosphere's different layers) might require knowledge-deepening activities like examining similarities and differences. The score 4.0 content (addressing what might happen to climatic patterns in a specific location under specific conditions) might require some knowledge application strategies, such as generating and defending claims. Finally, external instructional resources for proficiency scales might include directions and activities from some of the general instructional strategies, such as requiring students to elaborate on information or revise their knowledge.

Planning for Personal Tracking Matrices

While it is true that students can create personal tracking matrices for proficiency scales to better understand the content they are expected to master, it is also true that foundational planning can provide first-draft versions of personal tracking matrices derived from proficiency scales. Teachers can sometimes create personal tracking matrices by simply restating and reordering the same 2.0, 3.0, and 4.0 content on a proficiency scale. Figure 3.7 depicts a capacity matrix that is a simple restatement and reordering of the proficiency scale in figure 3.6.

LEVEL	INDICATOR	MY RATING			MY EVIDENCE
		I'm still confused about this topic.	I've learned some but not all of the topic.	I've got this now.	
4	I can provide evidence for my description of changes in climatic patterns.				
4	I can describe what might occur for climatic patterns in a specific location if a specific change occurred in a process of the water cycle.				
3	I can describe the effects of temperatures and pressures in different layers of the Earth's atmosphere.				
3	I can describe how climate changes are affected by the interaction among condensation, precipitation, surface runoff, percolation, and evaporation.				
3	I can describe the relationship among condensation, precipitation, surface runoff, percolation, and evaporation.				
2	I can explain the position of the troposphere in the Earth's atmosphere.				
2	I can describe the basic processes of the water cycle.				
2	I can provide an explanation of the term *troposphere*.				
2	I can provide an explanation of the term *stratosphere*.				
2	I can provide an explanation of the term *atmospheric layers*.				
2	I can provide an explanation of the term *climatic patterns*.				

Figure 3.7: Personal tracking matrix for atmospheric processes and the water cycle.

Planning for Assessments

Another type of foundational planning teachers should address is assessment of the various levels in each proficiency scale. We address this in depth in chapter 4 (page 97). Briefly, it is highly advisable to generate test items and tasks that can provide evidence of a student's proficiency at the score 2.0, 3.0, and 4.0 content of each scale. To illustrate, consider figure 3.8. During initial planning, these items and tasks do not have to constitute an exhaustive list since teachers will continually make additions throughout the year.

SCORE	GOAL STATEMENT	INSTRUCTIONAL ACTIVITIES AND ASSIGNMENTS	ASSESSMENT TASKS
Score 4.0	In addition to score 3.0 performance, the student demonstrates in-depth inferences and applications that go beyond what was taught.	The student reads real-life examples of using rounding of whole numbers in real-world contexts. With teacher-directed discussion, explicit connections are taught and noted.	The student explains how rounding whole numbers to the nearest 10 and 100 helps in figuring a family's grocery bill. The student cites other real-life examples, including explanations of how rounding whole numbers saves time and provides information.
Score 3.0	The student will "use place value understanding to round whole numbers to the nearest 10 or 100" (3.NBT.1; NGA & CCSSO, 2010d, p. 24).	The student will draw three cards from a deck of cards in which the non-number cards have been removed. The student will write down those numbers on a piece of paper to form a three-digit number. He or she will round that three-digit number to the nearest 10 and 100.	The student will solve three-digit place value problems on a pencil-and-paper test. Sample questions include: $900 + 50 +$ _____ $= 955$ $3 +$ _____ $+ 300 = 393$ The student will solve rounding problems on a pencil-and-paper test. Sample questions include: Round 421 to the nearest hundred. Round 956 to the nearest thousand. Please add the rounded numbers from the two problems together. The total is _____.

Score 2.0	The student will recognize or recall specific vocabulary, such as *nearest*, *place value*, *round*, and *whole number*. The student will use place value understanding to round whole numbers below 1,000 to the nearest 10 and 100 with visual support.	The student will complete a mix-and-match vocabulary game to review key terms. The student will use visual supports such as pictures to round three-digit numbers to the nearest 10 and 100.	The student will match vocabulary terms to their correct descriptions. The student will match a three-digit number to pictures representing the number rounded to the nearest 10 and 100.

Source: Adapted from Heflebower et al., 2014, p. 56.

Figure 3.8: Proficiency scale with sample test items.

The final issue teachers should also address during foundational planning is the flow of content throughout the year.

Planning for the Flow of Content

Recall that whole-class instruction is not as prominent in a competency-based system as it is in a traditional system because students move through content at their own pace. However, teachers can and should still develop plans for sequencing and pacing content. To illustrate, consider the following list of sixteen measurement topics for eighth-grade mathematics.

1. Exponents
2. Cube and square roots
3. Scientific notation
4. Rational and irrational numbers
5. Linear equations
6. Systems of linear equations
7. Quadratic equations
8. Concept of functions
9. Linear functions
10. Volume
11. Transformations, similarity, and congruence
12. Angles of two-dimensional figures
13. Line and angle constructions
14. Pythagorean theorem
15. Bivariate categorical data
16. Bivariate measurement data

During foundational planning, teachers identify the order in which they introduce measurement topics. For example, in the preceding list, the teacher has decided to begin instruction with the topic on exponents, then address cube and square roots, and so on. At the beginning of each year, if all students are starting at the same point, teachers could present the topics in a whole-class setting. As students start to move ahead of or fall behind the planned pace, there will be fewer and fewer opportunities for whole-class instruction on specific topics.

The issue of sequencing topics becomes exceedingly more complex when a teacher is dealing with more than one grade level. As mentioned previously, some manifestations of PCBE have teachers responsible for up to three levels of students in the same classroom. In such situations, it is very difficult to precisely predict a sequence of topics for multiple levels, simply because parts of some topics might overlap with parts of other topics, and one level of students might progress more quickly or slowly than anticipated. Consequently, teachers must always do foundational planning for flow of content with the realization that things might change during the year. Even with sound foundational planning, there will be a consistent need for teachers to plan on a weekly and daily basis.

Weekly and Daily Planning

Weekly and daily planning will take one of nine forms: (1) planning for whole-class instruction, (2) planning for small-group instruction, (3) planning for individual instruction, (4) planning for peer-to-peer instruction, (5) planning to update external instructional resources, (6) planning for engagement, (7) planning for relationships, (8) planning for communicating high expectations, and (9) planning for classroom management. These nine areas are highly dynamic and must be reconsidered on a systematic basis to meet the changing needs of students.

Planning for Whole-Class Instruction

On a weekly or daily basis, a teacher might make plans for whole-class instruction. For example, the pace of instruction articulated in foundational planning might have to be altered on a weekly basis based on student progress through the learning progressions.

One of the more common areas of emphasis during weekly planning for whole-class instruction is identifying previous topics on which a majority of students are experiencing difficulty reaching score 3.0 status. Teachers can use formal and informal observations to determine areas of focus and then review the identified material with the whole class. Once the review has been completed and teachers have collected feedback on the effectiveness of instruction, students can go back to their individual activities and pacing. To plan for whole-class instruction, a teacher might ask questions like the following.

- "What is the specific topic on which I will provide whole-class instruction?"
- "Will the lesson involve direct instruction, practicing and deepening, or knowledge application?"
- "What general instructional strategies will I use?"

Planning for Small-Group Instruction

On a weekly or daily basis, teachers will plan for instruction with ad hoc small groups. As the teacher recognizes that several students are having difficulty with the same topic, he or she can gather them together for small-group instruction. To plan for small-group instruction, a teacher might ask questions like the following.

- "What is the specific topic on which I will provide small-group instruction?"
  - "Will the lesson involve direct instruction, practicing and deepening, or knowledge application?"
  - "What general instructional strategies will I use?"

Planning for Individual Instruction

On a daily basis, teachers will identify students who need special attention on specific topics. This is a crucial aspect of a PCBE classroom. Teachers can use multiple forms of assessment to determine if individual students are effectively learning the content. We describe these in chapter 4. If issues come up, then teachers must use on-the-spot instruction. The development of SOPs can be extremely helpful for student self-checks and strategies for working through difficult content. Again, to help plan individual instruction, a teacher might ask questions like the following.

- "What is the specific topic on which I will provide individual instruction?"
- "Will the lesson involve direct instruction, practicing and deepening, or knowledge application?"
- "What general instructional strategies will I use?"

Planning for Peer-to-Peer Instruction

Peer-to-peer instruction—guided by SOPs—should be a common occurrence in a competency-based classroom. With the dynamic nature of a PCBE classroom, it is important that all students understand the SOPs so effective learning can take place. Even if the teacher is preoccupied with other students, peer-to-peer instruction can still take place. While peers should link up quite naturally in a competency-based system, teachers can facilitate such interaction. To help with such planning, a teacher might ask questions like the following.

- "Which students should I pair up?"
- "What should be the topic on which students interact?"
- "What should I do to facilitate the interaction?"

Planning to Update External Instructional Resources

Teachers will add external instructional resources to proficiency scales throughout the year. As teachers add new resources, they should make their students aware of them. To help plan for the incorporation of additional instructional resources, a teacher might ask questions like the following.

- "What new resources are available to students?"
- "How should I introduce them to students?"
- "Should I create SOPs for their use?"

Planning for Engagement

As described previously, in a PCBE system, we define *engagement* as students attending to activities that will help them reach the next level of performance on specific topics as opposed to paying attention to what the teacher is doing. This does not mean teachers can ignore the issue of overall student engagement. Indeed, teachers must continually monitor the extent that students are working on and advancing on specific topics. Daily or weekly goal setting can assist students who need more attention on a particular measurement topic. Additionally, there might be times when the teacher wants to pull students together to execute some whole-class engagement activity, if for no other reason than to foster a sense of cohesion. To facilitate such planning, a teacher might ask questions like the following.

- "What techniques or SOPs will I implement to ensure that all students are working and progressing on specific topics?"
- "Will I employ whole-class engagement strategies? If yes, what will they be?"

Planning for Relationships

Establishing relationships is typically a one-to-one endeavor in which a teacher interacts with specific students. PCBE provides many opportunities for such interaction. To help facilitate this type of planning, a teacher might ask questions like the following.

- "Which students are in need of personal attention from me?"
- "What type of interaction would benefit them most?"
- "How will I provide such interaction?"

Planning for Communicating High Expectations

As is the case with establishing positive relationships, teachers communicate high expectations one student at a time. This area in particular requires extra thought on the part of the teacher, since it involves self-understanding as well as an understanding of individual students. On the side of self-understanding, teachers must examine their own biases and low expectations about specific students and consistently identify and change their behaviors that might be adding to a student's perception of low expectations. On the side of student understanding, teachers must consider each student as a unique individual for whom some strategies might work well and others might not. To facilitate this type of planning, a teacher might ask questions like the following.

- "Which students need reinforcement of high expectations?"
- "What type of message should I communicate?"
- "How will I deliver that message?"

Planning for Classroom Management

As described previously, management in a competency-based system is very much student centered in that it involves the execution of SOPs and a code of cooperation. However, teachers (with student feedback) must still monitor the extent to which SOPs and codes of cooperation are being implemented and make adjustments as needed. To plan for classroom management, a teacher might ask questions like the following.

- "How will I monitor which SOPs students are following?"

- "Do I need to acknowledge that students are executing specific SOPs well or poorly? If yes, how will I do so?"

- "Which SOPs (if any) do I need to add or change?"

- "How will we monitor our use of the code of cooperation?"

- "How will we know if we need to revisit or adjust the code of cooperation?"

Summary

This chapter addressed the critical issue of instruction that supports student learning. While instruction in a PCBE classroom uses many of the same strategies as a traditional classroom, these strategies are typically executed in different ways. This chapter provided practical guidance for teaching in a PCBE classroom using the following nine strategies: (1) whole-class instruction, (2) small-group instruction, (3) individual instruction, (4) peer-to-peer instruction, (5) external instructional resources, (6) engagement strategies, (7) relationship strategies, (8) high expectations strategies, and (9) classroom management strategies. We discussed ways to use these strategies and compared their use in a traditional classroom to use in a PCBE classroom. Teachers should consider working with students to create and use personal tracking matrices, which translate learning targets or proficiency scales into tracking tools that use student-friendly language. Foundational planning is necessary for a successful PCBE classroom; it addresses external instructional resources, personal tracking matrices, assessments, and flow of content. Weekly and daily planning are necessary for teachers to make any needed updates and plans dealing with whole-class and small-group instruction, as well as several other important points mentioned previously. The next chapter deals with the important issue of determining student proficiency.

Chapter 4

How Will Teachers Measure Student Proficiency?

Measuring students' progress and current status is central to an effective PCBE system. It stands to reason that students must have access to accurate information about their status and growth on specific measurement topics to know what they need to do to improve. Similarly, teachers must have the same precise information to know how to alter instruction to facilitate student progress. A precise system that measures individual students' status and growth on specific topics makes the whole system run efficiently. Such a system does not occur by happenstance.

To begin, teachers must address some of the major issues that arise with assessment in a PCBE classroom. This chapter will discuss addressing unidimensionality through proficiency scales, creating reliability through multiple summative assessments, and replacing overtesting with measurement. Next, it will delve into how to use the measurement process for assessment and scoring, how to arrive at a summative score in a competency-based classroom, and how to check the accuracy of assessments. It also includes a brief overview of how to assess cognitive and metacognitive skills.

Addressing Assessment Issues in a PCBE Classroom

There are three major issues that arise with traditional assessment: (1) addressing unidimensionality through proficiency scales, (2) creating reliability through multiple summative assessments, and (3) replacing overtesting with measurement. This section will discuss how teachers may address these issues through the PCBE lens.

Addressing Unidimensionality Through Proficiency Scales

Unidimensionality is a foundational principle of test design, which states that assessments should measure a single dimension, particularly when a single score represents the student's status (Hambleton, 1993; Lord, 1953). A common pitfall of both PCBE and traditional assessment systems is when assessments violate this principle. When an assessment covers more than one specific topic, it is difficult to interpret the student's final score. To illustrate, consider the situation in table 4.1.

Table 4.1: Multiple Dimensions on a Test

	DIMENSION A	DIMENSION B	TOTAL SCORE
Student 1	2	10	12
Student 2	10	2	12
Student 3	6	6	12

Table 4.1 represents three students' scores on a twenty-item test that measures two dimensions, A and B. Each dimension involves ten items worth one point each for a total possible score of twenty points. Dimension A deals with the third-grade science topic of life cycles, and dimension B deals with the topic of food chains and webs. These topics are both covered in science at the third-grade level, but they have minimal content overlap. So, if a student knows a lot about life cycles, it doesn't follow that he or she will also know a lot about food chains and webs.

All three students in table 4.1 have the same total score, 12, yet their profiles relative to the two dimensions are quite different. Student 1 performed well on dimension B (that is, received 10 of 10 points) but not on dimension A (that is, received 2 of 10 points). Student 2 exhibited the opposite pattern, performing well on dimension A but not on dimension B. Student 3 had a moderate performance on both dimensions A and B. Because this test addressed two dimensions, the overall scores (traditionally the only information recorded) tell us little about the strengths and weaknesses of each student regarding the two dimensions. In effect, the information about the three students that the test scores provided cannot be generalized beyond this particular assessment. This is particularly problematic in a PCBE system focused on measuring students' competence on specific topics.

To solve this problem, we recommend that PCBE teachers use proficiency scales as described in previous chapters. Consider the scale in figure 4.1 on the topic of civic rights and responsibilities in a democracy.

Score 4.0	In addition to score 3.0 performance, the student demonstrates in-depth inferences and applications that go beyond what was taught.
Score 3.5	In addition to score 3.0 performance, partial success at score 4.0 content

Score 3.0	The student will demonstrate an understanding of important concepts, such as: • The influence of commonly held civic responsibilities on society in the United States (for example, explaining how engaging in different types of civic responsibility is important to a democracy)
Score 2.5	No major errors or omissions regarding score 2.0 content, and partial success at score 3.0 content
Score 2.0	The student will: • Recognize or recall specific vocabulary, including: *civic responsibility, civic duty, public service, democratic values.* • Understand different types of civic responsibilities, such as participation in government, church, and volunteer activities. • Understand the difference between a civic responsibility and a civic duty. • Identify and explain current issues involving civic responsibility, such as a local, state, or national election. • Identify opportunities for engaging in civic responsibilities in his or her city or state. • Identify ways he or she has engaged in civic responsibilities.
Score 1.5	Partial success at score 2.0 content, and major errors or omissions regarding score 3.0 content
Score 1.0	With help, partial success at score 2.0 content and score 3.0 content
Score 0.5	With help, partial success at score 2.0 content but not at score 3.0 content
Score 0.0	Even with help, no success

Source: Adapted from Marzano & Haystead, 2008.

Figure 4.1: Proficiency scale with a single element at score 3.0.

This scale has six elements at score 2.0 and one complex element at score 3.0. A specific score 4.0 target has not been identified, which allows students to develop their own assessments and evidence for achieving a score 4.0. As described in chapter 1 (page 11), the fulcrum for a proficiency scale is the score 3.0 content, which represents the single dimension that governs the entire scale. In this case, the score 3.0 content is the ability to describe the influence of commonly held civic responsibilities on society in the United States. The score 2.0 content includes the information and skills necessary to execute the central dimension identified at the score 3.0 level. In this case, such information and skills include some vocabulary terms such as *civic responsibility, civic duty,* and *public service.* Score 2.0 content also includes some basic understandings, such as identifying different types of civic responsibilities and related current issues.

When a teacher designs an assessment that addresses all three levels of content in this scale, he or she should not assume that items must be constructed for every element in the scale. Score 3.0 has one element only, but score 2.0 has multiple elements. When designing an assessment, the teacher would construct items that are representative of the score 2.0 content rather than specifically matched to each element at the score 2.0 level. To illustrate, consider figure 4.2 (page 100), which is an assessment based on the proficiency scale in figure 4.1.

Section A

1. Give a definition or explanation of civic responsibility. _____
_____
_____

2. In the following list, identify which is a civic responsibility and which is a civic duty.

Voting in an election _____

Paying taxes _____

Registering for selective service _____

Serving on a jury _____

Volunteering in the community _____

Attending school _____

Participating in a local caucus _____

Section B

Explain how donating time as a mentor at a youth center affects your local community. _____
_____
_____

Section C

Write a brief explanation of how, as a student who is not yet eighteen years old, you can engage various types of civic responsibility that have an important influence on your city or state. _____
_____
_____

Figure 4.2: Sample assessment.

Note that this assessment has three sections. Section A deals with score 2.0 content, section B deals with score 3.0 content, and section C deals with score 4.0 content. Section A, which addresses score 2.0, has two items, but they don't explicitly cover all six score 2.0 elements in the scale. Yet the teacher can assume that score 2.0 has been addressed (particularly over the course of multiple assessments) because multiple content statements at a given proficiency scale level should be related enough that they covary.

As described previously, the concept of covariance means that if a student knows one element, he or she will probably know another element. For example, if a student knows how to explain and calculate unit rate, he or she would probably know how to address comparing unit rates when comparing proportional relationships. When proficiency scales are constructed well, teachers can construct items that draw from multiple elements at a score level but don't cover every element. This circumstance is particularly the case for score 2.0 content where multiple elements are commonly listed.

The concept of covariance is particularly important when the score 3.0 level contains more than one element with accompanying score 2.0 elements. To illustrate, consider the proficiency scale in figure 4.3.

Score 4.0	Use measures of central tendency and variability of distributions to make decisions and predictions.
Score 3.5	In addition to score 3.0 performance, partial success at score 4.0 content
Score 3.0	The student will: 1. Use appropriate measures of central tendency and variability to describe a data set based on the shape of the data distribution and the context in which the data were gathered. 2. Calculate measures of center (mean, median) and variability (interquartile range, mean absolute deviation). The student exhibits no major errors or omissions.
Score 2.5	No major errors or omissions regarding score 2.0 content, and partial success at score 3.0 content
Score 2.0	The student will: 1.1. Understand that a set of data collected to answer a statistical question has a distribution which can be described by its center, spread, and overall shape. 1.2. Describe patterns and variations from patterns in a data set. 1.3. Know the following vocabulary terms and phrases: *central tendency, data distribution*. 2.1. Recognize that a measure of variation for a numerical data set describes how its values vary with a single number. 2.2. Recognize that a measure of center for a numerical data set summarizes all of its values with a single number. 2.3. Know that variability refers to how spread out a set of data is. 2.4. Recognize if a data set is more or less spread out than another data set. 2.5. Calculate the range of a set of data. 2.6. Know the following vocabulary terms and phrases: *mean, median, mode, variability, interquartile range, mean absolute deviation, outlier, deviation, dispersion*. The student exhibits no major errors or omissions regarding the simpler details and processes; however, the student exhibits major errors or omissions regarding the more complex ideas and processes.
Score 1.5	Partial success at score 2.0 content, and major errors or omissions regarding score 3.0 content
Score 1.0	With help, a partial understanding of some of the simpler details and processes and some of the more complex ideas and processes
Score 0.5	With help, partial success at score 2.0 content but not at score 3.0 content
Score 0.0	Even with help, no success

Figure 4.3: Proficiency scale on data distributions.

This scale has two elements at the score 3.0 level; for each of these elements, there are corresponding score 2.0 elements. A test designed for this proficiency scale is depicted in figure 4.4 (page 102).

Use the student survey data set to respond to the following items.

The student survey asked three questions.

1. On a scale from (1) like the least to (5) like the most, rate how well you like mathematics class.

2. Rate how comfortable you are participating in a large-group discussion in class: (4) very comfortable, (3) somewhat comfortable, (2) somewhat uncomfortable, (1) very uncomfortable.

3. Rank in order the following ways to learn, with 1 being your favorite and 5 being your least favorite: listen to the teacher talk, read about the subject, watch a video, work with classmates in a small group, work with one other person.

Part I

1. Calculate the range of the following group of numbers: 93, 17, 85, 66, 12, 35, 74, 75.

2. Explain the overall pattern of student responses to survey question 2.

3. Are the data for survey question 1 more or less variable than the data for survey question 3?

4. Define an outlier.

Part II

1. Calculate the mean, median, and mode for the student responses to survey question 1.

2. Using the student responses to survey question 2, calculate the mean absolute distribution of the data set.

3. Using the student responses to survey question 3, describe how the class likes best to learn in terms of the distribution of the data set.

Part III

In the survey, students were asked about their comfort levels in large-group discussions and their favorite ways to learn. Using the results of the survey, choose three types of learning activities that are most likely to help these students learn the material and enjoy mathematics class. Justify your choices in terms of the central tendencies and variability of the responses to each question.

Figure 4.4: Sample test for proficiency scale with two score 3.0 elements.

The assessment in figure 4.4 addresses all three levels of the scale in figure 4.3 (page 101)—part I focuses on the score 2.0 content, part II focuses on score 3.0, and part III focuses on score 4.0. While the proficiency scale has nine content statements at score 2.0, part I of the assessment has only four questions. However, these questions sample across the score 2.0 content to provide a complete picture of students' knowledge at that level. For example, the first question in part I ("Calculate the range of the following group of numbers") requires that students know the term *range* (element 2.6 on the scale) and be able to calculate it (element 2.5).

Part II of the assessment focuses on score 3.0 content. Questions 1 and 2 both assess students' knowledge of the second element at level 3.0 on the scale, while question 3 assesses the first element. Part III assesses the score 4.0 content, requiring students to apply their level 2.0 and 3.0 knowledge, make a decision, and defend it. Typically, when a proficiency scale contains two elements at score 3.0, the score 4.0 content requires students to integrate the two 3.0 elements. It is important to note that while constructing assessments from a proficiency scale that has two or more elements at the score 3.0 level and, therefore, two or more sets of elements at the score 2.0 level, it might become clear that the two sets of elements would be better represented as two distinct proficiency scales.

The requirement that an assessment address one dimension is built into the proficiency scale design. Indeed, a basic requirement of a proficiency scale is that its elements represent a single dimension. This makes scoring assessments designed using proficiency scales relatively straightforward for teachers. We discuss these issues in detail in subsequent sections of this chapter. Briefly though, a teacher would assign a score on the assessment in figure 4.4 using the proficiency scale. A score of 3.0 would mean that the student demonstrated competence in all the score 3.0 content and the score 2.0 content on the proficiency scale (as represented on the assessment) but not the score 4.0 content. A score of 2.0 would mean that the student demonstrated competence in the score 2.0 content on the proficiency scale (as represented on the assessment) but not the score 3.0 or 4.0 content. A score of 2.5 would mean that the student demonstrated competence on the score 2.0 content and partial competence with the score 3.0 content, and so on. In short, for the assessment in figure 4.4, each student would receive a single score that relates directly to the proficiency scale. We refer to this as the *measurement process* and discuss it later in the chapter.

Another problem frequently encountered in assessment is the use of a single score at one point in time to show a student's proficiency. This issue will be addressed in the following section.

Creating Reliability Through Multiple Summative Assessments

Another pitfall common in PCBE systems is relying too heavily on a single summative assessment. More specifically, many PCBE schools require students to obtain a passing score (sometimes referred to as a *cut score*) on a specific assessment to be considered proficient on a particular topic. Unfortunately, teachers should never use a single assessment as the sole criterion for determining a student's current status simply because all assessments are inaccurate to some degree. This idea is explicit in what might be thought of as the fundamental equation of classical test theory: *observed score = true score + error score*.

This equation indicates that the score a student receives on an assessment (referred to as the *observed score*) consists of two components: (1) a *true score* component and (2) an *error score* component. The student's true score represents his or her precise score regarding the topic being measured at a particular point in time on a particular test. The error score is the part of the observed score that is due to factors other than the student's level of understanding or skill. Four other factors might include the following.

1. The student guessed correctly on a few items.

2. The student misread a few items but knew the correct answer.

3. The teacher added up the student's points incorrectly, and the final score was higher than it should have been.

4. The teacher added up the student's points incorrectly, and the final score was lower than it should have been.

Factors 1 and 3 would produce an observed score for a student that is higher than the student's true score for the test. Factors 2 and 4 would produce an observed score that is lower than the student's true score. Any observed score probably has errors, rendering it higher or lower than the student's true score.

Reliability indices provide information about how precise students' scores on a particular test are. A reliability close to 0.0 means that the observed scores on a given test are highly inaccurate—they are comprised primarily of error. A reliability close to 1.00 means that the observed scores on a particular test are highly accurate—they are comprised primarily of true scores. In effect, the reliability of a test indicates how much error one might expect for any observed score. See table 4.2.

Table 4.2: Ninety-Five Percent Confidence Intervals

RELIABILITY	OBSERVED SCORE	LOWER LIMIT	UPPER LIMIT	RANGE
0.85	2.5	2.19	2.81	0.62
0.75	2.5	2.08	2.92	0.82
0.65	2.5	2.01	2.99	0.98
0.55	2.5	1.95	3.05	1.10

Note: The standard deviation of this test was 0.42, and the upper and lower limits have been rounded. For a detailed discussion of how to compute these intervals, see Marzano (in press).

Table 4.2 depicts how the accuracy of a single score changes across four levels of reliability: 0.85, 0.75, 0.65, and 0.55. Note the observed score (in the second column) is always the same—2.5. Consider the precision of an observed score of 2.5 when the reliability of an assessment is 0.85 (the first row). This is a typical reliability one would expect from a state or standardized test (Lou et al., 1996). The third and fourth columns represent the 95 percent confidence interval—a range of scores in which one is 95 percent confident that the true score actually falls. Examining the first row, we see that an observed score of 2.5 on an assessment that has a reliability of 0.85 has a 95 percent confidence interval of 2.19 to 2.81. In other words, one can be 95 percent sure that the accurate or true score for a student with an observed score of 2.5 is somewhere between 2.19 and 2.81. This is a fairly large spread, which becomes even larger as the reliability goes down. Consider what happens when the reliability is 0.55, which is what one might expect for a teacher-made assessment that was rather hastily put together. The 95 percent confidence interval is much larger: 1.95 to 3.05.

This example uses scores on a proficiency scale. The situation is the same when a one hundred–point scale, as opposed to the four-point scale, is used to score assessments. This is depicted in table 4.3. As indicated, an observed score of 75 on an assessment with a reliability of 0.85 has a 95 percent confidence interval between 68.63 and 81.37—a difference of 12.74 points. An observed score of 75 on an assessment with a reliability of 0.55 has a 95 percent confidence interval between 64.06 and 85.94— a difference of 21.88 points.

Table 4.3: Ninety-Five Percent Confidence Intervals Using the One Hundred–Point Scale

RELIABILITY	OBSERVED SCORE	LOWER LIMIT	UPPER LIMIT	RANGE
0.85	75	68.63	81.37	12.74
0.75	75	66.85	83.15	16.30
0.65	75	65.38	84.62	19.24
0.55	75	64.06	85.94	21.88

Note: The standard deviation of this test was 8.33, and the upper and lower limits have been rounded. For a detailed discussion of how to compute these intervals, see Marzano (in press).

Clearly, a single observed score on an assessment (regardless of whether one uses a four-point scale or one hundred–point scale) does not provide enough confidence in its accuracy to make a determination about a student's true competency, even when that assessment has a high reliability. For these reasons, it is almost always a bad idea to use a single score on a summative test as the indicator of whether a student is proficient regarding a specific learning target or measurement topic.

Teachers can solve the over-reliance on a single assessment problem by administering multiple assessments over time on the same topic. This approach, part of the measurement process described in the following section (page 106), allows the teacher and students to see growth on a particular topic. To illustrate, consider figure 4.5, which depicts one student's scores on a topic over a three-week period. The student began with a score of 1.5, but then moved up to a score of 2.5. This second score might have occurred a few days after the first assessment. The third score was also 2.5, occurring a week later, and so on, until the final score of 3.5.

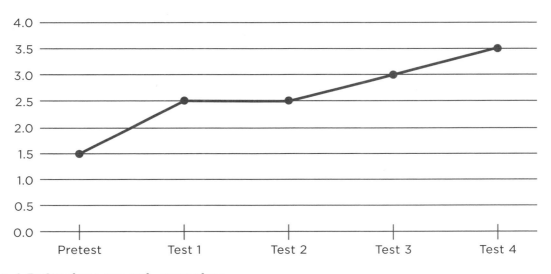

Figure 4.5: Student growth over time.

When teachers record scores for a particular student as shown in figure 4.5, teachers don't use one single assessment in isolation. Rather, teachers use all assessments as a set to determine the student's score at any point in time. We describe methods for computing the final score in depth in a subsequent section of this chapter (see Arriving at a Summative Score, page 122). Briefly, though, the final score in the series is not automatically the student's current or final score. Teachers can use previous scores to help compute a current score. For example, if a student had acquired three scores of 3.0 in a row, it would not make much sense that the student's next score would be a 2.0.

Tracking student progress as depicted in figure 4.5 (page 105) also provides a unique perspective on the concepts of formative and summative assessments. The concepts of formative and summative assessments became popular in the late 1990s, most probably due to the publication of "Inside the Black Box" in *Phi Delta Kappan* (Black & Wiliam, 1998). While these are powerful constructs, teachers have not used them in the most rigorous ways. Indeed, in some instances teachers use the constructs to reinforce some of the assessment problems discussed in this chapter, particularly the problem of over-reliance on a single test. Too often within a PCBE system, all assessment scores except for one are considered formative. In many cases, teachers consider formative scores as practice and do not even record the results. As described previously, this practice leads to the problem of over-reliance on a single test. The measurement process, described in the following section, uses all assessment scores to construct a summative score. Indeed, Marzano (2010) noted that it is more appropriate to refer to formative and summative *scores* as opposed to formative and summative assessments.

Replacing Overtesting With Measurement

The final trap educators in a PCBE system easily fall into is overtesting. To illustrate, consider again the following sixteen measurement topics for eighth-grade mathematics.

1. Exponents
2. Cube and square roots
3. Scientific notation
4. Rational and irrational numbers
5. Linear equations
6. Systems of linear equations
7. Quadratic equations
8. Concept of functions
9. Linear functions
10. Volume
11. Transformations, similarity, and congruence
12. Angles of two-dimensional figures
13. Line and angle constructions

14. Pythagorean theorem

15. Bivariate categorical data

16. Bivariate measurement data

There are sixteen measurement topics in this list. As described in chapter 1 (page 11), we recommend about fifteen to twenty-five measurement topics for each grade level. We also recommend that teachers articulate the specific content in each measurement topic as a proficiency scale. For example, figure 4.6 contains a proficiency scale for the mathematics topic of cube and square roots.

Score 4.0	The student will: • Estimate the square roots of non-perfect squares (for example, identify the nearest perfect squares above and below a given non-perfect square and identify the root of the non-perfect square as lying between the roots of the perfect squares).
Score 3.5	In addition to score 3.0 performance, partial success at score 4.0 content
Score 3.0	The student will: **_Evaluate the cube and square roots of perfect cubes and squares_** (for example, identify both the square root and the cube root of 64).
Score 2.5	No major errors or omissions regarding score 2.0 content, and partial success at score 3.0 content
Score 2.0	The student will recognize or recall specific vocabulary (for example, _base number, cube root, cube, degree, integer, perfect cube, perfect square, power, principal root, radical, radicand, raise, root, square root, square_) and perform basic processes such as: • Explain that raising a base value to an integer power represents repeated multiplication of the base value by itself. • Explain that the radical symbol is used to indicate the root of the radicand (the value beneath the radical). • Explain that a value raised to an even power has both positive and negative roots. • Explain that the positive root of a value is known as the principal root. • Explain that raising a value to the second power is known as squaring the value. • Explain that the root of a squared value is known as its square root. • Explain that a radical symbol without a specified degree indicates the square root of the radicand. • Identify perfect squares. • Explain that raising a value to the third power is known as cubing the value. • Identify perfect cubes.
Score 1.5	Partial success at score 2.0 content, and major errors or omissions regarding score 3.0 content
Score 1.0	With help, partial success at score 2.0 content and score 3.0 content
Score 0.5	With help, partial success at score 2.0 content but not at score 3.0 content
Score 0.0	Even with help, no success

Figure 4.6: Proficiency scale for the topic of cube and square roots.

As depicted in figure 4.6 (page 107), proficiency scales contain three levels of content (score 2.0 content, score 3.0 content, and score 4.0 content). If a school or district used the sixteen topics listed previously, eighth-grade mathematics would have forty-eight sets of content statements—three levels for each proficiency scale. If each of these forty-eight sets of content statements was considered in isolation, it would require an inordinate amount of testing, particularly in a PCBE system, simply because in such a system students are allowed many opportunities to demonstrate their proficiency. Multiple opportunities to demonstrate proficiency implies that students would have multiple chances to retest. If students averaged two tests before they demonstrated competency within a particular set of content at a particular level of a proficiency scale, they would take ninety-six tests for eighth-grade mathematics. If students averaged three assessments to demonstrate proficiency, then 144 tests would be required for each student in this content area and grade level, and so on. Obviously, this multiplier effect would render the assessment system completely impractical.

Teachers can solve this problem by conducting many different forms of assessment over time. By thinking of a test as only one form of assessment and instead integrating test scores with other assessment forms such as one-on-one discussion, group assessments, behavior observation, and so on, a teacher can develop a more accurate picture of a student's proficiency. In effect, the teacher is testing less but assessing more. This system is part of the *measurement process*, an approach which we will now discuss in greater detail.

Using the Measurement Process

Educators tend to think of classroom assessments as a series of independent events. Teachers administer, score, and enter those scores into a gradebook. The typical way to interpret these scores as an overall view of student achievement is to compute an average. But the average is usually an inaccurate perspective because students increase their understanding and skill over time. The mathematical process of averaging does not account for student growth. Fortunately, there is another more accurate and useful perspective. Some of the foundational terms and literature for this perspective are detailed in table 4.4.

Table 4.4: Definitions of Measurement-Related Terms

TERM	DEFINITION
Assessment	"Any systematic method of obtaining information, used to draw inferences about characteristics of people, objects, or programs; a systematic process to measure or evaluate the characteristics or performance of individuals, programs, or other entities for purposes of drawing inferences; sometimes used synonymously with *test*" (American Educational Research Association [AERA], American Psychological Association [APA], & National Council on Measurement in Education [NCME], 2014, p. 216)
Measurement	"The assignment of numerals to objects or events according to rules" (Stevens, 1946, p. 677)
Test	"A collection of tasks; the examinee's performance on these is taken as an index of his standing along some psychological dimension" (Lord, 1959, p. 472)

Score	"Any specific number resulting from the assessment of an individual, such as a raw score, a scale score, an estimate of a latent variable, a production count, an absence record, a course grade, or a rating" (AERA et al., 2014, p. 223)
Scale	"1. The system of numbers, and their units, by which a value is reported on some dimension of measurement. 2. In testing, the set of items or subtests used to measure a specific characteristic (e.g., a test of verbal ability or a scale of extroversion-introversion)" (AERA et al., 2014, p. 223)

The definitions in table 4.4 are technical ones. We present these technical definitions because there is so much misunderstanding and misuse of these concepts, particularly in K–12 education. Thorough understanding and application of these concepts solve many of the problems previously introduced. We begin with assessment.

In nontechnical terms, an *assessment* is any systematic way a teacher collects evidence regarding a student's level of knowledge or skill on a particular topic at a particular point in time. To a great extent, it is accurate to think of all types of assessments as evidence. As described in chapter 1 (page 11), the approach to PCBE refers to assessed topics as measurement topics. Assessments provide evidence of students' status and growth regarding these topics.

A *scale* is a system of units that describes progress along some continuum. In the system described in this book, a proficiency scale accompanies each measurement topic. Assessments provide evidence teachers can use to place students on a scale. In this case, the scale used has values that range from 0.0 to 4.0. *Measurement*, then, is the process of translating the evidence from an assessment into a number that is understandable on the scale (that is, proficiency scale). A *test* is a specific type of assessment that involves items or tasks. As noted in a subsequent section of this chapter, there are assessments other than tests that a teacher might use. Finally, the term *score* is the most ambiguous of the set in table 4.4. The term *score* can describe a student's status on a particular assessment. The term *score* can also describe a student's current status on a proficiency scale. Thus, a student can receive a score on an assessment that is then translated into a score on a proficiency scale.

To illustrate how these concepts interact, recall the proficiency scale in figure 4.3 (page 101) for the measurement topic on data distributions. At the beginning of a unit, a teacher gives a pencil-and-paper test on the score 2.0 content in the scale. As we have seen, a test is a type of assessment. The teacher assigns these test scores to students using the traditional one hundred–point or percentage scale. The teacher has established a score of 80 percent as the criterion score or cut score, indicating that a student should receive a score of 2.0 on the proficiency scale. Any student who receives a score of 80 percent or higher on the test receives a score of 2.0 on the proficiency scale. The system of scores on the test is different from the system of scores on the proficiency scale, but the teacher translates all assessment results into scores on the proficiency scale. A few days later, the teacher has a discussion with a specific student and asks questions about score 2.0 and 3.0 content on the proficiency scale. This discussion is also a type of assessment even though it is not a traditional test. The discussion qualifies as an assessment because it is gathering information about a particular student's status on a particular measurement topic. Based on this discussion, the teacher assigns a score of 2.5, indicating that the student understands the score 2.0 content and understands some but not all of the score 3.0 content.

These concepts and the way they interact provide a new perspective on testing and assessing students. See figure 4.7 for a visual of this measurement process. The sections of the measurement process will be discussed in detail below.

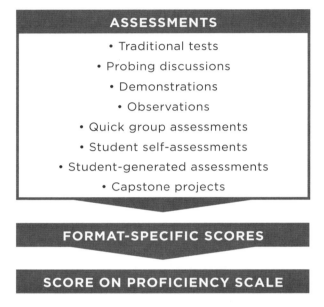

ASSESSMENTS
- Traditional tests
- Probing discussions
- Demonstrations
- Observations
- Quick group assessments
- Student self-assessments
- Student-generated assessments
- Capstone projects

FORMAT-SPECIFIC SCORES

SCORE ON PROFICIENCY SCALE

Figure 4.7: The measurement process.

Assessments

Assessments come in many forms (a traditional test being one). Assessments produce scores that are sometimes specific to the assessment format. For example, an assessment might be a quiz that yields a score of 1 to 10. An assessment might be a student presentation teachers score on a rubric that includes score values of *excellent, proficient, progressing,* and *needs work.* An assessment might be a rather long pencil-and-paper test that yields a score from 0 to 100. To be meaningful in terms of student learning, all these *format-specific* scores must be translated into a score on a common scale. In this case, the common scale is the proficiency scale for the topic teachers are measuring, which is why the topics we discuss in chapter 1 (page 11) qualify as *measurement topics.*

As can be seen in figure 4.7, there is a wide variety of assessments teachers can use to measure proficiency. In this section, we address eight types: (1) traditional tests, (2) probing discussions, (3) demonstrations, (4) observations, (5) quick group assessments, (6) student self-assessments, (7) student-generated assessments, and (8) capstone projects. The format-specific scores derived from these types of assessment are translated to general scores on the 0–4 scale and then recorded for the specific and related learning target or measurement topic. Understanding the variety of assessments available to teachers provides the opportunity to assess more but test less. We begin with traditional tests.

Traditional Tests

Traditional tests are only one type of assessment, but they are an important type. Commonly, traditional tests require students to record their responses in written form. Usually this is done in a pencil-and-paper format or electronically. Such tests include a variety of types of items and tasks. Next, we discuss the topics of (1) selected-response items, (2) short constructed-response items, and (3) extended constructed-response items.

Selected-Response Items

Many classroom tests employ selected-response items and tasks. The types of items and tasks in table 4.5 briefly exemplify a variety of selected-response items.

Table 4.5: Examples of Selected-Response Items

TYPE	EXAMPLE
Multiple Choice	Which of the following is an accurate statement about Venus? A. It is composed mostly of carbon dioxide. B. It is covered by thick clouds of sulfuric acid. C. It is believed to have had water that has all boiled away. D. It is surrounded by rings.

Matching	Match the state listed on the left with its most famous landmark listed on the right.
	
	1. District of Columbia A. The Alamo
	2. Arizona B. The Pentagon
	3. South Dakota C. The White House
	4. Texas D. Mount Rushmore
	   E. Everglades
	   F. Grand Canyon

Alternative Choice	On a number line, a negative seven can be found: A. To the right of zero B. To the left of zero
True or False	Quotation marks are at the end of sentences that are questions.
Multiple Response	Put a check next to the shapes for which you can find the volume. Circle Cube Square Sphere Octagon Prism
Fill-in-the-Blank	_____ was the first African American to hold the office of president of the United States.

Source: Adapted from Marzano, 2010.

Teachers most commonly use selected-response items like those in table 4.5 (page 111) to assess score 2.0 content. This is not to say that they can't also use those selected-response items for score 3.0 and 4.0 content, but in such cases they require a great deal of written explanation for students. For example, a teacher could construct a multiple-choice item to assess a student's use of the decision-making process as described in score 3.0 content. However, the stem for the item would have to provide a description of the alternatives, and the criteria teachers wanted students to use to select among the alternatives, and the relative importance of the criteria. To illustrate, assume a teacher wanted to design a selected-response item to assess students' abilities to use the decision-making process regarding the best place to build a nuclear reactor in the state. As part of the description of the task, the teacher would have to list the specific places the reactor might be located (that is, the alternatives; for example, near a certain forest, in a specific city, and so on), the criteria the students would use to select among the alternatives (for example, the potential impact on human and animal life, the creation of jobs, and so on), and the levels of importance for each criterion (for example, highly important, moderately important, and so on).

Short Constructed-Response Items

While selected-response questions require students to recognize the correct answer from a set of given options, short constructed-response questions prompt students to recall the answer from memory. Short constructed-response questions typically require written answers that range in length from a few words to a few sentences. For example, a high school social studies test might include the short constructed-response item, "Briefly explain the role that Alice Paul played in the American women's suffrage movement." Teachers commonly use short constructed-response items for score 2.0 and 3.0 content.

Extended Constructed-Response Items

An extended constructed response requires students to present a longer, more complex answer to a prompt or question. The most common form of this response type is an essay. Extended constructed-response items usually assess score 3.0 or 4.0 content and often require students to draw on multiple elements of content knowledge as they develop their answer over the course of several paragraphs. Extended constructed-response items might also pose multiple questions and prompt students to write an essay that answers all of them (Marzano, 2010). These items often incorporate content from all three levels of the proficiency scale, as depicted in the following example.

Read the passage and study the picture provided. Then answer the following questions.

A. Who is the artist this passage is about, and for what medium is he or she famous?

B. In what country and during what time period was this artist working?

C. What were the unique elements of the artist's work, and how did people initially react?

D. Compare this artist's work to one of the other artists we have studied. Who do you think is the superior artist and why?

This task addresses score 2.0, 3.0, and 4.0 content on a proficiency scale for art—score 2.0 focuses on knowing details about an artist's life and work, score 3.0 content focuses on understanding the unique features of an artist's style, and score 4.0 content focuses on comparing the work of different artists.

Probing Discussions

A probing discussion is a type of oral assessment. To use a probing discussion, a teacher meets one-to-one with a student to talk about a specific topic. The teacher begins with a broad prompt, and then, as the student explains the relevant concepts, the teacher asks more specific or in-depth questions to determine what the student knows and does not know about the topic. The teacher uses the proficiency scale for questioning; that is, the teacher determines a student's level of knowledge by asking questions that correspond to the levels of the scale.

Teachers commonly translate evidence directly from probing discussions into a proficiency scale score. That is, there is no need to assign a format-specific score and then translate that score into a proficiency scale score. For example, during a probing discussion with a student working on the fourth-grade science topic of properties of water, a teacher would ask questions pertinent to score 2.0, 3.0, and 4.0 content on the proficiency scale for that topic. At the end of the discussion, the teacher might conclude that the student demonstrated a thorough understanding of the score 2.0 content and a partial understanding of the score 3.0 content, thus assigning the student proficiency scale score of 2.5 for that assessment.

Demonstrations

Demonstrations are assessments that involve students carrying out a skill, strategy, or process. To assess a student using a demonstration, a teacher would simply ask the student to perform a specific skill, strategy, or process. For example, a social studies teacher might ask a student to demonstrate how to use the key on a map to interpret a particular map feature. The teacher can use demonstrations to assess both physical and mental skills and procedures. In the case of mental skills, the teacher can ask the student to think aloud or narrate the process as he or she performs it. Demonstrations can also be scored directly from a proficiency scale. For example, a student working on a fifth-grade English language arts measurement topic on using citations has prepared a demonstration of the process. As the student executes and explains the steps, the teacher might realize that he has demonstrated all the score 3.0 content with accuracy and assign that score to the demonstration.

Observations

While the assessment formats discussed thus far are all forms of *obtrusive assessments* (that is, they interrupt the normal flow of classroom activity), observations are often *unobtrusive*—that is, the student is not necessarily aware that the teacher is assessing him or her. Observations involve the teacher noticing a student demonstrating some level of proficiency and recording a score. Skills, strategies, and processes are most often the subject of observations; for example, a science teacher might notice a student independently executing the correct procedures for a specific aspect of a research project. Informational knowledge, however, might also be the subject of an observation. For example, a student might use a piece of information in a class discussion that represents score 2.0 content on a scale. The teacher would recognize that the student understands that content. Again, observations are scored directly from a proficiency scale.

Quick Group Assessments

As the name implies, teachers administer quick group assessments to the entire class at once. They usually focus on score 2.0 content teachers can assess easily with selected-response items. For example, assume that a particular science proficiency scale on the topic of energy conversion has the following three elements of score 2.0 content.

1. Explain that an object's energy is a combination of kinetic energy and potential energy.

2. Use the law of conservation of energy to explain why energy is always transferred from place to place or from form to form.

3. Describe various forms of energy (for example, chemical, elastic, electrical, light, mechanical, nuclear, sound, and thermal).

The teacher might consider a number of selected-response items like the following.

1. **Fill-in-the-blank:** An object's energy is a combination of _____ energy and _____ energy.

2. **Select the best answer:** The law of conservation of energy says that:

    A. Energy is constant in a closed system.

    B. Energy can change form, but it can't be created or destroyed.

    C. Both A and B

    D. Neither A nor B

3. **Select any items in this list that are *not* forms of energy:** chemical, sound, electrical, practical, heat, weight.

Teachers would simultaneously display each of these items to all students, perhaps using a PowerPoint slide. Students would record their answers on response cards and hold them up so that the teacher could see them. The teacher would keep track of the students who answered correctly, perhaps using a seating chart. Over the course of a class period, the teacher might administer ten items and keep track of students' individual responses. By the end of the class, the teacher would have scores for each student on a ten-item assessment of score 2.0 content. Another option is for the teacher to use electronic voting devices, sometimes referred to as *clickers*. If teachers have devices that allow students to connect to the Internet, they can use free websites or software, such as Kahoot! (getkahoot.com), Quizzizz (quizzizz.com), or Socrative (socrative.com) to gather students' responses.

Student Self-Assessments

With student self-assessments, students score themselves using personal tracking matrices, and teachers then translate these student-generated scores into proficiency scale scores. To illustrate, consider the personal tracking matrix in figure 4.8.

LEVEL	INDICATOR	MY RATING			MY EVIDENCE
		I'm still confused about this topic.	I've learned some but not all of the topic.	I've got this now.	
Score 4.0	I can show situations in which solving a linear equation is best done through graphing versus situations in which it is best done algebraically.	/////			
Score 3.0	I can find the point that will satisfy two linear equations by graphing both equations.	/////	/////		
Score 2.0	I can verify the point of intersection by inserting the coordinates into each linear equation.	/////	/////	/////	Practice activity 4
Score 2.0	I can determine the intersection point of the graphs of two linear equations.	/////	/////	/////	Practice activity 3
Score 2.0	I can graph a linear equation on a coordinate plane.	/////	/////	/////	Practice activity 2
Score 2.0	I can convert a linear equation into its slope-intercept form.	/////	/////	/////	Practice activity 1
Score 2.0	I can provide an explanation of the term *intersection point*.	/////	/////	/////	Vocabulary worksheet
Score 2.0	I can provide an explanation of the term *coordinate plane*.	/////	/////	/////	Vocabulary worksheet

Figure 4.8: Personal tracking matrix.

continued →

LEVEL	INDICATOR	MY RATING				MY EVIDENCE
Score 2.0	I can provide an explanation of the term *slope-intercept form*.					*Vocabulary worksheet*
Score 2.0	I can provide an explanation of the term *linear equation*.					*Vocabulary worksheet*

Figure 3.4 (pages 84–85) depicted this personal tracking matrix for the topic of solving linear equations through graphing. Recall that a teacher created the matrix by unpacking the elements of the proficiency scale for this topic into rather discrete elements. Specifically, the teacher assigned all the score 2.0 elements, including vocabulary, a row in the matrix. The teacher also coded each row for its level on the proficiency scale. Finally, there is a self-rating scale ranging from "I'm still confused about this topic" to "I've got this now" in the columns of the matrix.

The student has used the scale to self-assess each element. Note that the student has assigned himself the value of "I've got this now" for all the score 2.0 content. The student has assigned the value of "I've learned some but not all of the topic" for the score 3.0 element and has assigned himself the value of "I'm still confused about this topic" for the score 4.0 content. In the column My Evidence, the student has briefly noted the activities and assignments he completed as support for his self-ratings.

For the teacher to use the matrix as an assessment, the student would have to provide more evidence for the score he assigned. This evidence might be in a folder the student keeps with related assignments and assessments or evidence that has been archived electronically. The teacher would examine the student's self-assessment represented in the personal tracking matrix and the supporting evidence and translate it into a proficiency scale score. The personal tracking matrix analysis often accompanies a brief conversation with the student. While interacting with the student, the teacher might decide that the student's self-assessment warrants a score of 2.5 on the proficiency scale at this point in time. As described previously, teachers can directly score some assessment types using a proficiency scale. For example, a teacher can score a probing discussion directly using a proficiency scale.

Student-Generated Assessments

Student-generated assessments involve students themselves deciding what they will do to demonstrate proficiency. While underutilized, this process is extremely powerful because students take responsibility for demonstrating their learning. When a student feels that she has achieved a particular level of proficiency, she goes to the teacher and explains how she will demonstrate her knowledge or skill. If students are having difficulty generating ideas for assessments, it is highly useful for the teacher to brainstorm possibilities with the class or even generate a list of ways students might document their competence. Students commonly use such assessments to provide evidence of competence at a specific level of a scale.

For example, a student might propose that she will make a timeline of civil rights events to show her understanding of that topic at the 2.0 level on a proficiency scale.

Capstone Projects

One of the most flexible forms of assessment is the capstone project. According to *The Glossary of Education Reform for Journalists, Parents, and Community Members*,

> [A] **capstone project** is a multifaceted assignment that serves as a culminating academic and intellectual experience for students, typically during their final year of high school or middle school, or at the end of an academic program or learning-pathway experience. While similar in some ways to a college thesis, capstone projects may take a wide variety of forms, but most are long-term investigative projects that culminate in a final product, presentation, or performance. (Capstone project, 2016)

Students at any level can work on capstone projects. In fact, we recommend that every student is engaged in some type of capstone project each year. It is important that students have a maximum level of control over the project content and design. As indicated by the preceding definition, capstone projects are often investigations about areas of interest to students. For example, a high school student who is interested in the culinary arts as a potential career path might research a certain style of cooking and practice making dishes, perhaps even interning with a local chef. A middle school student might research his favorite animal, observe it at the zoo, and write a paper describing the species' behavior. An elementary student might create a poster about a specific type of dinosaur. With guidance from the teacher, students identify which academic, cognitive, and metacognitive skills they are demonstrating in their projects. Additional information about capstone projects can be found in Scott and Marzano (2014).

Once a teacher has decided the types of assessments to administer in the classroom, attention should be turned to scoring student proficiency.

Format-Specific Scores and Proficiency Scores

As the measurement process indicates in figure 4.7 (page 110), the ultimate goal of a PCBE teacher is to record all students' scores on proficiency scales. Of the assessment formats listed, teachers can score demonstrations, observations, and student-generated assessments directly using a proficiency scale.

Traditional tests, however, usually require some type of format-specific score that teachers then translate to a proficiency scale score. To illustrate, consider tests (like those in figure 4.2, page 100, and figure 4.4, page 102) that each have three sections—one section with items focusing on score 2.0, another section with items focusing on score 3.0, and another with items focusing on score 4.0. Assume that the items on the test include selected-response items and short constructed-response items. There are two ways to score tests like these and translate the format-specific scores into proficiency scale scores: (1) using percentage scores and (2) using response codes.

Using Percentage Scores

This method involves determining what percentage of available points a student earned and using that percentage to assign an appropriate proficiency scale score. To illustrate, consider figure 4.9.

SECTION	ITEM NUMBER	POSSIBLE POINTS PER ITEM	OBTAINED POINTS PER ITEM	SECTION PERCENTAGE
Score 2.0	1	5	5	22/25 = 88 percent
	2	5	4	
	3	5	3	
	4	5	5	
	5	5	5	
	Total	25	22	
Score 3.0	6	10	7	15/30 = 50 percent
	7	10	4	
	8	10	4	
	Total	30	15	
Score 4.0	9	10	1	3/20 = 15 percent
	10	10	2	
	Total	20	3	

Source: Adapted from Marzano, Heflebower, Hoegh, Warrick, & Grift, 2016, p. 56.

Figure 4.9: The percentage approach to scoring assessments.

Figure 4.9 compares the available points on each section of an assessment to the points a student obtained. For example, there were twenty-five points available in the score 2.0 section, and this student earned twenty-two. This ratio is then converted into a percentage to make it easier to assess the student's overall success in each section. The teacher examines the percentage for each section to determine a proficiency scale score. In figure 4.9, the student earned 88 percent in the score 2.0 section, indicating that he or she knows most of that content. The student also earned 50 percent in the score 3.0 section, indicating that he or she knows only half of that content. Based on this evidence, the teacher would likely assign a proficiency scale score of 2.5—no major errors or omissions with the basic content and partial success with the target content.

Using Response Codes

With this method, the teacher marks a student's responses to each item *correct*, *partially correct*, or *incorrect* and then examines the pattern of responses to determine the student's proficiency level. To illustrate, consider figure 4.10.

SECTION	ITEM NUMBER	CORRECT, PARTIALLY CORRECT, OR INCORRECT?	SECTION PATTERN
Score 2.0	1	C	Correct
	2	C	
	3	C	
	4	C	
	5	C	
Score 3.0	6	PC	Partially Correct
	7	C	
	8	PC	
Score 4.0	9	I	Incorrect
	10	I	
Overall Score			2.5

Source: Adapted from Marzano, 2010.

Figure 4.10: The response codes approach to scoring assessments.

This student provided all correct responses for the score 2.0 items, so the overall pattern for the section is recorded as *correct*. In the score 3.0 section, he or she gave one correct answer and two partially correct answers, leading to a section pattern of *partially correct*. Both items in the score 4.0 section were marked incorrect, so the overall pattern for that section is *incorrect*. Because these patterns indicate complete understanding of score 2.0 and partial understanding of score 3.0, this student would receive an overall score of 2.5.

One of the growing problems in many PCBE systems is that teachers must record not only scores on assessments but also assignments and activities. This task becomes untenable quite quickly when one considers all the student assignments, activities, and assessments in a PCBE system. The issue of what gets recorded can make or break a system.

Recording Scores in a PCBE System

Teachers must always record students' scores on proficiency scales. However, this does not mean that teachers record every format-specific score. For example, as described previously, a teacher might administer an assessment with three sections pertaining to score levels 2.0, 3.0, and 4.0 on a proficiency scale. Each of these sections might have its own score, but teachers do not record them. Instead, the teacher examines the score pattern across the three sections to assign an overall proficiency scale score for the assessment. It is this overall proficiency scale score that is recorded, not the format-specific score. Similarly, a teacher administers a ten-point quiz on score 2.0 content. Teachers might score this quiz using a percent-correct method. Any student scoring 80 percent or higher would receive a score of 2.0 on the scale, and the teacher would record the score 2.0.

A PCBE system that only keeps track of proficiency scale scores requires no more record-keeping than a traditional system. To illustrate, assume that a particular level or grade level contains twenty proficiency scales. Teachers generate multiple proficiency scale scores for each student. Ideally, over the course of the year, the teachers would generate three to five scores for each student on each measurement topic. If we assume an average of four scores per measurement topic, this amounts to eighty scores for each student over the course of the year. If we assume an average of six scores per measurement, this amounts to 120 scores for each student over the course of a year.

This is about the same number of scores per student typically recorded in a traditional system. For example, in a traditional system, a teacher records quizzes, formal tests, homework, various assignments, and extra credit points for a single student each quarter. If a quiz is given every week, homework or assignments are recorded twice per week, and a test is given halfway through the quarter and at the end of the quarter, then the teacher would record twenty-nine scores (nine quizzes, eighteen homework assignments, and two tests) per student per quarter. This would mean 116 entries each year per student. The critical feature of recording in a PCBE system is that format-specific assessment scores do not have to be recorded. However, teachers always record proficiency scale scores that they derived from various assessments.

While it is true that teachers are only required to record proficiency scale scores, an individual teacher might wish to record data regarding assignment completion rates, homework completion rates, classroom behavior, and even some format-specific scores. If a teacher does wish to record such data, it is important to remember that they should never mix with the proficiency-scale data. As mentioned previously, one option is to have students keep notebooks or folders with completed assignments, assessments of all types, and the like. Teachers may or may not choose to record proficiency scores for cognitive and metacognitive skills. We discuss these topics next.

Assessing Cognitive Skills

If a teacher wishes to record cognitive skill mastery, proficiency scales should be created for each cognitive skill. A sample scale for the cognitive skill of presenting and supporting claims is depicted in figure 4.11.

Score 4.0	The student is able to explain the overall logic of his or her argument.
Score 3.0	The student executes the four-step process and describes the overall logic of his or her final argument.
Score 2.0	• The student recognizes and recalls basic vocabulary, such as: *argument*, *claim*, *grounds*, *backing*, and *qualifier*. • The student is able to explain and exemplify the following steps: (1) describe your claim; (2) identify and describe the grounds that support your claim; (3) identify and describe the backing that supports your grounds; and (4) identify and describe any qualifiers for your overall argument.

Figure 4.11: Scale for presenting and supporting claims.

Teachers would use the proficiency scales to guide their formal instruction of these skills. We also recommend assessing cognitive skills in the same fashion as academic measurement topics. Teachers record students' scores and consider the students proficient when a student has earned a reliable score of 3.0 on the proficiency scale for a specific reasoning skill. Of course, this approach would require designing various types of assessments for the various cognitive skills. While time-consuming, the effort would yield useful results.

Another option is to assess students and record scores on cognitive skills but use performance tasks as the primary or alternative assessment method. In this case, students would be invited to create projects of their own design that demonstrate their competence in specific reasoning skills. Capstone projects (page 117) are useful tools to this end.

Assessing Metacognitive Skills

Metacognitive skills should also have proficiency scales. As described in chapter 1 (page 11), such scales have a slightly different structure. To illustrate, consider figure 4.12, which depicts a proficiency scale for the metacognitive skill of resisting impulsivity. Again, score 4.0 performance involves conscious decisions by students to utilize the particular disposition.

Score 4.0	The student makes conscious decisions to resist impulsivity in appropriate situations involving making decisions or forming conclusions.
Score 3.0	The student executes the four-step process for resisting impulsivity and describes the outcomes of his or her efforts.

Figure 4.12: Scale for resisting impulsivity.

continued →

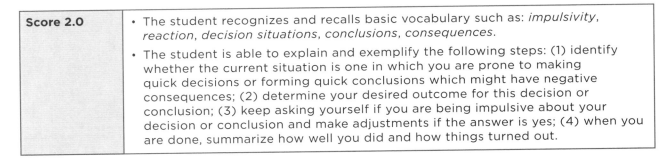

| Score 2.0 | • The student recognizes and recalls basic vocabulary such as: *impulsivity, reaction, decision situations, conclusions, consequences.*
• The student is able to explain and exemplify the following steps: (1) identify whether the current situation is one in which you are prone to making quick decisions or forming quick conclusions which might have negative consequences; (2) determine your desired outcome for this decision or conclusion; (3) keep asking yourself if you are being impulsive about your decision or conclusion and make adjustments if the answer is yes; (4) when you are done, summarize how well you did and how things turned out. |

Whether students should be expected to demonstrate proficiency at the score 3.0 level is a difficult question. As discussed in chapter 1 (page 11), teachers can design the scales for metacognitive skills so that score 3.0 status means that a student has demonstrated the ability to execute the underlying skill. In this case, demonstrating proficiency does not force students into making specific decisions about how they wish to live their lives. Teachers should expect students to achieve proficiency only if the scales students use for measurement do not require them to make decisions about their use outside of school. Individual district and school leaders should make decisions that represent local community values. In any event, it is probably best to assess metacognitive skills in the context of long-term capstone projects (page 117).

Once the teacher is armed with proficiency scores on several different measures, each student must be allocated a final, summative grade. How to arrive at this grade is discussed in the following section.

Arriving at a Summative Score

At any point in time, every student should have a score indicating his or her current status on each measurement topic. Recall from the previous discussion that scores (not assessments) should be thought of as formative or summative. At some point in time, a teacher must assign a summative score to a student. All the preceding scores are considered formative. There are four basic methods to generating summative scores for students: (1) using most recent scores, (2) using mounting evidence, (3) using mathematical models, and (4) beginning with score 4.0 tasks.

Using Most Recent Scores

An obvious approach to computing a student's current status is to use the last score recorded for a specific measurement topic. To illustrate, assume that a student has a set of proficiency scale scores for a specific measurement topic as shown in figure 4.13.

Date	February 14	February 28	March 10
Score	2.0	2.5	3.0

Figure 4.13: Student scores on a proficiency scale.

The student began with a score of 2.0 on February 14, the next score was 2.5 on February 28, and the third score was 3.0 on March 10. Given that the most recent score is 3.0, it is assumed to be a reliable estimate of the student's true status; therefore, it is considered the student's summative score. While this approach has some intuitive appeal, it has at least two weaknesses.

We discussed the first weakness at the beginning of this chapter. Any single score has a great deal of error associated with it. To illustrate, reconsider tables 4.2 and 4.3 (pages 104 and 105) from the section of this chapter that discussed reliability. We saw that the 95 percent confidence interval for a single score was rather large, even for scores that had a rather high reliability. Table 4.6 depicts the 95 percent confidence intervals for a summative score of 3.0 when considering only the last score.

Table 4.6: Ninety-Five Percent Confidence Intervals for Summative Score of 3.0

RELIABILITY	OBSERVED SCORE	LOWER LIMIT	UPPER LIMIT	RANGE
0.85	3.0	2.69	3.31	0.62
0.75	3.0	2.58	3.41	0.82
0.65	3.0	2.51	3.49	0.98
0.55	3.0	2.45	3.55	1.10

Clearly, the final observed score of 3.0 could include a great deal of imprecision or error. If the reliability of that score was 0.55, the 95 percent confidence interval would be between 2.45 and 3.55. Even if the reliability of that third score was 0.85, the range would still be between 2.69 and 3.31.

A second weakness of using only the most recent score as the summative score is that it does not address the problem of proficiency scores that are lower than previous proficiency scores. To illustrate, assume that on March 15 the student was assigned a score of 2.5—half a point lower than the score assigned on March 10. This situation can occur when summative scores assigned on a particular date are not dependent on previous scores. For these reasons, we strongly advise against using only the most recent score as the summative score.

Using Mounting Evidence

With the method of mounting evidence, the teacher stops assessing at a particular score level once he or she is convinced that a student has achieved that status. To illustrate, consider the following five scores for a specific student: 1.5, 2.0, 2.5, 2.5, 3.0.

The teacher might have gathered these scores over a three-week period. Notice that the second score of 2.0 is underlined. This indicates that at this point in time, the teacher is convinced that the student has achieved a measurement score of 2.0 on the proficiency scale. Thus, the teacher does not have to assess the student at that level anymore. Similarly, the fifth score of 3.0 is underlined. This indicates that at this point, the teacher is convinced the student has achieved a score of 3.0. Therefore, the teacher does not have to assess the student at this level anymore.

The main difference between this approach and the method of most recent scores is that the method of mounting evidence always includes an examination of the previous scores. In fact, this approach is sometimes referred to as a *preponderance of evidence* (Marzano, 2000, 2010; Marzano & Kendall, 1996). When a teacher becomes convinced that a student has received a specific score value on the proficiency scale, the teacher no longer gathers assessment data about that score value or lower score values. In this situation, records of students' activities and assignments become useful. A teacher examines all of that information and when he or she concludes that the preponderance of evidence indicates that the student's score is at least a 2.5 (for example), the teacher records the score and marks it in some fashion.

While an electronic gradebook should allow for this process, we illustrate the process using a handwritten grade sheet. This is depicted in figure 4.14 (find a reproducible version of this form on page 131). This grade sheet has room for five measurement topics. In this case, the measurement topics are from science at the fourth-grade level. Each cell depicts scores for a specific student on a single topic, and there is a column at the right of each cell with four boxes labeled 4.0, 3.0, 2.0, and 1.0. Scores are entered to the left. When the teacher is convinced a student has accrued enough evidence to demonstrate competence at a specific level, the appropriate scores on the right are shaded in. If a teacher judges a student to be at a half-point level, the appropriate cell is only half shaded or marked with a diagonal line.

	ENERGY		MOTION		LIGHT AND VISION		WAVES		INFORMATION TRANSFER
Chayla	1.5 2.0	4.0		4.0		4.0		4.0		4.0
		3.0		3.0		3.0		3.0		3.0
		2.0		2.0		2.0		2.0		2.0
		1.0		1.0		1.0		1.0		1.0
David	2.0 2.5 3.5	4.0		4.0		4.0		4.0		4.0
		3.0		3.0		3.0		3.0		3.0
		2.0		2.0		2.0		2.0		2.0
		1.0		1.0		1.0		1.0		1.0
Burke	3.0 3.0 3.5	4.0		4.0		4.0		4.0		4.0
		3.0		3.0		3.0		3.0		3.0
		2.0		2.0		2.0		2.0		2.0
		1.0		1.0		1.0		1.0		1.0

| Eryn | 2.5
2.0
2.0 | 4.0
3.0
2.0
1.0 | | 4.0
3.0
2.0
1.0 | | 4.0
3.0
2.0
1.0 | 4.0
3.0
2.0
1.0 | | 4.0
3.0
2.0
1.0 |
| Alicia | 3.0
4.0 | 4.0
3.0
2.0
1.0 | | 4.0
3.0
2.0
1.0 | | 4.0
3.0
2.0
1.0 | 4.0
3.0
2.0
1.0 | | 4.0
3.0
2.0
1.0 |

Figure 4.14: Sample grading sheet.

To illustrate, consider the first student, Chayla, and the first measurement topic, energy. Chayla has two raw scores: 1.5 and 2.0. The teacher has shaded in the column on the right-hand side of the cell up through the score of 2.0. This shading indicates that at this point in time, the teacher judges Chayla to be at score 2.0 status. From this point on, the teacher will assess Chayla at score 3.0 and 4.0 only. Raw scores will be entered in the left-hand side of the column, progressing sequentially from top to bottom. When the teacher is convinced that Chayla has demonstrated score 3.0 competence, the entire score 3.0 box will be shaded.

Using Mathematical Models

This method requires the use of mathematical models that Marzano (2006) described. Teachers cannot do recordkeeping by hand using this method. Rather, teachers must employ an electronic gradebook that utilizes the appropriate algorithms. The manner teachers use to analyze scores makes this method unique. To illustrate, consider figure 4.15.

	1	2	3	4	5
Wally	1.5	2.0	3.0	3.5	4.0
Manuel	2.0	2.0	3.0	2.5	
Enrique	2.5	3.0	3.0		
Jake	2.0	2.5	1.5	2.5	
Olivia	3.0	3.0	3.0	3.5	
Raymond	3.0	3.0	2.0	3.0	
Serena	2.5	2.5	4.0	3.5	
Nadya	3.0	3.5	2.5		
June	1.5	2.0	3.0		

Figure 4.15: Student scores for a measurement topic on fractions.

Note that not all students have the same number of scores. Wally has five, Enrique has three, and Raymond has four. This is an important aspect of the PCBE system. Teachers can assess students at different times, with different types of assessments, and with different frequencies. When implemented, the method of mathematical models produces reports like the one in figure 4.16.

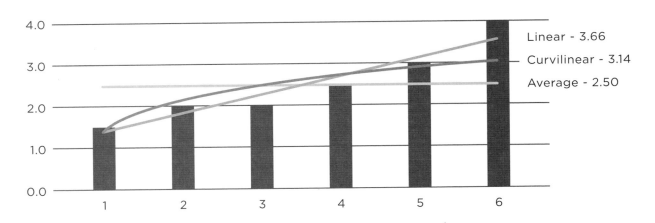

Figure 4.16: Mathematical models.

Figure 4.16 depicts one student's scores on a specific measurement topic. The bars represent the observed scores. The student began with an observed score of 1.5 and ended with an observed score of 4.0. Figure 4.16 also depicts three ways of computing a summative score, represented by the three lines through the student's observed scores. The straight horizontal line represents the average. If we used the average to summarize the student's scores, the summative score would be 2.50. The average makes sense if no learning has occurred from assessment to assessment. The straight line increasing at equal intervals from left to right represents the linear trend in the student's scores. If we use this to estimate the student's summative score, the student would receive a score of 3.66. The linear trend makes sense if a student's true learning increases at the same rate as time goes on. The curved line represents what is referred to as the *curvilinear trend*. If a teacher used this model to compute the student's summative score, the student would receive a score of 3.14. The curvilinear trend makes sense if a student's learning increases rapidly in the beginning and then flattens out as the student becomes more proficient.

Perhaps the most powerful aspects of these models is that teachers can mathematically evaluate each in terms of how well they represent or *fit* the observed scores (Marzano, 2006). In this case, the linear trend best fits the observed scores. Therefore, from the perspective of mathematical models, the summative score of 3.66 would be the estimate of the student's true final status. Marzano (in press) reports on formulas that can be used to compute these mathematical models using readily available software, such as Microsoft Excel.

Beginning With Score 4.0 Tasks

In some situations, the measurement process in a PCBE classroom can be very simple. Specifically, students might exhibit a high level of content knowledge without any instruction in a specific measurement topic. If a teacher senses that a student already knows the topic, the teacher can verify this perception by asking the student to complete a score 4.0 task for a given topic. To illustrate, consider this score 4.0 task for a measurement topic on the Pythagorean theorem: The student will use the Pythagorean theorem to solve problems in the real world—for example, given that a 32-inch television (measured diagonally) is twelve inches high, determine how wide a shelf would have to be in order to accommodate it.

The teacher would ask the student to design and solve a similar problem from his or her own experience. If the student was successful in designing and completing such a task, the teacher would still seek further information since this task is a single assessment with inevitable built-in errors. The teacher would also query the student regarding some 3.0 content. For example, the teacher might ask the student to calculate the distance between two points on a coordinate plane using the Pythagorean theorem. If the student could not perform these tasks, the teacher would guide the student through the content progression in the proficiency scale (that is, beginning with 2.0 content and then moving up the scale accordingly). If the student demonstrated competency on these tasks, the teacher could reasonably conclude that the student should be assigned a score of at least 3.0 and possibly a 3.5 or 4.0 if warranted by the student's performance.

Once a teacher has assessment formats selected and scoring mechanisms in place, he or she may wish to check the reliability of the assessment measures. We discuss this in the following section.

Checking Accuracy of Assessments

If a school or district uses the recommended methods of computing a summative score, that school or district can be fairly certain that these scores are reliable. However, additional methods can help establish the accuracy of assessments. The following sections discuss the use of safety net assessments and state assessments in checking accuracy.

Using Safety Net Assessments

As the name implies, safety net assessments ensure that students' summative scores on measurement topics are true reflections of their status. They can be thought of as final quick checks on the accuracy of the summative scores. Safety net assessments cover multiple topics, and teachers can easily administer them. Many secondary schools have developed end-of-course tests. These can serve well as safety net assessments. However, we advise that you design such assessments in addition to end-of-course assessments and certainly for courses or grade levels for which end-of-course assessments do not exist. This is often the case for elementary grades.

Safety net assessments are intended to ensure that a student's summative score is not an overestimate of a student's true score. As such, a district or school might decide that teachers must use safety net assessments with all students, or they might decide to have teachers administer safety net assessments at their own discretion on a case-by-case basis.

It is best to have safety net assessments for clusters of measurement topics at each level. For example, assume that grade 4 (or level 4) science involves the following measurement topics.

- Energy
- Motion
- Light and vision
- Waves
- Information transfer
- Geographic features
- Earth changes
- Earth's history
- Natural hazards
- Natural resources
- Plant needs
- Animal needs
- Defining engineering design problems
- Solutions for engineering design problems
- Scientific method

Figure 4.17 depicts a sample safety net assessment for the topic of animal needs. Note that every item deals with score 3.0 content. The items are not comprehensive but do represent a final check on a student's understanding.

1. Which of the following are adaptive features of a polar bear's fur?
    A. It helps the polar bear stay warm in the cold environment.
    B. It helps the polar bear blend in with its surroundings.
    C. It protects polar bears' feet from the snow and helps them walk on slippery surfaces.
    D. All of the above

2. Match the following adaptations with the correct purpose.

I. Colorful feathers or plumage II. Sharp teeth and claws III. Stripes or spots on fur IV. Gills V. Webbed feet VI. Scales	A. Help predators attack and eat their prey B. Camouflage animals in their environment C. Allow fish to absorb oxygen from the water D. Help animals swim or paddle in water E. Attract mates F. Hold in moisture and protect animals from injury

3. How does a snake's tongue help it understand its environment?
A. The tongue allows a snake to collect scents and identify objects through smell.
B. The tongue allows a snake to lick and identify objects through taste.
4. Identify three internal or external features of a fish that help it survive underwater. Explain how each feature is similar to or different from the features of an animal that does not live underwater.
5. Identify two adaptations prey use to protect themselves from predators, and explain how each adaptation helps the prey survive.

Figure 4.17: Animal needs safety net assessment.

It is also possible to combine multiple topics into a single safety net assessment. For example, teachers might combine the measurement topics of plant needs and animal needs to form one safety net assessment.

Using State Assessments

Another way to assess the accuracy of the measurement process is to compare student classroom results with state assessments. If students are receiving high scores on proficiency scales for measurement topics, they should also be receiving high scores on their state assessments. A school or district can readily determine this. To illustrate, consider table 4.7.

Table 4.7: Validity Study in an Elementary School

MEASUREMENT TOPICS MASTERED	NUMBER OF STUDENTS	PERCENT PROFICIENT OR ABOVE
0	12	0
1	2	0
2	6	0
3	13	0
4	8	0
5	13	23
6	29	21
7	12	42
8	29	52
9	29	76
10	29	48
11	40	86
12	44	84
13	227	96

Source: Adapted from Haystead, 2016.

The data in table 4.7 (page 129) represent the relationship between scores on proficiency scales for third-grade mathematics and the results of a state assessment. The first column, Measurement Topics Mastered, reports the number of measurement topics on which a student received a summative score of 3.0 or higher. The second column represents the number of students. Thus, twelve students did not demonstrate mastery of any of the thirteen mathematics measurement topics at third grade. However, 227 students mastered all thirteen topics. The third column, Percent Proficient or Above, reports the percentage of students who scored proficient or higher on the state test. Of those twelve students who did not demonstrate mastery on any of the measurement topics, none were proficient on the state test. The same can be said for those students who mastered only one, two, three, or four of the measurement topics—none demonstrated proficiency on the state test. Of the thirteen students who mastered five measurement topics, 23 percent demonstrated proficiency on the state test. At the bottom of the table, of the 227 students who mastered all thirteen measurement topics, 96 percent scored proficient or higher on the state test. It is critical that schools and districts keep these types of data to continually monitor the precision and utility of their proficiency scales used for measurement.

Summary

This chapter presented a case for testing less while assessing more by utilizing the measurement process, an approach that we assert is critical for a successful PCBE system. Using proficiency scales can help a PCBE system avoid violating the principle of unidimensionality, while taking a measurement perspective can help a PCBE system avoid problems associated with overtesting and relying too heavily on a single assessment. Schools must take into account methods of integrating format-specific scores and proficiency scores to arrive at a single summative score. Teachers can use safety net or state assessments to check the reliability of their assessment and scoring. The next chapter addresses scheduling in a PCBE system.

Sample Grading Sheet

	Topic:		Topic:		Topic:		Topic:	
Name:		4.0		4.0		4.0		4.0
		3.0		3.0		3.0		3.0
		2.0		2.0		2.0		2.0
		1.0		1.0		1.0		1.0
Name:		4.0		4.0		4.0		4.0
		3.0		3.0		3.0		3.0
		2.0		2.0		2.0		2.0
		1.0		1.0		1.0		1.0
Name:		4.0		4.0		4.0		4.0
		3.0		3.0		3.0		3.0
		2.0		2.0		2.0		2.0
		1.0		1.0		1.0		1.0
Name:		4.0		4.0		4.0		4.0
		3.0		3.0		3.0		3.0
		2.0		2.0		2.0		2.0
		1.0		1.0		1.0		1.0
Name:		4.0		4.0		4.0		4.0
		3.0		3.0		3.0		3.0
		2.0		2.0		2.0		2.0
		1.0		1.0		1.0		1.0
Name:		4.0		4.0		4.0		4.0
		3.0		3.0		3.0		3.0
		2.0		2.0		2.0		2.0
		1.0		1.0		1.0		1.0

Chapter 5

How Will Scheduling Accommodate Student Learning?

In a PCBE system, the primary dynamic is that students move at their own pace through the required content. With this shift, a teacher transitioning from a traditional classroom to a PCBE system might quietly consider the worst-case scenario and ask, "How do I manage thirty different students doing thirty different things?" (For strategies that discuss how to deal with this concern, please see chapter 3, page 69.) Taken at face value, this concern seems valid. However, in a well-run PCBE system, scheduling should produce an environment where any given teacher is dealing with students who are at or close to the same level of competence for a particular subject area. This approach actually makes teaching in a PCBE system more efficient since in the traditional system, students organized by age typically produce grade-level classes with students spanning a wide range of levels of expertise. In the traditional system, then, each teacher must differentiate curriculum, instruction, and assessment for a wide range of students. In a PCBE system, a teacher is dealing with either only one level of student competence or a few relatively well-defined levels of competence.

Depending on the level of school, scheduling is handled in different ways. Elementary schools usually have a less difficult transition to a PCBE system because teachers are certified as generalists who cover all content areas. If a middle school is organized like an elementary school, it is generally easier to transition; if teachers have content certification requirements as in high school, issues with certification arise, which bring unique challenges. In some of the approaches described in this chapter, there is an elementary example and a high school example. Those interested in middle schools can reference either example depending on which one best fits their situation.

There is no single best way to create a PCBE schedule. As a result, this chapter describes multiple approaches. These approaches range from relatively small modifications of a traditional schedule to completely rethinking the schedule to fit a PCBE philosophy. Now, we will discuss the importance of assigning initial placements, transitioning to a PCBE schedule, going beyond the traditional schedule, and addressing social issues.

When a student enters a PCBE system, the first order of business is to place him or her accurately relative to each subject area.

Assigning Initial Placements

In a traditional system, placing students accurately is not problematic because students' ages automatically determine their placement for all subject areas. Table 5.1 displays a typical chart that a district might create relating ages to when students start grade levels.

Table 5.1: Grade Level Versus Age

GRADE	TYPICAL AGE RANGE
K	4.9–5.8
1	5.9–6.8
2	6.9–7.8
3	7.9–8.8
4	8.9–9.8
5	9.9–10.8
6	10.9–11.8
7	11.9–12.8
8	12.9–13.8
9	13.9–14.8
10	14.9–15.8
11	15.9–16.8
12	16.9–17.8

Initial placement in a PCBE system, however, comes with a unique set of challenges since students may be at differing levels of proficiency with different topics. The relatively easy task of placing students in a traditional system can be quite labor intensive in a PCBE system because teachers must make decisions separately for each subject area. When first transitioning, some districts use state-testing data for initial student placement. Such placements are approximations, but they do provide a starting place. If students are proficient in a given subject area on a state test, they are assigned to their chronological grade level. If they are less than proficient, they are assigned to a lower grade level; if they are beyond proficient on the state test, they are assigned to a higher level.

District- or school-designed placement tests can enhance the precision of initial placements. Part of the registration process for students may include taking placement tests in reading, writing, mathematics, and science that the district designed to be aligned with their measurement topics. These tests can be based on safety net assessments, as described in chapter 4 (page 97).

Whatever process the district or school uses, initial placements have room for error simply because information about the appropriateness of the placements will be forthcoming as soon as students begin classes. For example, based on placement tests administered during registration and examination of the student's scores on state assessments, an eighth-grade student transferring in from another district might be placed in a sixth-grade mathematics class. The sixth-grade teacher would receive the student, but might soon determine that the initial placement level was inaccurate. The teacher would move the student to a more suitable level, using professional expertise and recently collected assessment data on specific measurement topics.

Having a system that allows for moving students if they are placed at the wrong level takes pressure off initial placement assessments. In fact, if effective placement tests are not in place, a district or school might follow a traditional system and simply assign students to the grade level per their age. Teachers can then move students up or down one or more levels based on their performances in class in specific subject areas. Schools should establish standard operating procedures for initial placement and for adjusting the initial placement.

In the transition to a PCBE system, it is not uncommon for questions to arise when teachers initially place students in specific levels. Parents and guardians are familiar with traditional age-based placement but not with competency-based placement. In answering these questions, it is useful to keep in mind that a PCBE system has obvious advantages over a traditional system. In a traditional system, students are grouped by age, and teachers attempt to reach the students who are struggling and encourage the students who want to move ahead. In effect, the traditional system forces teachers to teach to the middle of the distribution of students in their classes and try their best for the rest of the students. In a PCBE system, there may still be multiple levels of students in the classrooms, but these levels are more accurate and easier to manage.

One question that frequently arises is, Isn't this new placement system simply a form of tracking students? This concern is largely due to a misunderstanding of the differences between a PCBE system and a traditional system relative to what happens to students when they do not demonstrate proficiency at a particular grade level in the allotted period of time. In a traditional system, an elementary student would be held back if he or she did not receive a passing grade in a majority of the content areas at a particular grade level. That student would have to take all content areas over again, even the parts in which he or she had already demonstrated proficiency. In high school, if a student does not pass a course, he or she must take the entire course over—even the parts he or she already knows. In a PCBE system, students only need to work on the material on which they have not yet demonstrated proficiency.

This thinking breaks the mold of a set 180-day school year with defined start and end times for learning. Because the general public (and even some educators) does not widely understand PCBE, it is useful to construct answers to some common questions that arise, particularly around the issues of scheduling and transitioning students from one level to another. Following are some other questions K–12 teachers and leaders commonly encounter with regard to a PCBE schedule, as well as responses to those questions.

- **Can schools still use grade levels in a PCBE system?** The answer to this question is yes, but systems must allow students who are chronologically at one grade level to work at lower or higher grade levels for specific subject areas based on their needs. For example, at the beginning of the year in an elementary school a teacher may have three third graders doing well enough in mathematics that they should be in a fourth-grade mathematics class. The teacher may also have four fifth graders who would benefit from being in a fourth-grade classroom because they have not mastered some of the content at that level. Additionally, there is a group of seventeen fourth graders who should stay in fourth-grade mathematics. The "fourth-grade" mathematics class would include three third graders, seventeen fourth graders, and four fifth graders. In this approach, the teacher can focus on fourth-grade content while simultaneously adjusting and refining grouping and instructional opportunities to meet the needs of the third-grade and fifth-grade students who are also focusing on the fourth-grade content.

- **What if a student only needs to demonstrate proficiency with a few topics in a given level of a subject area at the beginning of a scheduling time interval?** In this case, the teacher would move the student to the next level up, and the teacher at that level would work with two levels of content until that student completes the requirements. The teacher would then help the new student catch up with the general pace of the other students.

- **What if a student finishes a content level just prior to the end of a scheduling time interval (such as a semester)?** The student could move to the next-level class right away or begin working on the new level in the class that he or she is currently in. This is not simple enrichment of the content previously addressed. Rather, it involves starting work on new content at the next level. A move could take place, but if there are only a few weeks remaining before scheduled changes, it might be best not to move the student. The student may have established strong peer relationships in the current class, and it would not make sense to burden the student with the task of building new relationships in a new class right before scheduled changes will occur.

- **Should you put a nine-year-old student with fourteen-year-old students just because she is working on the same content level?** There is no simple answer to this question because social and emotional factors must be taken into account. Teachers should address questions like the following: Is the nine-year-old socially ready to be with fourteen-year-olds? Will the fourteen-year-olds resent the younger student? If it is determined through conversations with the student and parents that it would be best to have the nine-year-old be with other students closer to his or her age, then a compromise is necessary.

Transitioning to a PCBE Schedule

Many schools start moving toward a PCBE system incrementally, by tweaking their current systems. Other transitions include more radical shifts in thinking. The next section will discuss ways schools can implement PCBE systems by discussing the following six topics: (1) tweaking a traditional schedule, (2) focusing on small groups of students, (3) implementing focused instruction time, (4) using advisory systems, (5) teaching in teams, and (6) transitioning between buildings.

Tweaking a Traditional Schedule

In this transition to a PCBE system, teachers and administrators examine the traditional schedule to find the best places for slight alterations. These alterations reduce the number of levels per classroom so students get as much teacher attention and as many resources as possible. To illustrate at the elementary level, assume that with a traditional schedule, three teachers teach English language arts at the same time during the day. Consequently, students break into three groups based on their performances on specific measurement topics. The three classrooms shuffle the students around, with certain teachers focusing on material to fill in gaps for some students, stay on pace with others, and address accelerated needs with others. Consider the following example.

- Teacher A has two groups; the first group is second graders who need to fill in gaps for kindergarten and first grade, and the second group is students on pace for second-grade English language arts.

- Teacher B has one group on pace for second grade.

- Teacher C has two groups; the first group is second graders on pace for English language arts, and the second group is students working on the beginning of third-grade English language arts.

At the high school level, the modifications are the same as long as two or more teachers are teaching the same subject at the same time. Each teacher would use student data regarding performance on measurement topics to shuffle the students between the classrooms according to their needs. Because the students' course schedules have not changed, the scheduling office only needs to adjust students' classroom locations rather than altering the courses they are enrolled in or the order of their classes.

Modifying a pre-existing schedule has limited utility simply because it requires that two or more teachers have scheduled classes at the same time on the same content. However, it allows a school to transition to a PCBE schedule in small increments. Pilot teachers can try it out using student performance on specific measurement topics to reorganize their students. Opportunities to apply new thinking around scheduling can cause increased motivation for change, which can then spark schoolwide modifications. The next five options represent new thinking regarding scheduling.

Focusing on Small Groups of Students

For teachers interested in making a greater move toward a PCBE system, one option is focusing PCBE initially on small groups of students. One small group on which to focus is students *on the bubble*, which are (1) students who need more time to complete the course work and (2) students who are ready to move to the next level early. We typically interpret the idiom "on the bubble" as "on the brink." We use the term *on the bubble* for these two groups because one is on the brink of falling behind their peers, and the other is on the brink of moving ahead of their peers to the next level of content. Both groups require special attention. The students who fall into one of these two groups usually become obvious by the second half of the school year. Scheduling for these students involves providing time and resources to move them through specific measurement topics so that they may move to the next level as quickly as possible.

One approach to accommodating these students' needs is to establish time before or after school when they can receive help on specific measurement topics—for example, a forty-five-minute period before or after school that provides students with extra instruction and on-demand assessment opportunities for specific measurement topics on a rotating basis. Another approach is to build this time into the school day. For example, twice a week, classes might begin thirty minutes later in the morning and end thirty minutes early so teachers can provide extra support for students on the bubble (both ahead and behind typical pace). Students not in these bubble groups (that is, students working at a traditional pace) work on topics or projects independently (with teacher supervision). Finally, summer school is a useful tool for assisting students on the bubble. Since by definition these students have needs related to specific measurement topics, summer school offerings can meet those specific needs. Some students might have to attend summer school for only a week or two because they are working toward proficiency on a few measurement topics only. Other students might have to attend longer because they are working on a number of measurement topics.

Implementing Focused Instruction Time

In this approach, a chunk of time is set aside for all students to have access to teachers and resources. Granting students full access to all teachers for a particular time period provides them with opportunities to complete activities or work on advanced material. Each student can go to the appropriate classroom or instructor for support. Focused instruction time might be thought of as a more structured study hall based on students' needs. Focused instruction time plays out differently at the elementary and high school levels.

Focused Instruction Time in Elementary Schools

If the elementary school is set up with different content-area teachers, then scheduling focused instruction time would be similar to the high school schedule. Figure 5.1 depicts a version of focused instruction time in a departmentalized K–5 elementary school. As figure 5.1 indicates, the term *WIN time* (What I Need time) is this school's term for focused instruction time. In figure 5.1, notice that students go to content-area classes at the same time. For example, after homeroom, each day starts with English language arts, so students go to the classroom for their level. Because all teachers are teaching English language arts at the same time, students can move through levels as necessary. To accommodate WIN time, half of the students (group A) attend lunch while the other half of the students (group B) attend WIN time. During the next period, the schedule is reversed. This schedule allows students to visit classrooms for needed support in any subject area, as teachers will be available for help across levels and subjects.

BLOCK	MONDAY	TUESDAY	WEDNESDAY	THURSDAY	FRIDAY
8:15 a.m.	Homeroom	Homeroom	Homeroom	Homeroom	Homeroom
8:30 a.m.	English Language Arts	English Language Arts and Spelling	English Language Arts	English Language Arts and Spelling	Independent Work on Projects
9:00 a.m.	English Language Arts				
9:30 a.m.	Literacy or Reading				
10:00 a.m.	Physical Education	Music	Social Studies	Physical Education	Art
10:30 a.m.	Mathematics				
11:30 a.m.	A Lunch B WIN Time	A Lunch B WIN Time	A Lunch B WIN Time	A Lunch B WIN Time	A Lunch B WIN Time
12:00 p.m.	A WIN Time B Lunch	A WIN Time B Lunch	A WIN Time B Lunch	A WIN Time B Lunch	A WIN Time B Lunch
12:30 p.m.	Science				
1:00 p.m.	Science	Health	Science	Media	Media
1:30 p.m.	Social Studies	Physical Education	Physical Education	Social Studies	Physical Education
2:00 p.m.	English Language Arts	English Language Arts	Mathematics	English Language Arts	Mathematics
2:30 p.m.	Dismissal				

Figure 5.1: Focused instruction time in a departmentalized elementary school.

If an elementary school is set up so one teacher teaches one group of students for a majority of the content areas, then each teacher can set his or her own focused instruction time. For example, a teacher could set aside one daily thirty-minute block of time for students to work on a content area they need the most support on. To illustrate, consider figure 5.2. In figure 5.2, the teacher has scheduled a thirty-minute period each day called *flex time*, when students can work independently, in pairs, or in small groups on topics they need to catch up on or in areas where they are moving ahead of pace. With this schedule, the teacher can support groups and individuals as time allows but must also have resources and activities prepared for students to use independently.

BLOCK	MONDAY	TUESDAY	WEDNESDAY	THURSDAY	FRIDAY
8:00 a.m.	Homeroom	Homeroom	Homeroom	Homeroom	Homeroom
8:15 a.m.	Mathematics Workshop	Mathematics Workshop	Mathematics Workshop	Mathematics Workshop	Mathematics Workshop
9:15 a.m.	Art	Recess	Music	Recess	Health
9:45 a.m.	Reading Workshop	Reading Workshop	Reading Workshop	Reading Workshop	Reading Workshop
10:45 a.m.	Science	Social Studies	Science	Social Studies	Science
11:30 a.m.	Lunch	Lunch	Lunch	Lunch	Lunch
12:00 p.m.	Flex Time	Flex Time	Flex Time	Flex Time	Flex Time
12:30 p.m.	Writing Workshop	Writing Workshop	Writing Workshop	Writing Workshop	Writing Workshop
1:00 p.m.	Physical Education	Media	Physical Education	Media	Physical Education
1:30 p.m.	English Language Arts	English Language Arts	Mathematics	English Language Arts	Mathematics
2:15 p.m.	Dismissal				

Figure 5.2: Focused instruction time in a self-contained elementary classroom.

Focused Instruction Time in High Schools

To illustrate focused instruction time at the high school level, assume that a high school has a seven-period day. The school creates a sixty-minute period in the middle of the day during which students are scheduled twenty minutes for lunch (alternating times to accommodate the student body) and the rest of the time is available for them to go to teachers' classrooms for additional support. Teachers create SOPs to make that focused instruction more beneficial for all students. In figures 5.3 and 5.4, the schools call focused instruction time *power hour* and *academy time*. Other common terms include *FIT period* (focused instructional time period), or *WIN time* (What I Need time) as noted in elementary school. Some schools may name this time after their mascot—for example, *Warrior Time*.

First Bell	7:15 a.m.
Tardy Bell	7:20 a.m.
Period One	7:20–8:10 a.m.
Period Two	8:15–9:05 a.m.
Period Three	9:10–10:00 a.m.
Period Four	10:05–10:55 a.m.
Power Hour	10:55–11:55 a.m. (Lunch + FIT)
Period Five	11:55 a.m.–12:45 p.m.
Period Six	12:50–1:40 p.m.
Period Seven	1:45–2:35 p.m.

Figure 5.3: Power hour.

FIRST BELL: 8:20 A.M.				
BLOCK	ONE-MINUTE BELL	TARDY BELL	START TIME	END TIME
First	8:24 a.m.	8:25 a.m.	8:25 a.m.	9:55 a.m.
Second	9:59 a.m.	10:00 a.m.	10:00 a.m.	11:25 a.m.
Academy	11:29 a.m.	11:30 a.m.	11:30 a.m.	12:00 p.m.
Third	12:04 p.m.	12:05 p.m.	12:05 p.m.	1:55 p.m.
Fourth	1:59 p.m.	2:00 p.m.	2:00 p.m.	3:25 p.m.

Figure 5.4: Academy time.

Using Advisory Systems

When thinking about scheduling at the building level, school leaders can use an advisory system to manage many issues that might arise within a PCBE system. The basic purpose of the advisory system is to ensure that every student perceives that he or she is known and understood as an individual. Operationally, this means that at least one adult in the building knows each student's background, receives information about the student, is available to the student, and is an advocate for the student. Advisory systems are common at the middle school and high school levels but not at the elementary level. Because students at the elementary level commonly have one teacher with whom they spend the majority of their time, in effect, that teacher becomes the advisor for the students in his or her class.

Advisory systems can have a variety of purposes in a PCBE system, including the following.

- **To facilitate ongoing work for content-area subjects:** When students need more time to complete measurement topics, advisory can be a structured time for individual instruction, small-group instruction, and peer tutoring or mentoring opportunities.

- **To address independent learning plans for specific students:** Learning plans are an important aspect of PCBE because they outline the students' work flow through the measurement topics. Students need to be coached in the creation of their plans, including determining the appropriate pace of learning and incorporating student voice and choice opportunities. The advisor also needs to monitor and revise learning plans, a function that advisory can support.

- **To register students for new initiatives:** Students can be invited to take new short, rotating elective classes (called *wheel classes*) in the next quarterly rotation. These courses are typically on special interest topics that are not necessarily a part of the formal academic curriculum. For example, one district with which we have worked had wheel classes for karate, fishing, canoeing, and the like. Students took these courses because of their interest in the topics, but also as vehicles to practice and demonstrate their acumen with specific cognitive and metacognitive skills.

- **To facilitate student-to-student instruction:** In some cases, teachers use an advisory system to facilitate the use of peer-to-peer instruction. During advisory, teachers ask students if they would prefer more or less student-to-student instruction and about preferences they might have regarding with whom they would like to work.

- **To teach students specific goal-setting procedures that they can use inside and outside of school:** Students can establish long- and short-term goals and utilize advisory to monitor their progress toward each goal. When advisors establish close ties with students (as is the intent of an advisory system), they can help students set personal goals, monitor progress, and celebrate success. These goals can go beyond academic content and deal with more personal goals for which students might want support.

- **To support college and career readiness and monitor progress toward graduation requirements:** Sometimes teachers use advisory simply to ensure that all necessary paperwork and documentation are in place for students to move to their next levels. This becomes particularly important as students move toward graduation.

- **To provide opportunities for speakers to present to students about topics they are interested in:** Perhaps one of the more creative uses of advisory is to identify topics in which a group of students has interest. Once teachers identify these topics, they might invite guest speakers to present in person or virtually.

An advisory system can also support teachers. This is particularly the case when all teachers have one set of students they are in charge of when it comes to scheduling and learning needs and goals. Teachers can rely on each other when they have questions about a particular student by going to that student's advisor. This is not to say that students' regular teachers should not strive to build relationships with their students, but with an advisory system in place, there is additional and intentional time (and a person) set aside for discussing students' life goals and concerns outside of academics.

In addition to these traditional advantages of an advisory system, such a system can provide guidance for students regarding their progress on specific measurement topics. While an advisor teacher might not be able to provide help regarding the content in a particular measurement topic, the teacher can always help students identify the areas in which they need help and the resources that might be available.

There are many ways to place students within advisory structures. These include creating groups based on students' approximate readiness levels in English language arts, mathematics, and science; grade level (that is, ninth, tenth, eleventh, and twelfth grades), ensuring that the students stay together over several years; or mixed-age groups, ensuring that graduating students have an advisor focused on graduation. At the middle school level, a school might have advisors who work with students in some groupings for grades 6–8 in addition to an advisor who attends to the needs of students working on high school content.

A final characteristic regarding advisory is its schedule. There are many options, including the following.

- The school views advisory as an individual course and scheduled exactly like a course would be in a traditional system. Advisory would have the same time frame as all of the other courses.

- The advisory process takes place once a week for a long period of time (perhaps two to three hours). This chunk of devoted time is essentially taken out of the schedule for that day.

- Advisory occurs once a week, replacing a class for a particular period. The school can choose to rotate the advisory period so that one content area does not continually miss a class each week.

- The advisory process occurs three times per week for one class period but focused instruction time is used one of those times.

- Schools schedule advisory daily for shorter periods of time. Some schools choose to replace homeroom with an advisory period, which keeps with a traditional schedule and makes advisory easier to incorporate.

- Advisory time takes place at the beginning or end of a scheduling period. For example, when a new quarter or semester starts, schools can schedule advisory to establish learning plans and goals for upcoming courses. At the end of a quarter or semester, schools can schedule advisory to review student learning plans and goals to determine what to celebrate and to establish next steps.

- Advisory serves as the morning launch pad for intensive classes. For example, the school holds a unique one-month schedule featuring intensive classes that the normal schedule doesn't offer. Rather than change the entire building schedule, for one month the students start each day in advisory and then go to their intensive classes. The scheduling office communicates with advisors for locations throughout the day.

- Advisory happens two times per week at a set time so all students are in advisory at the same time. This approach provides opportunities for students to move throughout the building to receive appropriate resources when needed. This is similar to scheduling focused instruction time.

- Advisory has a check-in and check-out format, so every day begins and ends with advisory. This approach provides opportunities for students to create daily goals and revisit them at the end of the day.

Figure 5.5 provides a visual depiction of a schedule with advisory every Monday and Thursday. This is similar to a typical schedule for advisory in a traditional system. The school has placed students into readiness levels for the entire day. Elective classes address multiple levels of students and several content areas, but, depending on the readiness level of students, may not be appropriate for all students; therefore, advisors guide and assist students during elective registration using a course catalog so students can see which levels and content areas each elective course addresses.

2014–2015 BELL SCHEDULE					
	MONDAY	TUESDAY	WEDNESDAY	THURSDAY	FRIDAY
7:30–9:25 a.m.	Block 1				
9:30–10:30 a.m.	Advisory	Elective	Skills	Advisory	Elective
10:30–11:05 a.m.	Lunch				
11:10 a.m.–12:10 p.m.	Skills	Elective	Block 2 Humanities Early release at 1:00 p.m.	Elective	Skills
12:15–2:00 p.m.	Block 2 Humanities			Block 2 Humanities	

Figure 5.5: Sample schedule with advisory on Mondays and Thursdays.

In figure 5.6, students participate in personal work time (PWT); this course is meant to give students additional time to address measurement topics from their classes or to address topics through new independent projects in a structured environment. Note that in this schedule, advisory occurs at the end of each day. Depending on the focus for advisory, there are many advantages to holding advisory as the final class, such as checking in with students about their current goals and any responsibilities that surfaced during that day. The consistency provides students with routine support.

Teaching in Teams

The premise behind team teaching and scheduling is there are more teachers available in the same room to address the different levels of student needs. The scheduling modifications mentioned in the previous sections should work in concert with team teaching.

	TEACHER 1	TEACHER 2	TEACHER 3	TEACHER 4	TEACHER 5	TEACHER 6	TEACHER 7	TEACHER 8	TEACHER 9
Period 1	Electives	Writing 1 and 2	Mathematics 1	Science 4	Prep Block	Science 3	Mathematics 5	Social Studies 4	Reading 1 and 2
Period 2	Social Studies 2	Writing 1 and 2	Mathematics 3	Electives	English Language Arts 3	Prep Block	Mathematics 4	Prep Block	Reading 1 and 2
Period 3	Social Studies 1	Electives	Mathematics 3	Prep Block	English Language Arts 4	Science 4	Mathematics 4	Social Studies 4	Electives
Period 4	Electives or PWT	Electives or PWT	Electives or PWT	Electives or PWT	Electives or PWT	Electives or PWT	Electives or PWT	Electives or PWT	Electives or PWT
Period 5	Social Studies 2	Prep Block	Prep Block	Science 4	English Language Arts 3	Science 5	Mathematics 5	Social Studies 4	Reading 1 and 2
Period 6	Social Studies 2	Writing 1 and 2	Mathematics 1	Chemistry	English Language Arts 1	Science 3	Prep Block	Electives	Reading 1 and 2
Period 7	Prep Block	Writing 1 and 2	Mathematics 2	Electives	English Language Arts 2	Electives	Electives	Social Studies 4	Prep Block
Period 8	Advisory	Advisory	Advisory	Advisory	Advisory	Advisory	Advisory	Advisory	Advisory

Figure 5.6: Sample schedule with personal work time.

To illustrate, assume there are four teachers team teaching at the elementary, middle, or high school level: (1) English language arts, (2) mathematics, (3) science, and (4) social studies. The four teachers plan all their lessons around one common theme or project even though they are responsible for different measurement topics. Each teacher takes a turn being the lead teacher based on the content, and the other teachers support and make connections to the other content areas. With four teachers in the room, they can begin with whole-group instruction and then move to small-group work with each teacher moving around to assist students. All four classes can be taught together or paired off depending on the content of the lesson and the size of the available space. Some classes have removable walls or common areas for instruction to make this more effective. Pairing off puts two teachers in one room and the other two in another room. This pairing should be flexible—for example, mathematics and science teachers together and English language arts and social studies teachers together for some portions of the unit, then mathematics and English language arts teachers and science and social studies teachers for other portions.

Schools can also use team teaching to distribute students at different levels across the content areas. For example, assume a unit of study is addressing a social studies theme and all students need focused instruction in reading while learning about a particular topic. Teams give schools the ability to spread students across teachers for that particular lesson so more personalized instruction in reading skills can occur.

Transitioning Between Buildings

If data show that a majority of students are underprepared for the upcoming content, or, conversely, that they have advanced beyond the upcoming content, then teachers need to make specific modifications. These modifications might play out differently at the elementary and secondary levels.

At the elementary level, assume a group of second-grade students is moving to a building for grades 3–5. An analysis of student data shows that a large number of students are weak in mathematics. Using all student data (including social-emotional learning data), teachers group students to focus on mathematics areas in which they need to improve. Once students reach proficiency in those areas, the group starts the next level of mathematics with the same teacher. With this approach, the focus and resources can target gap areas. When students do move buildings and get to the third-grade material, they will be prepared to move more efficiently through the content.

This is similar to focusing on small groups of students (as discussed previously). The difference here is that students on the bubble will be moving to another building (if they are ahead of their peers) or will be prohibited from moving to another building (if they are behind their peers). This increases the importance of addressing the needs of these two groups of students as quickly as possible.

At the high school level, assume a group of eighth graders is moving into high school. Regular course requirements include algebra 1. Data reveal that a large group of students is not prepared for algebra 1. Consequently, teachers create an entry-level minicourse (a course that is perhaps two to four weeks in duration) for those students based on their specific gaps in mathematics (for example, one group might include students who need additional practice with inequalities and one-step equations). Teachers would customize each entry-level minicourse to the students' needs based on their previous performance, with the end goal being to have all students prepared for algebra 1 content as quickly as possible. Students leave the minicourse and begin the algebra 1 content as soon as they are ready. The time teachers and students spend filling in the students' gaps makes future learning more efficient and saves time in the long run.

Going Beyond the Traditional Schedule

The previous discussion assumes that a school or district wishes to implement a PCBE system by modifying—minimally or more radically—a traditional schedule. A more direct and effective approach is to completely rethink the schedule. There are two things to keep in mind as you embark on this task: (1) teaching one subject per period, and (2) considering the technology solution.

Teaching One Subject Per Period

The most straightforward approach is for the district or school to schedule only one subject to be taught per period. Previously, we addressed the utility of taking advantage of two or more teachers teaching the same content at the same time. Here, we consider this type of scheduling as the primary structure. For example, all mathematics courses are taught at the same time each day, all reading courses are taught at the same time, and so on. The longer this type of scheduling is in place, the tighter the grouping of students becomes because teachers do not push students through the system with unaddressed content gaps. The students arrive at the next level prepared for the material, and teachers spend no time reviewing content below their current level. Another advantage to this type of scheduling is that more teachers are available to provide support to individuals and small groups of students.

To illustrate how this type of scheduling might manifest, assume there are six hundred students and twenty-one teachers in a grades K–5 elementary school. Table 5.2 represents the students' grade levels by chronological age.

Table 5.2: Grade Level by Chronological Age

GRADE LEVEL BY AGE	STUDENTS PER GRADE BASED ON AGE
K	89
1	104
2	111
3	97
4	116
5	83

As indicated in table 5.2 (page 147), scheduling by age produces a rather even distribution of students. Table 5.3 depicts these same students distributed by content needs.

Table 5.3: Students Distributed by Content Needs

GRADE-LEVEL CONTENT	NUMBER OF STUDENTS PER GRADE BASED ON CONTENT NEEDS
PreK	14
K	75
1	120
2	107
3	90
4	98
5	87
6	9

In table 5.3, there is a much wider distribution of students. This is because some students are not ready for kindergarten content and others have surpassed the requirements for fifth-grade content. Another option is in table 5.4.

Table 5.4: Grade-Level Bands

BUILDING	CONTENT LEVELS COVERED
Grades 6–8	High school Grade 8 Grade 7 Grade 6 Below grade 6
Grades 3–5	Above grade 5 Grade 5 Grade 4 Grade 3 Below grade 3
Grades K–2	Above grade 2 Grade 2 Grade 1 Kindergarten Below kindergarten

Table 5.4 depicts a scheduling structure that spans three different buildings that address different grade levels: K–2, 3–5, and 6–8. In all three schools, one subject is taught every class period. Of course, this

approach allows students to move up or down easily from their chronological grade level. In addition, every school ensures that instruction is available to students who are above or below the grade-level band. To illustrate, consider the 3–5 grade-level band. During the common period for teaching science, a fourth-grade student (chronologically) who is at the fifth-grade level in science would attend instruction in the fifth-grade class during science. A fourth-grade student operating at the sixth-grade level in science would go to the classroom focused on above-fifth-grade content. A fourth-grade student operating at the second-grade level in science would attend instruction in the below-third-grade class.

A high school can follow a similar schedule if it organizes courses into levels. For example, a high school might have English language arts content organized into the following levels: pre-English, English 1, English 2, English 3, English 4, and English 5. The pre-English course would address English language arts content for those students operating below the ninth-grade level. English 1 through English 4 would address ninth through twelfth grades, respectively. English 5 would address advanced content above and beyond high school graduation requirements. Again, if all English language arts classes are taught at the same time, students can easily move to the appropriate levels.

Employing traditional courses, scheduling becomes more complex since many courses will not be neatly organized into sequential levels. In a comprehensive high school that offers a wide variety of courses, the constraints of offering leveled courses at the same time become prohibitive. In such cases, when possible, teachers of courses like algebra 1 and algebra 2 teach the classes at the same time.

Considering the Technology Solution

The well-developed use of technology in a PCBE system can transform scheduling because teachers no longer need to present all content to students. Recall from chapter 3 (page 69) that teachers should develop tutorials for score 2.0, 3.0, and 4.0 content for each measurement topic. This predeveloped content releases teachers from the time-consuming role of continually presenting students with new content (usually at the score 2.0 level) since it can be done quite efficiently with teacher- and student-designed screencasts and readily available content from the Internet (for example, the Khan Academy or other free educational resources). Teachers can also design other forms of tutorials for score 3.0 and 4.0 content.

Figure 5.7 (page 150) identifies the online lessons and activities associated with score 2.0, 3.0, and 4.0 learning targets. Ideally, teachers will load these into a learning management system so students can access them electronically. Notice that the teacher identified some ready-made lessons and activities—that is, lessons or activities that she reviewed, aligned with the proficiency scale, and linked to the proficiency scale targets. Some of the lessons and activities the teacher adapted from online lessons and then linked for students to access. For all activities, it is likely that some teacher guidance will help students use them more efficiently. For example, some of the games identified for this proficiency scale are intended for small groups. In this case, the teacher will provide basic instructions with the activity link in the learning management system to help students organize themselves. In addition, for some lessons and activities, the teacher may link readings, a short podcast, or a screencast that provides instructions, an introduction, or a brief direct instruction lesson to accompany the identified online resources.

	ONLINE INSTRUCTIONAL RESOURCES	
Score 4.0	In addition to score 3.0 performance, the student demonstrates in-depth inferences and applications that go beyond what was taught.	Lesson developed from iCivics Lesson Plan: A Trip Around the World www.oercommons.org/courses/icivics -lesson-plan-a-trip-around-the-world
Score 3.0	The student will demonstrate an understanding of important concepts, such as: • The influence of commonly held civic responsibilities on society in the United States (for example, explaining how engaging in different types of civic responsibility is important to a democracy)	iCivics Game: Activate www.oercommons.org/courses /icivics-game-activate/view iCivics Game: Responsibility Launcher www.oercommons.org/courses/icivics -game-responsibility-launcher iCivics Game: Cast Your Vote www.oercommons.org/courses /icivics-game-cast-your-vote iCivics Game: Represent Me! www.oercommons.org/courses /icivics-game-law-craft iCivics Game: Counties Work www.oercommons.org/courses /icivics-game-counties-work Lesson developed from iCivics Lesson Plan: Students Engage www.oercommons.org/courses /icivics-lesson-plan-students-engage Lesson developed from iCivics Lesson Plan: Interest Groups www.oercommons.org/courses /icivics-lesson-plan-interest-groups
Score 2.0	The student will: • Recognize or recall specific vocabulary, including *civic responsibility*, *civic duty*, *public service*, *democratic values* • Understand different types of civic responsibilities, such as participation in government, church, and volunteer activities • Understand the difference between a civic responsibility and a civic duty • Identify and explain current issues involving civic responsibility, such as a local, state, or national election • Identify opportunities for engaging in civic responsibilities in their city or state • Identify ways he or she has engaged in civic responsibilities	Seize the Vote! www.oercommons.org/courses/just-vote Quizlet: Civic Duties and Responsibilities https://quizlet.com/21594590/civic -duties-and-responsibilities-flash-cards Lesson developed from iCivics Lesson Plan: Citizen Me www.oercommons.org/courses/icivics -lesson-plan-citizen-me Lesson developed from Youth Leadership Initiative www.oercommons.org/courses/youth -leadership-initiative/view Lesson developed from Learning to Give www.learningtogive.org/teach/lessons Lesson developed from My Civic Responsibility www.learningtogive.org/units/we-are -government/my-civic-responsibility Lesson developed from the Carolina Database of K–12 Resources http://database.civics.unc.edu

Figure 5.7: Scale with technology resources.

With technology-based content in place, many of the previous scheduling structures take on new power. For example, consider focused instruction time. Students now do not have to wait until a teacher is available to get help or learn new content. Rather, students can work on any topic at any level independently. Indeed, students can work on measurement topics even outside school hours, assuming they have access to technology. Figure 5.8 depicts a sample high school schedule that incorporates independent online learning on a daily basis.

	MONDAY	TUESDAY	WEDNESDAY	THURSDAY	FRIDAY
7:30–8:15 a.m.	Zero-Hour Classes (optional) Open Lab, Collaboration, or Teacher Office Hours				
8:15–9:50 a.m.	Announcements The Cockpit The Flight Deck The Command Center	Announcements The Cockpit The Flight Deck The Command Center	Announcements The Cockpit The Flight Deck The Command Center	Announcements The Cockpit The Flight Deck The Command Center	Announcements The Cockpit The Flight Deck The Command Center
9:50–9:55 a.m.	Break				
9:55–11:20 a.m.	The Cockpit The Flight Deck The Command Center	The Cockpit The Flight Deck The Command Center	The Cockpit The Flight Deck The Command Center	The Cockpit The Flight Deck The Command Center	The Cockpit The Flight Deck The Command Center
11:20–11:45 a.m.	Lunch				
11:45 a.m.–12:45 p.m.	Physical Education	Elective or Credit Recovery	Physical Education	Elective or Credit Recovery	Outdoor Education
12:45–12:55 p.m.	Break				
12:55–2:00 p.m.	Elective or Credit Recovery Announcements	Project-Based Learning Announcements	Elective or Credit Recovery Announcements	Project-Based Learning Announcements	Outdoor Education
2:00–3:00 p.m.	Study Hall, Open Lab, Collaboration, or Teacher Office Hours (Required for students assigned to academic support or on a learning contract)				

Note: **The Cockpit**—*Students work online, silently and independently.* **The Flight Deck**—*Students work in collaborative peer groups, learning from each other.* **The Command Center**—*Students work in a traditional, teacher-led small-group setting.*

Figure 5.8: Sample high school schedule with independent online learning time.

This particular school uses individualized instruction as well as experiential and project-based learning opportunities to prepare students for postsecondary success. As depicted in figure 5.8, the schedule includes traditional, direct instruction sessions (The Command Center) as well as a combination of online, independent learning (The Cockpit) and collaborative work in peer groups (The Flight Deck). The use of technology allows greater flexibility in the schedule and assists teachers in individualizing instruction; developing students' cognitive skills; providing topic recovery in smaller, targeted groups; extending lesson concepts; and developing metacognitive skills (such as collaboration, communication, and problem solving).

Addressing Social Issues

As we discussed in the section on assigning initial placements, implementing a PCBE system can give rise to many questions. For example, some teachers, parents, and others may ask, Is a personalized competency-based classroom the right approach for all students? They may wonder if this approach is just a different term for tracking students. Others will want to know how teachers are supposed to deal with students who drag their feet on meeting learning goals and do not seem to want to take ownership of their learning.

While these are all valid questions, we assert that a personalized competency-based classroom is the best approach for meeting the needs of all students. One reason is transparency. In a PCBE system, students, their teachers, and their parents are aware of the knowledge and skills students have mastered and the knowledge and skills they need to continue working on. With the use of proficiency scales, as recommended in this handbook, students, their teachers, and their parents also have information that will help students progress on the measurement topics they have not mastered. The proficiency scale provides detailed information about the foundational knowledge and skills a student should address to become skilled at the learning targets. In a traditional system, even when students earn "good" grades—a B, for example—the students, their teachers, and their parents do not know what knowledge or skills are missing. When students move on under this system, those missing pieces of knowledge and skills will likely hinder further learning of more advanced concepts and materials.

Another reason is personalization. A PCBE system does not label students as *fast* learners or *slow* learners. Each learner has individual interests, needs, strengths, challenges, and motivations. Each learner will demonstrate proficiency on some topics more quickly than on others. In this way, all learners are both fast and slow learners. A PCBE system, by design, seeks to meet each student where she or he is relative to those interests, needs, strengths, challenges, and motivations by providing supports and challenges. At times, students will work together when they have overlapping needs and interests. At times, a student will work one-on-one with a teacher, peer, or tutor to tackle a particular challenge. At times, students will create their own challenges with learning experiences and projects they find motivating and engaging.

Finally, by design a PCBE system seeks to ensure that *all* students feel successful. In a traditional system, when students receive test scores or semester grades, only the "best" students—those earning As and Bs—have the distinction of feeling successful. The rest of the students experience feelings of being mediocre (Cs), less than average (Ds), and like failures (Fs). A PCBE system motivates students. In a PCBE system that reports students' current status and growth on topics, all students receive concrete evidence of their ability to learn and grow. Frequently assessing students using a variety of assessments and providing ongoing and frequent feedback can make students feel successful on a regular basis. Feeling successful engenders motivation. And in a PCBE classroom, failure is not an option—students will not get moved along with a C or a D; they receive feedback and try again.

As described in this handbook, personalizing instruction and allowing students choice and control in how they learn and how they demonstrate their learning are also powerful ways to motivate and engage them. Importantly, we do not just assume if we tell students they now own their learning, they will understand what that means or jump at the opportunity to experience teaching and learning in a different way. Rather, we show teachers ways to support students in developing the skills they need—planning for goals and making adjustments, staying focused, and pushing the limits of one's knowledge and skills, for example—to learn to control their actions, and, in turn, their learning. When schools start selling something students want to buy—feeling successful and making progress (Christensen, Horn, & Johnson, 2011)—we wager students will be motivated to spend their time, engage their efforts, and own their learning.

Summary

This chapter presented a variety of methods for scheduling in a PCBE system, including methods for working within a traditional system and suggestions for going beyond a traditional schedule. Focused instructional time—a block of time set aside for students to have access to teachers and resources to address individual needs—is an important part of a PCBE system. This time allows students to address their individual needs, such as catching up on a topic or moving on to more advanced material. Schools can use several strategies, such as team teaching, to provide students with greater access to expertise and resources across topics, and should use data and creative scheduling to support students as they transition to new grade levels, different buildings, or advanced courses. Using technology allows schools greater flexibility in scheduling to support students in a PCBE system. In the next chapter, we discuss reporting methods that can support student learning.

Chapter 6

How Will Reporting Facilitate Student Learning?

Like scheduling, reporting in a PCBE system can involve significant changes from current practice. One of the biggest changes is that it is difficult to assign overall (omnibus) grades or scores to students. As is the case with scheduling, there is no single best way to report learning in a PCBE system. In this chapter, we present multiple examples of reporting systems or report cards. While they all share commonalities, each example has some unique features. Here, we discuss four options: (1) levels, (2) grade levels and courses, (3) pace, and (4) standards-referenced reports.

Levels

One option is to report students' current status of progression through levels as opposed to grade levels and courses. See figure 6.1 (page 156). Figure 6.1 represents a school system that has gotten rid of traditional grade levels. Note that most subject areas include levels 01 through 10. Level 10 represents mastery of a subject area sufficient for a general high school diploma. However, not all subject areas include ten levels. For example, art has six levels, technology has seven levels, and personal or social skills has five levels. Each content area, then, contains as many or as few levels necessary to describe progression up to high school graduation. Also, note that some subjects contain levels above and beyond that required of a general high school diploma. For example, mathematics has three advanced levels, as do language arts and science. Art has one advanced level, and technology has two.

Finally, note that figure 6.1 displays the level a student is currently working on for each subject area, as well as the areas where the student has already demonstrated mastery. For example, in mathematics, the student is working on level 04. The proportion in the cell is $21/35$. Of the thirty-five measurement topics at that level, the student has demonstrated proficiency (that is, obtained a score of at least 3.0 on the scale) on twenty-one of the topics. Also, note that at level 03 in mathematics, the student has a recorded score of 3.0. This means that the student received a 3.0 or higher on all measurement topics, but the majority of scores were 3.0. At levels 02 and 01, the student received a 3.0 or higher on all measurement topics,

LEVEL	ART	CAREER LITERACY	MATH	PERSONAL/ SOCIAL SKILLS	LANGUAGE ARTS	SCIENCE	SOCIAL STUDIES	TECHNOLOGY
(Advanced) 3								
(Advanced) 2								
(Advanced) 1								
10								
09								
08								
07								
06								
05								
04		2 of 16	21 of 35		3 of 36	17 of 25		
03	9 of 10	3.0 (Proficient)	3.0 (Proficient)	4 of 6	4.0 (Advanced)	3.0 (Proficient)	13 of 15	7 of 8
02	3.0 (Proficient)	3.0 (Proficient)	4.0 (Advanced)	3.0 (Proficient)	3.0 (Proficient)	3.0 (Proficient)	3.0 (Proficient)	4.0 (Advanced)
01	3.0 (Proficient)	3.0 (Proficient)	4.0 (Advanced)	3.0 (Proficient)	3.0 (Proficient)	3.0 (Proficient)	3.0 (Proficient)	3.0 (Proficient)

Note: Shaded cells indicate levels that do not apply to the subject area.

Figure 6.1: A report card with levels.

but the majority of scores were 4.0, so the student has a recorded score of 4.0 at this level. An alternative to this convention is to report the average score across measurement topics. For example, instead of an overall score of 4.0 for level 02 mathematics, the student might have received a 3.68. It is important to note that, in all cases, this average score across the measurement topics would always be at least a 3.0 because students must obtain a score of at least 3.0 before they can move on to the next level. Once a student has completed a level, the teacher drops the proportional scores, and all the teacher reports is the overall score for the measurement topics of that level.

Grade Levels and Courses

As described previously, a PCBE system could be well executed and still use the convention of grade levels and courses. From grades K–8, this is simply a change in labels. Instead of using the term *levels*, the term *grades* is used. Figure 6.2 depicts a K–8 report card that utilizes grade levels.

GRADE	ART	CAREER LITERACY	MATH	PERSONAL/ SOCIAL SKILLS	LANGUAGE ARTS	SCIENCE	SOCIAL STUDIES	TECHNOLOGY
8								
7								
6								
5			4 of 32					
4		7 of 11	3.0 (Proficient)		7 of 31	2 of 23		
3		3.0 (Proficient)	4.0 (Advanced)	2 of 6	3.0 (Proficient)	4.0 (Advanced)		
2	9 of 10	3.0 (Proficient)	3.0 (Proficient)	3.0 (Proficient)	4.0 (Advanced)	3.0 (Proficient)	2 of 15	7 of 8
1	3.0 (Proficient)	3.0 (Proficient)	4.0 (Advanced)	3.0 (Proficient)	3.0 (Proficient)	3.0 (Proficient)	3.0 (Proficient)	4.0 (Advanced)
K	3.0 (Proficient)	3.0 (Proficient)	4.0 (Advanced)	3.0 (Proficient)	3.0 (Proficient)	3.0 (Proficient)	3.0 (Proficient)	3.0 (Proficient)

Figure 6.2: Sample report card that maintains grade levels.

Figure 6.2 is basically identical to figure 6.1. The primary difference is that it reports grade levels, which top out at eighth grade. The K–8 PCBE school report card in figure 6.2 would operate in the same way as a PCBE school that used levels. The only difference is that activities and procedures would be in place to ensure that students maintained a grade-level identity. For example, students in fifth grade might begin and end the day in brief advisory periods (for example, fifteen-minute classes with their grade-level cohort). They might take certain minicourses on unleveled topics (for example, topics about local history or specific metacognitive skills) with their grade-level cohort.

School systems that keep grade levels are likely to keep a course structure at the high school level. See a high school report card in a PCBE system in figure 6.3.

SUBJECT AREA	COURSE	SCORE
Mathematics	Calculus	
	Geometry	
	Algebra 2	12 of 24
	Algebra 1	3.0 (Proficient)

Figure 6.3: High school report card.

continued →

SUBJECT AREA	COURSE	SCORE
Science	AP Environmental Science	
	Physics	
	Chemistry	6 of 22
	Biology	3.0 (Proficient)
Social Studies	Economics	
	World History	11 of 21
	U.S. History	4.0 (Advanced)
	Geography	3.0 (Proficient)
Language Arts	Shakespeare	
	Ancient Literature	13 of 22
	European Literature	3.0 (Proficient)
	U.S. Literature	3.0 (Proficient)
Art	Orchestra	
	Performing Arts	9 of 21
	Painting	3.0 (Proficient)
Technology	Web Design	
	Computer Science Analysis and Design	17 of 22
	Foundations of Computer Science	4.0 (Advanced)

Source: Adapted from Marzano, 2010.

Figure 6.3 contains a high school report card that a system would use if it kept traditional grade levels in grades K–8 and courses at the high school level. In figure 6.3, courses in each subject area are listed from simple to complex. For example, in mathematics, algebra 1 addresses simpler content than algebra 2 and so on. Some sets of courses might not exhibit a strict hierarchical structure. It might be that, in technology, students don't have to take Foundations of Computer Science before Web Design. In all cases, a student receives a credit only after all measurement topics in the course have been mastered (that is, the student receives a score of 3.0 or higher). If the majority of a student's scores were 4.0, then the student's final score for the course would be 4.0; if the majority of scores were 3.0, then the final score would be 3.0. Again, the alternative to this convention is that the average of all measurement topic scores could serve as the final score for the course.

Pace

One problem in a PCBE system is that some students might assume that they can procrastinate (when in the traditional system they could not). One can understand how such an inference might occur. In a PCBE system, the emphasis is not on handing in assignments on time. Indeed, in a traditional system, if students turn in assignments late, they lose points and their grades go down. In a PCBE system, the emphasis is on demonstrating proficiency, not being on time. Consequently, some students might adopt the attitude that they don't have to continually progress through the measurement topics since there is no penalty for progressing rather slowly. Such a perspective is risky and could cause students to fall further and further behind.

The solution to this problem is to report concretely and systematically on each student's pace relative to the expected pace if the student is to graduate on time, which can be accommodated in an effective reporting system. To illustrate, consider figure 6.4.

Jimmy Kaufman			Grade Level: 4 Report Date: March 14, 2016		
Mathematics Level 4 Ten measurement topics, seven complete		Student has mastered 70 percent of this year's learning!	Language Arts Level 3 Seven measurement topics, four complete		Student has mastered 60 percent of this year's learning!
		On pace			Trending to complete this year on pace, but one level below
		Zero of ten learning targets demonstrated at score 4.0			Four of seven learning targets demonstrated at score 4.0
Science Level 5 Five measurement topics, three complete		Student has mastered 60 percent of this year's learning!	Social Studies Level 3 Four measurement topics, three complete		Student has mastered 75 percent of this year's learning!
		On pace			Trending to complete this year ahead of schedule, but one level below
		Zero of five learning targets demonstrated at score 4.0			One of four learning targets demonstrated at score 4.0

Figure 6.4: Progress report for learning pace.

continued →

Physical Education Level 5 Seven measurement topics, six complete	🏆	Student has mastered 85 percent of this year's learning!	Health Level 4 Seven measurement topics, four complete	🏆	Student has mastered 60 percent of this year's learning!
	⏱️	Trending to complete this year one month ahead of schedule		⏱️	On pace
	💡	Three of seven learning targets demonstrated at score 4.0		💡	Two of seven learning targets demonstrated at score 4.0
World Languages Level 4 Four measurement topics, two complete	🏆	Student has mastered 50 percent of this year's learning!	Visual and Performing Arts Level 4 Six measurement topics, four complete	🏆	Student has mastered 65 percent of this year's learning!
	⏱️	Trending to complete this year two weeks behind schedule		⏱️	On pace
	💡	Two of four learning targets demonstrated at score 4.0		💡	Zero of six learning targets demonstrated at score 4.0

In figure 6.4, the student is in the fourth grade chronologically. The report card depicts the student's status in eight subject areas: mathematics, language arts, science, social studies, physical education, health, world languages, and visual and performing arts. The number under each subject area is the level on which the student is currently working. As indicated, the student is working at the fourth-grade level for mathematics, health, world languages, and visual and performing arts. The student is operating at the third-grade level in language arts and social studies, and at the fifth-grade level in science and physical education.

For each subject area, the report indicates the number of measurement topics for the specified level and how many of the measurement topics have been mastered (that is, the student has received a score of 3.0 or higher). To illustrate, in mathematics, there are ten measurement topics that students must master at the fourth-grade level. According to the report, the student has received a score of 3.0 or higher on seven of the ten topics. There are also three icons in the report: a trophy, a speedometer, and a light bulb. The trophy highlights how many measurement topics the student has mastered, the speedometer explains the extent to which the student is on pace, and the light bulb highlights how many measurement topics the student has mastered at the score 4.0 level.

Figure 6.5 depicts a section of a high school report card that includes pace.

LEVEL 9 SCIENCE	PROGRESS
Understands how waves act and interact. Understands that the behavior of waves is caused by reflection, refraction, and absorption. Understands how reflection and absorption of light produce color.	2.5
Understands the properties and uses of different parts of the electromagnetic spectrum. Understands the concept of wave intensity (energy delivered or area). Understands the properties of different types of radiation.	1.5
Understands the evidence for the age, origin, and process of formation of the universe as currently understood by science. Understands the tools and technology used by astronomers to gather information about the universe.	3.0
Current Course Score	2.5
Percent Course Completed	75 percent
Student Pace	On pace
LEVEL 9 LITERATURE AND COMPOSITION	**PROGRESS**
Understands how rhetoric advances point of view and purpose for a specific audience.	2.0
Understands advanced research includes conducting an advanced search, using multiple print and online sources, adjusting strategies as appropriate, citing information, and creating a properly formatted bibliography.	—
Is skilled at using patterns of word changes to indicate different meanings or parts of speech.	—
Understands the rules for using devices that indicate pause.	—
Current Course Score	2.0
Percent Course Completed	13 percent
Student Pace	Behind pace

Figure 6.5: High school report card including pace.

The report card in figure 6.5 is organized by courses and reports on all of the current course measurement topics in progress. It also shows overall scores on the measurement topics and percentage of standards completed in the course. Student pacing indicates whether the student is on an appropriate pace for graduation. In this example, the student is on pace in science but behind pace in literature and composition.

Standards-Referenced Reports

As schools contemplate moving to a PCBE system, many view the change as too drastic. A viable course of action for such schools is to implement a standards-referenced system as a stepping stone to a PCBE system. A standards-referenced system maintains grade levels and overall grades or scores on report cards. To illustrate, consider figure 6.6 (pages 162–165).

Name	Lora Fedorovski
Address	1230 Blueberry Street
City	Anytown, CO 80000
Grade Level	5

Subject	Score	Grade		Skill	Score	Grade
Language arts	2.56	B–		Generating conclusions	2.70	B
Mathematics	3.18	A–		Navigating digital sources	3.50	A
Science	2.56	B–		Staying focused	3.00	A–
Social studies	2.94	B+		Seeking accuracy	3.00	A–
Art	2.75	B				

English Language Arts	Score	0.5	1.0	1.5	2.0	2.5	3.0	3.5	4.0
Decoding	2.5								
Analyzing text organization and structure	1.5								
Analyzing ideas and themes	2.0								
Analyzing claims	3.5								
Analyzing narratives	2.5								
Comparing texts	1.0								
Analyzing words	2.5								
Generating text organization and structure	3.0								
Generating sentence structure	3.0								
Generating claims	3.0								
Using citations	2.5								
Generating narratives	2.5								
Generating point of view and purpose	3.0								
Writing for a specific audience	3.0								
Using specific words and parts of speech	3.0								
Punctuation, capitalization, and spelling	2.0								
Revision and editing	3.0								
Average for English Language Arts	2.56								

Cognitive Skills (English Language Arts)										
Generating conclusions	2.5									
Navigating digital sources	3.5									
Metacognitive Skills (English Language Arts)										
Staying focused	3.0									
Seeking accuracy	3.0									
Mathematics										
Decimals	3.0									
Fractions	3.0									
Area	3.0									
Volume	2.5									
Multiplication	3.5									
Division	3.5									
Comparison symbols	4.0									
Exponents	3.0									
Ordered pairs and coordinate systems	3.0									
Addition and subtraction	4.0									
Perimeter	4.0									
Data representation	3.0									
Central tendency in data sets	3.0									
Numerical patterns	3.0									
Probability	3.0									
Symmetry	3.0									
Two-dimensional figures	4.0									
Basic functions	2.5									
Factors and multiples	2.5									
Measurement	3.0									
Average for Mathematics	3.18									
Cognitive Skills (Mathematics)										

Figure 6.6: Standards-based report card.

continued →

Generating conclusions	3.0
Navigating digital sources	3.5
Metacognitive Skills (Mathematics)	
Staying focused	3.5
Seeking accuracy	3.5
Science	
Matter and its interactions	2.5
Motion and stability: Forces and interactions	3.0
Energy	3.0
From molecules to organisms: Structures and processes	2.5
Ecosystems: Interactions, energy, and dynamics	2.0
Earth's place in the universe	2.0
Earth's systems	2.0
Earth and human activity	3.0
Engineering design	3.0
Average for Science	2.56
Cognitive Skills (Science)	
Generating conclusions	2.5
Navigating digital sources	3.5
Metacognitive Skills (Science)	
Staying focused	2.5
Seeking accuracy	2.5
Social Studies	
History: Analyze and interpret historical sources	3.5
History: Historical eras, individuals, groups, ideas, and themes in regions of the Western Hemisphere	3.5
Geography: Use geographic tools	3.0

Geography: Human and physical systems	3.0									
Economics: Different economic systems	2.5									
Economics: Personal financial literacy	3.0									
Civics: Connection of the United States to other nations	2.5									
Civics: Multiple systems of government	2.5									
Average for Social Studies	2.94									
Cognitive Skills (Social Studies)										
Generating conclusions	3.0									
Navigating digital sources	3.5									
Metacognitive Skills (Social Studies)										
Staying focused	3.0									
Seeking accuracy	3.0									
Art										
Perceptual skills and visual arts vocabulary	3.0									
Art elements and principles of design	3.0									
Skills, processes, materials, and tools	2.5									
Communication and expression through original works of art	2.5									
Average for Art	2.75									
Cognitive Skills (Art)										
Generating conclusions	2.5									
Navigating digital sources	3.5									
Metacognitive Skills (Art)										
Staying focused	3.0									
Seeking accuracy	3.0									

In figure 6.6 (pages 162–165) the teachers compiled the overall grades at the top of the report card by translating the final score on measurement topics for a given subject area into an overall letter grade. To illustrate, consider the final scores for the subject area of English language arts. The bar graph for each measurement topic has a dark portion and a light portion. The dark portion represents the student's initial status; the light portion represents the student's current status. For the measurement topic of decoding, the student started with a score of 1.0 (the dark part of the bar graph) but reached a score of 2.5 by the end of the grading period. Thus, the student grew by 1.5 score points and had a final or summative score of 2.5. The report in figure 6.6 also contains measurement topics for cognitive and metacognitive skills. These are treated in the same manner as academic content: each subject area reports status and growth for each specific measurement topic. Note that at the top, this report card includes traditional letter grades. Summative proficiency scale scores can be converted to letter grades using the conversion scale in table 6.1.

Table 6.1: Conversion From Proficiency Scale Scores to Letter Grades

AVERAGE PROFICIENCY SCALE SCORE	LETTER GRADE
3.75–4.00	A+
3.26–3.74	A
3.00–3.25	A–
2.84–2.99	B+
2.67–2.83	B
2.50–2.66	B–
2.34–2.49	C+
2.17–2.33	C
2.00–2.16	C–
1.76–1.99	D+
1.26–1.75	D
1.00–1.25	D–
Below 1.00	F

Source: Adapted from Marzano, 2010.

There is a sound logic to the conversion scale in table 6.1. Since a score of 3.0 on a proficiency scale represents proficiency with the content, an average of 3.0 or above puts a student in the A category. An average score of 2.50 to 2.99 puts a student in the B category. A score of 2.5 would indicate that across the topics the student knew the simpler content and had partial knowledge of the target content. Table 6.2 translates proficiency scale scores into percentage scores.

Table 6.2: Conversion From Proficiency Scale Scores to a One Hundred–Point Scale

AVERAGE PROFICIENCY SCALE SCORE	ONE HUNDRED–POINT SCALE SCORE
4.0	100
3.5	95
3.0	90
2.5	80
2.0	70
1.5	65
1.0	60
Below 1.0	50

Source: Adapted from Marzano, 2010.

Table 6.3 (page 168) contains a comprehensive conversion system from proficiency scale scores to both letter grades and percentage scores.

Just as the report card in figure 6.6 (pages 162–165) lists overall grades for each subject area at the top of the report card, it also reports overall grades for cognitive and metacognitive skills. Teachers use the same conversion system to calculate the grades for the cognitive and metacognitive skills, using an average of the scores across all subject areas. For example, the scores for generating conclusions are as follows: English language arts, 2.5; mathematics, 3.0; science, 2.5; social studies, 3.0; and art, 2.5. The average of these scores is 2.70, which translates to a B.

There is another approach to computing overall grades: the *conjunctive approach* (Marzano, 2010). In a conjunctive approach, teachers establish minimum scores for each measurement topic for specific grades. To illustrate, consider the measurement topics for mathematics in table 6.4 (page 169). Each of these measurement topics has a proficiency scale, and the teacher introduced nine topics in the first trimester. However, for three of these topics, the class did not progress beyond the score 2.0 content. In addition, students only just started learning about score 3.0 content in two topics. Given that for three topics students did not receive instruction beyond score 2.0 content and for two topics they received only partial instruction on the score 3.0 content, the teacher might establish criteria for a grade of A as depicted in table 6.4.

Table 6.3: Comprehensive Conversion System

SCALE SCORE	PERCENTAGE	GRADE	SCALE SCORE	PERCENTAGE	GRADE	SCALE SCORE	PERCENTAGE	GRADE	SCALE SCORE	PERCENTAGE	GRADE
4.00	100	A	2.30 to 2.34	76	C	1.30 to 1.31	50	F	0.73 to 0.75	25	F
3.90 to 3.99	99	A	2.25 to 2.29	75	C	1.28 to 1.29	49	F	0.70 to 0.72	24	F
3.80 to 3.89	98	A	2.20 to 2.24	74	C	1.26 to 1.27	48	F	0.67 to 0.69	23	F
3.70 to 3.79	97	A	2.15 to 2.19	73	C	1.24 to 1.25	47	F	0.64 to 0.66	22	F
3.60 to 3.69	96	A	2.10 to 2.14	72	C	1.22 to 1.23	46	F	0.61 to 0.63	21	F
3.50 to 3.59	95	A	2.05 to 2.09	71	C	1.20 to 1.21	45	F	0.58 to 0.60	20	F
3.40 to 3.49	94	A	2.00 to 2.04	70	C	1.18 to 1.19	44	F	0.55 to 0.57	19	F
3.30 to 3.39	93	A	1.95 to 1.99	69	D	1.16 to 1.17	43	F	0.52 to 0.54	18	F
3.20 to 3.29	92	A	1.90 to 1.94	68	D	1.14 to 1.15	42	F	0.49 to 0.51	17	F
3.10 to 3.19	91	A	1.85 to 1.89	67	D	1.12 to 1.13	41	F	0.46 to 0.48	16	F
3.00 to 3.09	90	A	1.80 to 1.84	66	D	1.10 to 1.11	40	F	0.43 to 0.45	15	F
2.95 to 2.99	89	B	1.75 to 1.79	65	D	1.08 to 1.09	39	F	0.40 to 0.42	14	F
2.90 to 2.94	88	B	1.70 to 1.74	64	D	1.06 to 1.07	38	F	0.37 to 0.39	13	F
2.85 to 2.89	87	B	1.65 to 1.69	63	D	1.04 to 1.05	37	F	0.34 to 0.36	12	F
2.80 to 2.84	86	B	1.60 to 1.64	62	D	1.02 to 1.03	36	F	0.31 to 0.33	11	F
2.75 to 2.79	85	B	1.55 to 1.59	61	D	1.00 to 1.01	35	F	0.28 to 0.30	10	F
2.70 to 2.74	84	B	1.50 to 1.54	60	D	0.98 to 0.99	34	F	0.25 to 0.27	9	F
2.65 to 2.69	83	B	1.48 to 1.49	59	F	0.96 to 0.97	33	F	0.20 to 0.24	8	F
2.60 to 2.64	82	B	1.46 to 1.47	58	F	0.94 to 0.95	32	F	0.19 to 0.21	7	F
2.55 to 2.59	81	B	1.44 to 1.45	57	F	0.91 to 0.93	31	F	0.16 to 0.18	6	F
2.50 to 2.54	80	B	1.42 to 1.43	56	F	0.88 to 0.90	30	F	0.13 to 0.15	5	F
2.45 to 2.49	79	C	1.40 to 1.41	55	F	0.85 to 0.87	29	F	0.10 to 0.12	4	F
2.40 to 2.44	78	C	1.38 to 1.39	54	F	0.82 to 0.84	28	F	0.07 to 0.09	3	F
2.35 to 2.39	77	C	1.36 to 1.37	53	F	0.79 to 0.81	27	F	0.04 to 0.06	2	F
			1.34 to 1.35	52	F	0.76 to 0.78	26	F	0.01 to 0.03	1	F
			1.32 to 1.33	51	F				0.00	0	F

Table 6.4: Scoring Criteria for a Grade of A for First Trimester

MEASUREMENT TOPIC	EXPOSURE TO CONTENT	CRITERIA
Decimals	Complete	3.0 or above
Fractions	Just started score 3.0 content	2.5 or above
Area	Score 2.0 content only	2.0 or above
Volume	Score 2.0 content only	2.0 or above
Multiplication	Complete	3.0 or above
Division	Complete	3.0 or above
Ordered Pairs and Coordinate Systems	Score 2.0 content only	2.0 or above
Addition and Subtraction	Complete	3.0 or above
Perimeter	Just started score 3.0 content	2.5 or above

Notice that in this scheme, a student can receive a grade of A with scores of 2.0 on the measurement topics of area, volume, and ordered pairs and coordinate systems, and a score of 2.5 on fractions and perimeter.

For a grade of B, the teacher might use the minimum scores depicted in table 6.5.

Table 6.5: Scoring Criteria for a Grade of B for First Trimester

MEASUREMENT TOPIC	EXPOSURE TO CONTENT	CRITERIA
Decimals	Complete	2.5 or above
Fractions	Just started score 3.0 content	2.0 or above
Area	Score 2.0 content only	1.5 or above
Volume	Score 2.0 content only	1.5 or above
Multiplication	Complete	2.5 or above
Division	Complete	2.5 or above
Ordered pairs and coordinate systems	Score 2.0 content only	1.5 or above
Addition and subtraction	Complete	2.5 or above
Perimeter	Just started score 3.0 content	2.0 or above

The teacher would use a similar approach to set minimum scores for grades of C, D, and F. As these examples illustrate, the conjunctive approach can be useful in a standards-referenced system when students have not been exposed to all of the score 2.0 and score 3.0 content for some measurement topics during a grading period.

Summary

When transitioning to a PCBE system, a school must consider the reporting needs of students, families, and teachers, and identify, adapt, or create a system that meets these needs. Transparency is central to the functioning of a PCBE system, and the reporting system should reflect this principle by reporting progress on measurement topics, including cognitive and metacognitive skills. Schools should also determine a method for reporting on pace so that students do not fall behind and risk not graduating on time. Finally, as a step toward implementing a true PCBE system, schools might consider using standards-referenced reporting, which maintains grade levels and overall grades. In the next chapter, we consider approaches for transitioning to a PCBE system.

Chapter 7

How Do Schools and Districts Transition to a PCBE System?

Transitioning to a PCBE system is not a straightforward process. It can look quite different from district to district and school to school depending on organizational factors such as commitment to change, resources, culture, and so on. One of the most important factors a district or school must consider when transitioning to a PCBE system is how quickly they wish to implement the rule that every student must achieve proficiency on each measurement topic before moving on to the next level. Implementing this rule too quickly can send shock waves through a system. To illustrate, assume that a high school has decided that all students must show proficiency in all measurement topics before they can move to the next course. For seniors, this could mean that many students do not graduate on time since they previously have not been required to meet such high expectations. Indeed, in the past, the graduation requirements were credit based, which meant that students only had to pass a certain percent of courses. The plan for transitioning to PCBE requirements is one of the most important aspects of PCBE implementation.

We'll discuss a two-staged transitional approach comprising (1) the ramp-up phase, and (2) the rollout phase. We'll also discuss how to implement PCBE in a single classroom, for teachers who wish to incorporate PCBE in a school or district still adhering to a traditional model.

The Ramp-Up Phase

The ramp-up phase is designed to develop and vet all the necessary components of the PCBE system that will be implemented across the school or district. It will typically last about two years.

Year One

We recommend seven steps for the first year of PCBE ramp-up.

1. Establish a shared vision.

    2. Begin working on measurement topics and proficiency scales.

    3. Select a small group of vanguard teachers to begin experimenting with PCBE concepts.

    4. Experiment with a different reporting system in vanguard classrooms.

    5. Design the instructional model.

    6. Begin designing the assessment system.

    7. Begin selecting a learning management system.

These seven steps will involve different sets of constituents, including district and school administrators, teachers, nonteaching staff, parents and guardians, community members, and students. While there will certainly be groups that naturally and obviously should be involved in specific steps, we recommend that you invite all constituent groups to give input at every step. Appendix B (page 207) provides some direct guidance as to how to interact with various constituent groups. Leading the effort should be a design team that represents all constituent groups. Certainly district and school administrators should be on the team, as well as teacher leaders. Members of the design team should be willing to serve through the ramp-up phase at least.

Establish a Shared Vision

A shared vision provides a sense of direction. It helps members of the school community answer questions such as, What do we want to accomplish? Why are we doing this? and How will we work together to make our vision happen? The process of developing a shared vision engages the school community—administrators, teachers, nonteaching staff, students, parents and guardians, business representatives, and other community members—in developing common understandings and commitments. A shared vision gathers multiple perspectives to create a picture of how the school can better prepare students for the future relative to how the school currently prepares students.

The process for developing a shared vision does not need to be complicated, but should include the following characteristics.

- Include as many stakeholders as possible from as many diverse groups as possible.

- Facilitate so that participants have direction and feel that the process is purposeful.

- Share relevant data and information, such as student achievement data and current research.

- Be transparent so that everyone understands his or her role and how the process will work.

Creating a shared vision for a district or school involves six steps: (1) identify stakeholder groups, (2) create guiding questions to generate input, (3) gather input from stakeholder groups, (4) prioritize and synthesize input, (5) take a final vote, and (6) deploy the shared vision.

Step 1: Identify Stakeholder Groups

As mentioned, the shared vision process should engage many stakeholders from diverse groups. The goal of developing a shared vision is to invite, hear, and include everyone's voice so that all constituents will feel a part of and support the hard work required to achieve the vision. Stakeholders to consider including in the shared vision process are certified staff (for example, teachers, media specialists, guidance counselors, and instructional coaches), classified school staff (for example, teacher aides, and maintenance, custodial, cafeteria, transportation, health, and clerical or administration staff), students, parents and guardians, community members, and representatives from local businesses.

Step 2: Create Guiding Questions to Generate Input

Essential questions should guide the work of generating a shared vision. Those questions should help participants explore ideas, experiences, assumptions, and preconceived notions about the school's purpose, how teaching and learning happen, and what students need to be successful in school and beyond. Questions should focus on the current state of the school and the community's vision for the future, as exemplified by the following.

- According to current test scores, how are our students doing?

- What happens to our students once they leave our K–12 system?

- Why do we come to school? Why is school important?

- What do we want our students to know and be able to do?

- What does a successful student look like?

- What does an ideal school look like, feel like, and prioritize?

Step 3: Gather Input From Stakeholder Groups

The next step in developing a shared vision involves gathering input from participants through a series of hosted conversations. *Hosted conversations* are discussions with specific stakeholder groups (for example, students, parents and guardians, teachers and noncertified staff, administrators, business representatives, and so on). Although separate meetings should be held for different stakeholder groups in order to tailor the questions and examples to their perspectives and needs, the meetings should be held within a short time frame to ensure all stakeholders have the opportunity to provide input without losing momentum for creating the shared vision. Appendix B (page 207) provides suggestions for working with different groups, examples of scenarios and data that might work best with certain groups, essential questions, and activities.

Step 4: Prioritize and Synthesize Input

This step involves reviewing all the input, categorizing the ideas, and creating statements to capture the input. First, the design team should assess the input from all groups. This team might include staff and volunteers who facilitated conversations, school leaders, and parent volunteers. Next, combine similar ideas and create categories based on the types of ideas (for example, environment, academics, character). Narrow the ideas within each category by identifying the most common or overarching concept that represents various ideas. Finally, with the narrowed ideas, create several examples of vision statements that embody the concepts, ideally in one or two sentences.

Step 5: Take a Final Vote

After the initial team has crafted possible shared vision statements, it is important to engage stakeholders and seek input again to continue building a community of understanding and collaboration. During this step, remind participants of the process the school used to gather input; describe the processes the team used to synthesize the input and craft possible vision statements; and help participants connect their roles with the work of achieving the shared vision. A voting process (such as power voting) allows each group to have input into the final statement that best represents its vision for the school.

Step 6: Deploy the Shared Vision

It is important to ensure that all stakeholders know the results of the vote. Those who create or identify opportunities should communicate the visioning process whenever possible. Additionally, multiple representations of the shared vision (such as graphics, posters, and messaging in newsletters) communicate the vision statement. Continually invoke the vision by using it to drive decision making (for example, Will this decision help us achieve our vision?) and to bring clarity and focus to setting strategic goals, objectives, and outcomes.

Begin Working on Measurement Topics and Proficiency Scales

It is important to start work on identifying measurement topics and developing related proficiency scales right at the outset (we discuss this process in detail in chapter 1). Initially, scales should be developed for English language arts, mathematics, and science. Subject-matter teachers or curriculum specialists (if the district is large enough to include specialists in various subject areas) first identify the measurement topics at each grade level and subject area using the processes described in chapter 1 (page 11). They then construct proficiency scales by identifying score 2.0, score 3.0, and score 4.0 content.

Resources to support this process include the Critical Concepts measurement topics (Simms, 2016). For example, schools and districts might use the Critical Concepts measurement topics as a starting point for creating proficiency scales or use the set of Critical Concepts proficiency scales and customize them. Alternatively, Heflebower and her colleagues (2014) outlined processes for analyzing and prioritizing state or district standards and writing proficiency scales. Additional resources include several books that provide guidance and ready-to-use proficiency scales, such as *Proficiency Scales for the New Science Standards* (Marzano & Yanoski, 2016) and *Using Common Core Standards to Enhance Classroom Instruction & Assessment* (Marzano et al., 2013), as well as a free online database of proficiency scales available on the Marzano Resources website (MarzanoResources.com/resources/proficiency-scale-bank).

As teachers create proficiency scales, it is important to tag existing instructional resources (including electronic or Internet-based instructional resources) to the content at scores 2.0, 3.0, and 4.0, along with assessment items.

Select a Small Group of Vanguard Teachers to Begin Experimenting With PCBE Concepts

Vanguard teachers should be volunteers who wish to pilot PCBE strategies in their classrooms. Vanguard teachers should begin by creating a learner-centered classroom environment that facilitates the development of student agency as described in chapter 2 (page 37). This process starts with creating classroom-level goals aligned with the school's shared vision, designing and implementing a code of cooperation for the class, and establishing standard operating procedures with students. Although students should participate in each of these activities, as a group, the vanguard teachers might develop and implement some common elements. For example, vanguard teachers and their students might develop some common SOPs that provide consistency for prevalent activities or issues, such as how to get help, lead a parent conference, and use bathroom sign-outs. Using common SOPs for activities such as these can build student confidence and increase efficiency across the classrooms of vanguard teachers.

As described in chapter 2 (page 37), vanguard teachers should also institute procedures to provide students with voice and choice. Again, vanguard teachers should start small and increase options as students begin to develop confidence and independence. The vanguard teachers should also start using proficiency scales and personal tracking matrices. Vanguard teachers should be part of the team that creates the proficiency scales and might decide as a group how to introduce the scales to students. As with the code of cooperation and SOPs, consistent use of proficiency scales across vanguard classrooms will develop student confidence in using them and build momentum for expanding their use throughout the school. As they begin to use proficiency scales with students, vanguard teachers will identify additional instructional resources that can be tagged to the content at scores 2.0, 3.0, and 4.0. Teachers should share these resources and add to the learning management system so the database of resources continues to grow.

Experiment With a Different Reporting System in Vanguard Classrooms

Given that vanguard classrooms use proficiency scales, teachers must report each student's status and growth for each measurement topic. See chapter 6 (page 155) for descriptions of reporting approaches.

Even though the vanguard team is using proficiency scales, it might still be advisable to translate scores on those scales into a traditional overall grade or percentage score simply because parents might still expect traditional grades. To do this, a district or school can use the conversion systems depicted in chapter 6 (page 155).

Design the Instructional Model

An effective PCBE system must have an effective instructional model. Although called an *instructional model*, it should not be limited to instructional strategies alone. In fact, as defined in this book, an instructional model addresses essential components of the classroom, including effective instructional strategies, classroom management or environment, and assessment and feedback. It addresses all aspects of teaching, not just the cognitive levels associated with learning the academic content in standards, and reflects the complex interactions of all the component parts. For school staff, an instructional model serves several purposes, including the following.

- Developing shared understanding and a common language about teaching and learning among leaders, teachers, and staff

- Creating schoolwide consistency in instructional design and delivery by identifying practices to use in all classrooms, and allowing teachers to implement the *science* of instruction while maintaining the *art* of instruction

- Outlining the role assessment plays in the classroom and in student achievement

- Defining essential components of the learning environment

While we sometimes refer to the model that a school defines as a *common* model, common does not mean that all teachers have to teach the same way. Rather, the model introduces a framework and language (based on current best practices) that can guide teachers as they plan units and lessons and engage in collegial conversations around effective pedagogy across all levels and subject areas. The instructional model assists teachers in aligning their current instructional practices with what research tells us about effective teaching and learning.

An instructional model is not intended to limit creativity; teachers are allowed to shape, adjust, and customize the model in unique ways to meet their students' needs. In addition to being a planning tool, an instructional model can assist teachers in reflecting on their current practices. The model also provides a structure for organizing and scaffolding professional development experiences, as well as direction for coaching teachers in their efforts to improve their current practice.

We recommend that an instructional model include the following elements.

1. Feedback

    a. Providing and communicating clear learning goals

    b. Conducting assessment

2. Content

    a. Conducting direct instruction lessons

    b. Implementing practicing and deepening lessons

    c. Implementing knowledge application lessons

    d. Using strategies that appear in all types of lessons

3. Context

    a. Using engagement strategies

    b. Implementing rules and procedures

    c. Building relationships

    d. Communicating high expectations

For additional detail on these elements, please see chapter 3 (page 69) and appendix A (page 191). Vanguard teachers can begin the design of the basic elements of the instructional model as they implement various pieces throughout the school year.

Begin Designing the Assessment System

A district or school must weigh several factors when designing an assessment system to measure student proficiency. The design team should ask a number of questions, such as the following.

- Will we use proficiency scales or another method for identifying learning targets?

- How will we avoid overtesting our students?

- Will we use summative assessments to determine a current score or another method, such as most recent scores, mounting evidence, or mathematical models?

- How will we design and score assessments consistently?

- What recording guidelines will we provide teachers?

- Will we use safety net assessments?

- How will we assess cognitive and metacognitive skills?

As we discussed in chapters 1 and 4 (pages 11 and 97), our strong preference is for using proficiency scales as the basis for the assessment system. Proficiency scales provide consistency for teachers and students and foster precision in measurement. To support vanguard teachers and prepare for bringing in additional teachers, we suggest that teacher teams work together to design assessments. This process serves several purposes. Working together helps teachers build an assessment bank that others can draw from. The process also enables teachers to refine their understanding of key assessment issues, such as distinctions among the terms *measurement*, *assessment*, *test*, *score*, and *scale* and what each looks like in the classroom, and how to design and score various assessment types using a proficiency scale. A school may determine that teachers should administer some common assessments, particularly if a school opts to use safety net assessments or summative assessments. Finally, developing assessments together prepares teachers to work together on issues related to scoring assessments, reviewing student work, and determining current scores.

Once teachers design an initial assessment system, we recommend that schools document key tenets of the system, including the measurement method the school will use to determine current scores. As teachers begin to use the assessment system, they will identify areas that may need further discussion and refinement.

Begin Selecting a Learning Management System

Teachers must begin the process of selecting a learning management system. Ultimately, an electronic learning management system must be in place that allows for easy data entry and easy access to a variety of reports. There are a number of systems that can support a PCBE system, including Buzz by Agilix (http://agilix.com), various Edgenuity (www.edgenuity.com) products, Empower Learning (www.empower-learning.com), and PEAK by Fuel Education (www.getfueled.com/peak). The one we have worked most closely with is Empower Learning.

The field of options is constantly evolving. There are several good sources that can support the decision-making process for selecting a learning management system, including the report and infographic in *Getting Smart on Next-Gen Learning Platforms* (Getting Smart Staff, 2015) which contain decision-making tips, desired features, and snapshots of existing platforms. The report reviewed progress on digital learning platforms and adaptive learning applications and provided information on the features schools look for in a learning management system. The report noted that many school and district leaders want a system that:

- Powers and tracks personal learning plans;
- Manages assignments and dynamic grouping;
- Supports development of standards-aligned projects;
- Makes it easy to combine proprietary, open, district and teacher-developed content;
- Combines formative assessments in a standards-based gradebook;
- Incorporates social, collaborative, productivity, and presentation tools;
- Integrates with other systems, provides single sign-on for lots of apps; and
- Connects students, parents, and teachers anywhere on any device. (Getting Smart Staff, 2015, p. 1)

The report concluded that "some platforms meet the needs of traditional schools moderately well. However, no platform currently meets all the needs of schools attempting personalized and competency-based models" (Getting Smart Staff, 2015, p. 44). However, the report also indicated that most platforms are improving quickly.

Another iNACOL report (Glowa & Goodell, 2016) attempted to collect information on student-centered learning and technology to comprehensively address "what student-centered learning means for each end user segment and . . . the fundamental requirements for the technologies needed to support end users' needs" (p. 4). The report addressed the following core considerations for a well-designed student-centered learning system:

- A reference framework for aligning learning experiences, resources, assessment and reporting to the competencies

- Customized learner profiles that combine data from source systems and input from students, parents, educators and others who work with the student

- Personalized learning plans that are responsive to the learner as he or she progresses and changes

- A variety of learning experiences within and beyond the school setting and calendar plus the collection of associated data to inform student progress

- Access to content, digital resources, human resources and tools through a user-centric interface

- Meaningful, timely feedback during the learning process

- Multiple ways of demonstrating and assessing mastery towards competency

- Relationships, collaboration and communication

- Dashboards that reveal in real time which concepts and objectives students struggle with, pinpoint at-risk students and enable targeted intervention

- Analytic tools to support data-informed practices (learning, teaching, administration)

- Integration of multiple systems and data flows using data and interoperability standards and practices (Glowa & Goodell, 2016, p. 6)

Because the systems and platforms are constantly evolving, a school or district should consult sources such as Getting Smart (www.gettingsmart.com) and iNACOL (www.inacol.org) to support the process of selecting the system that best meets its needs.

Year Two

In the second year of ramping up, a school should build on the steps started in year one. There are seven steps we recommend for the second year. Again, the design team should seek input from all constituent groups.

1. Expand the vanguard group.

2. Create proficiency scales for other subject areas.

3. Design the reporting system.

4. Finalize the instructional model.

5. Finalize the assessment system.

6. Select the learning management system and train vanguard teachers.

7. Train all teachers who will be involved in the first tier of implementation.

Expand the Vanguard Group

In the second year, the design team should expand the vanguard group to include more teachers in different grade levels and subject areas. As the year-one vanguards did, these teachers should implement similar structures and processes for creating more learner-centered classroom environments that facilitate student agency. They should also institute procedures to provide students with voice and choice. One key to expanding the vanguard group is to provide numerous opportunities for year-one vanguards and year-two vanguards to collaborate and learn from each other. Although they will be at different places in their understanding and implementation, year-two vanguard teachers will have much to learn from what worked (and what did not work) in year one. In addition, year-two vanguards will most likely be teachers who spent time during year one familiarizing themselves with the basic tenets of the school's approach, discussing aspects of the classroom with year-one vanguards, and preparing to transition their own classrooms. Thus, these teachers may have new ideas to contribute and may experience some successes quicker than teachers did in year one. The vanguard teachers should also be involved in developing proficiency scales (step 2) and should start using the proficiency scales and the personal tracking matrices that accompany them with students.

Create Proficiency Scales for Other Subject Areas

While in year one, the vanguard group focused on developing proficiency scales for core subject areas like English language arts, mathematics, and science. In year two, subject-matter teachers or curriculum specialists should follow the steps to create proficiency scales for other subject areas such as social studies, health, physical education, and art. That is, these teachers and specialists should first identify the measurement topics at each grade level and subject area using the processes described in chapter 1 (page 11). They can then construct proficiency scales by identifying score 2.0, 3.0, and 4.0 content.

As teachers develop proficiency scales, they should continue to build the database of resources (including electronic and online resources) and assessments that align with the proficiency scales by tagging them to scores 2.0, 3.0, and 4.0. The more resources developed, adapted, or identified during this year, the better prepared the district or school will be to roll out to all teachers and students.

Design the Reporting System

In year two, the vanguard teachers and school leaders should begin designing a schoolwide reporting system. The reporting system will depend greatly on other decisions that the school makes, such as whether to keep grade levels and courses or shift to reporting levels and whether (and how) to report on student pace (see chapter 6, page 155).

As discussed in chapter 6, reporting in a PCBE system will most likely involve significant changes from current practice. A school can, and probably should, make an intentional decision and a phased plan to gradually move to a full standards-based reporting system. For example, one approach that can make the shift easier for many stakeholders—principals, teachers, students, and parents alike—is to continue using omnibus letter grades for a specified time frame. Although assigning an overall grade or score to students can be challenging, a school may find the decision to abandon overall grades overnight even more challenging.

For this reason, as the district or school design team works through the various options for reporting and the required decisions that must be made, administrative leaders and vanguard teachers should engage other teachers and staff, students, and parents and guardians in discussions. It will be important to understand concerns from each perspective and work to address these concerns as the system is designed. The vanguard teachers should use the system as it is being designed in order to identify and address any problems and to allow ample time for teachers, students, and parents to provide input. This testing phase also allows the school time to document the different elements of the system and the rationale for its design and use.

Whether a district or school gradually implements the new reporting system in stages or all at once, it will be important to be consistent and transparent across the school. All teachers should use the same reporting system, measurement method, and conversion schema to calculate overall grades (if the reporting system will include an overall grade). It is also important that the system is documented and available to all stakeholders. The school or district can accomplish this by posting all relevant documents on the school or district website.

Finalize the Instructional Model

Vanguard teachers started developing the instructional model in year one. The model is an adaptation of the one presented in chapter 2 (page 37) and should be clear and transparent across the school. Since vanguard teachers tested pieces of the instructional model in year one, they must bring any suggestions for additions, deletions, and refinement to the process for finalizing the model in year two. As discussed previously, the instructional model should provide clear and consistent guidance for instruction as it relates to feedback, content, and context in an environment that is both personalized for students and based on achieving competency in knowledge and skills before moving on to the next level.

The instructional model will offer a platform for coaching and providing feedback to teachers and engaging them in conversations focused on teaching and learning in a personalized competency-based system. It will also help school leaders and teacher teams identify areas where some or all teachers require professional development supports. For example, if a school conducts a short survey of all teachers on the specific elements of the instructional model, the results should indicate areas where teachers feel confident with specific strategies and areas where teachers may need assistance to further develop knowledge and skills. Collecting perception data from teachers and students, conducting observations of teaching and learning in the school, and engaging in conversations around the model are all important ways of gauging the level of implementation and continuing to develop teachers as experts.

That said, teachers should review the instructional model as an adaptable aspect of the system. That is, as the personalized competency-based system develops over time, the school staff should periodically review the instructional model to discuss what is working well, what is not working well, and what changes might be appropriate.

Finalize the Assessment System

Vanguard teachers began developing an assessment system in year one. That work should continue with the additional vanguard teachers in year two so that the assessment system is in place for the rollout phase. To begin the process of finalizing the assessment system, teachers who used the system in year one should provide feedback on what is working well and what needs to be revised. School leaders and vanguard teachers should also review each decision that influenced the design of the assessment system to ensure it is aligned with the school's shared vision for personalized competency-based learning and meets the needs of students. In year two, the larger group of vanguard teachers should make and test adjustments to the assessment system.

Other work in year two should focus on designing additional assessments aligned with proficiency scales at score 2.0, 3.0, and 4.0 to continue to build the assessment bank for all teachers. As in year one, we suggest that, when possible, teacher teams work together to design assessments, which assists teachers in refining their understanding of key issues surrounding assessment and honing their skills for designing and scoring various types of assessments using a proficiency scale. This is also a good time to develop and administer additional common assessments, particularly if a school has decided to use safety net assessments or summative assessments. Finally, vanguard teachers should spend time together scoring assessments, reviewing student work, and determining current scores, all of which build their capacity and prepare them to support other teachers during the rollout phase.

Finally, we recommend that schools document (or refine the documentation started in year one) the key tenets of their assessment system, including the method of measurement the school will use to determine current scores. Such documentation will provide critical support for teachers during the rollout phase.

Select the Learning Management System and Train Vanguard Teachers

In year one, school leaders and vanguard teachers researched and experimented with different learning management systems. In year two, school leaders and vanguard teachers should review the test run findings of the different systems, familiarize themselves with any planned updates to possible solutions, and finalize the criteria for making a decision. A school should always rely on a set of criteria to assist in the process of selecting a viable learning management system. We recommend a learning management system that fulfills the following requirements.

- Computes an estimated current true score using the method the school has selected (for example, using mathematical models)

- Mathematically determines which estimate of the true score best fits the data

- Allows for the entry of measurement topics and associated proficiency scales and tagging resources, activities, and assessments to the score 2.0, 3.0, and 4.0 content

- Provides easy access for parents and guardians

- Tracks and reports student progress on measurement topics across multiple levels, whether reporting levels or grade levels

- Supports the development and use of individual learning paths (for example, playlists, and personalized learning plans) and facilitates student choice

- Provides a student-centered and student-friendly dashboard and interface

As explained in the discussion of the year one ramp-up phase, there are many resources schools can and should access for information to support decision making in this area. In addition, we recommend that schools ask for references from schools and districts currently using the system under consideration and speak to teachers who have firsthand experience.

It is important to train all vanguard teachers to use the system, preferably to the point that they can serve as in-house resources for other teachers during the rollout phase.

Train All Teachers Who Will Be Involved in the First Tier of Implementation

The school should ensure that all vanguard teachers have the support they need to implement the major components of the PCBE system. This support may include professional development that addresses shifting from a teacher-centered to a student-centered approach; developing and using measurement topics and proficiency scales as the foundation for curriculum, instruction, and assessment; and understanding and using methods for assessment and measurement. We recommend that initial training focus on establishing a student-centered climate and culture that set the stage for students to take ownership of their learning as described in chapter 2 (page 37).

The Rollout Phase

At the end of the two-year ramp-up period, a district or school will have the following elements in place.

- Proficiency scales for each subject area and each grade level, with online resources and assessment items for score 2.0, 3.0, and 4.0 content in each scale

- A student recordkeeping and management system that:
  - Allows teachers to enter student measurements
  - Provides teachers with access to assessment items keyed to each measurement topic
  - Provides students with access to online resources for each measurement topic
  - Reports students' current status and growth on measurement topics

- An instructional model designed for use in a PCBE system

- A group of first-tier implementation teachers trained in the major components

At this point, a district or school is ready for a formal rollout. There are at least five approaches schools may use to accomplish a PCBE rollout. They are:

1. Lowering the number of measurement topics

2. Starting with certain content areas

3. Starting with certain grade levels

4. Creating demonstration classrooms

5. Jumping in headfirst

Next, we will discuss each of the five approaches.

Lowering the Number of Measurement Topics

In this approach, the district or school delineates tiered expectations for graduation based on the amount of time students will spend in the PCBE system. For example, eighth graders would have to demonstrate proficiency on 100 percent of the measurement topics to graduate because they would have five years to fill in learning gaps and learn new content. The ninth-grade class would be responsible for completing 75 percent of the graduation requirements because they would only have four years to complete the work and fill in gaps. The tenth-grade class would be required to complete at least 50 percent, the eleventh-grade class would be expected to complete at least 25 percent, and the twelfth-grade class would meet graduation requirements in the traditional system. This plan involves a five-year rollout and eases into full implementation. It allows staff, students, and parents to become familiar with the PCBE system while honoring their past accomplishments.

A variation on this approach is that teacher expectations for scores on measurement topics start low and then gradually increase as students have more time in the system. The first year of implementation, students would be expected to receive a minimum score of 2.0 on all topics. The second year, minimum expectations would be raised to a score of 2.5. The third year, expectations for minimum scores would rise to a score of 3.0.

Another variation is that for each graduating class, a certain number of measurement topics is non-negotiable; that is, all students must demonstrate proficiency on these topics in order to graduate. This approach is similar to the tiered approach described previously (eighth graders must demonstrate proficiency on 100 percent of the measurement topics, ninth graders must demonstrate proficiency on 75 percent, and so on). The difference in this method is that all students must demonstrate proficiency on 100 percent of topics designated as non-negotiable. As students progress through the system, the number of non-negotiable measurement topics increases. For example, eighth graders must demonstrate proficiency on all measurement topics. For grades 9, 10, 11, and 12, the school or district would define the set of non-negotiable measurement topics for each grade. For example, grade 12 might have nine measurement topics on which students must demonstrate proficiency: three in English language arts, three in mathematics, and three in science. Grade 11 might have fifteen measurement topics on which students must demonstrate proficiency: five in English language arts, five in mathematics, and five in science. Grade 10 might have eighteen measurement topics on which students must demonstrate proficiency: six in English language arts, six in mathematics, and six in science. Grade 9 might have twenty-one measurement topics on which students must demonstrate proficiency: seven in English language arts, seven in mathematics, and seven in science. Unlike the tiered percentage approach, under this system all students are responsible for demonstrating proficiency on the same set of measurement topics that the school or district deems critical and therefore non-negotiable.

Starting With Certain Content Areas

This approach is geared more toward elementary school. As mentioned previously, one key difference between elementary and secondary schools is that elementary teachers are normally generalists, meaning they teach multiple subject areas instead of focusing on one subject area as is common for high school and middle school teachers. Capitalizing on this difference, a transition plan could be set up for teachers to start implementing PCBE requirements in only one or two content areas first and then expand to other areas in the following school years. Normally, English language arts and mathematics are the two areas that start the transition to PCBE. The length of the transition plan might be four years, with the first year involving teachers implementing PCBE in English language arts across the school. In the second year they might incorporate mathematics, the third year science, and the fourth year the remaining content areas. After a year or two, the rate of implementation can speed up, given that the structures and strategies are similar across content areas and teachers are more familiar with developing and using them.

Starting With Certain Grade Levels

This approach can begin at the elementary level and extend through high school. Administrators select a particular grade level or levels to be the first group of students to move through the PCBE system. Each of the teachers trained in PCBE within the chosen grade level is expected to implement aspects throughout all of his or her classes. The next year, the students move to the next grade, and that group of teachers implements the PCBE system. This continues until all grade levels are implementing PCBE.

Alternatively, the rollout can move progressively through elementary, middle, and high school. That is, the first year of the rollout phase is focused on the elementary level. One or more years after that, the district initiates the rollout at the middle school level, and one or more years after that the district initiates the rollout at the high school level.

Creating Demonstration Classrooms

As mentioned previously, a group of pilot teachers can opt into implementing a PCBE system in their classrooms. This vanguard team receives training and support for implementing all the PCBE components. Teachers use these pilot classrooms as demonstration classrooms so other teachers can observe and learn from them. The classrooms also constitute innovation zones where teachers develop and vet new procedures, tools, and strategies. In this approach, the teachers are generally motivated and eager to try new things, which is of great advantage to the entire district or school because the pilot teachers act as in-house examples and experts to support the remaining staff when full implementation occurs.

Jumping in Headfirst

This approach is exactly what it sounds like. Within one to two years, the district or school jumps into a PCBE system. Teachers develop and use assessments to place students in each subject area. Teachers place the students into classes or levels for each subject according to their needs. Strong leadership is critical to the success of this type of plan. The leader will be the shield for the staff and students from questions, concerns, and complaints that will arise. Providing advanced training and resources for staff, students, and parents is also crucial to the success of this approach.

PCBE in a Single Classroom

Growing numbers of teachers want to implement a PCBE system but are in a district or school that does not have or intend to develop one in the near future. It is still possible for these teachers to create a PCBE system for the students in their classes.

Such teachers must first create proficiency scales for the required content. As described in chapter 1 (page 11), a teacher should identify between fifteen and twenty-five topics for the entire year. These topics should come from school- or district-prescribed standards but can also be informed by the Critical

Concepts identified by Marzano Resources (Simms, 2016). Ideally, the teacher engages in this type of planning during the summer months and has all his or her scales ready for the beginning of the school year.

When the school year starts, the teacher begins by ensuring all students are aware of the new system. Key points to stress might include the following.

- Students can demonstrate their current status on any proficiency scale in many ways, including discussions with the teacher and coming up with ways of their own to demonstrate their understanding or skill.

- Relative to any proficiency scale, students can expect to receive low scores initially, but low scores in the beginning in no way hinder their ability to obtain high scores later on. A student could start with a score of 0.0 and end with a score of 4.0.

- The teacher and fellow students are all sources of help and support.

After proficiency scales, standard operating procedures should be the next order of business. As discussed in chapter 2 (page 37), teachers should develop SOPs with students so the students feel ownership. Of course, SOPs can and should be modified over time. Additionally, teachers should develop new SOPs as new issues and situations arise. At the beginning of the year, teachers should create SOPs for the following areas.

- What to do when you need help

- How to enter and leave the classroom

- What to do if you missed class

- If appropriate, how to work with devices (for example, for young students, how to carry and handle devices, or for older students, how and when to use devices and what to do with them when class ends)

The teacher may also want to create a code of cooperation with students as described in chapter 2. This code assists students with the shift to becoming more responsible for their own learning and provides a tool for holding themselves and each other accountable for classroom behaviors. Together, the SOPs and code of cooperation ease the transition within the classroom from a space where all students are listening to the teacher and working on the same activity to a space where more students are engaging in different types of activities; working together in small groups, in pairs, or individually; and directing more of the activities associated with teaching, learning, and assessing.

The beginning of the year starts with the teacher presenting all students with the same measurement topics. When a teacher first introduces topics, he or she will need to spend time with students explaining what a proficiency scale is and how it supports their learning. This process may involve unpacking proficiency scales with students or developing personal tracking matrices. As teachers introduce new topics, students are able to improve their scores on measurement topics addressed previously. This process, of course, is employed in a standards-referenced system. In addition, the teacher would allow students to move ahead on measurement topics that teachers will address in the future.

This approach will require the teacher to adjust instruction to allow for a flexible learning environment. As noted previously, a simple way to get started is to use classroom learning centers and have students rotate among the centers. For example, a teacher might organize the classroom around three learning centers. In one center, she could provide direct instruction to a small group of students who are working on the same learning target. While she is providing instruction to this group of students, another group could be working together in pairs on an activity or long-term project, while a third group might use computers or other devices individually to practice a skill or deepen their knowledge on a particular proficiency scale. The students would rotate through each learning center during the class period.

The teacher will also want to create or use an existing recording and reporting system that allows for scoring on measurement topics. This system might be as simple as a spreadsheet or a Google Doc that resembles the report in figure 6.6 (pages 162–165). Determining and sharing students' status on measurement topics are critical, so the system or approach a teacher chooses must allow students to see their current status and growth. The teacher might also share the reports with parents periodically (such as when report cards go out) to provide additional information about what students are learning and how they are progressing. Communication with parents should begin early in the year and continue throughout the school year. The teacher might introduce the basics of the approach during a family night at the beginning of the year and work with students so they lead conferences with parents and guardians during the year.

Summary

This chapter discussed considerations and approaches for transitioning to a PCBE system. Schools must determine the best approach for getting started and rolling out the system within a school or across a number of schools. We recommend a two-phase approach that includes (1) a ramp-up phase and (2) a rollout phase. Using a systematic process to address the design questions addressed in this book will assist schools in a successful transition.

Epilogue

As demonstrated in this handbook, the process of moving to a PCBE system is not magical, mystical, or even unknown. We assert that the previous chapters provide the necessary guidance at the necessary level of detail to take any traditional district or school to a PCBE format. We also believe that, while the concept of PCBE has been discussed and even attempted for decades, this is a new era in which all the pieces are in place for an easier, more straightforward implementation than was previously possible. This is not to say that such a transition is simple; it is to say that such a transition is eminently doable.

While this book presents the practical steps for shifting to a PCBE system, school administrators and teacher leaders must cultivate their own beliefs in order to successfully carry out such a transition. Without certain foundational assumptions among those leading a PCBE initiative, the process can become tedious and overbearing—probably more work than it appears to be worth. However, when these foundational beliefs are in place, the process can become a labor of love and, in some cases, the fulfillment of the tacit promise most educators make to themselves when they choose to enter the profession in the first place—the promise to help all students reach their full potential.

The first requisite belief is that this change is not only necessary but inevitable. The current system that keeps students at one level of performance dictated by their age simply can't stand. The current system that moves students ahead even when they haven't mastered the content simply can't stand. In effect, the current system simply does not work anymore, and we hear calls for its replacement all across the country. The shift to a PCBE system *is* the future of K–12 education. It is not a temporary fad. The only question is how quickly the shift will occur. Armed with this belief of inevitability, educational leaders are more likely to start the journey right now.

The second belief is that this change is a moral imperative—a requirement to do the right thing—on the part of K–12 educators. This seems rather obvious: changing to a system that will benefit all students in a variety of ways certainly is the right thing to do. If educators are the only ones who can effect this change, it is a necessity that they lead the effort. Armed with this belief, educational leaders feel more compelled to embark on the change journey.

The third belief is that your particular district or school can make this shift. We believe that leaders within a district or school commonly underestimate the willingness and desire of the educators and other constituents in their system to make substantive change. All too often we hear comments like, "It's a great idea, but we're not ready for it here." In our experience, the speed of a transformation like PCBE is more of a function of the will and perseverance of the leadership, than it is the perceived readiness of the constituents in the district or school.

These three beliefs and the step-by-step approach outlined in this book make PCBE a goal that any district or school can achieve.

Appendix A

A Model of Effective Instruction

This appendix outlines the specific instructional strategies associated with *The New Art and Science of Teaching* (Marzano, 2017). The model organizes the research-based strategies into a comprehensive instructional framework. That framework involves three overarching categories: (1) feedback, (2) content, and (3) context. Marzano (2017) described these categories:

> *Feedback* refers to the information loop between the teacher and the student that provides students with an awareness of what they should be learning and how they are doing. *Content* refers to lesson progression, which allows students to move from an initial understanding of content to application of content while continuously reviewing and upgrading their knowledge. *Context* refers to the following student psychological needs: engagement, order, a sense of belonging, and high expectations. (p. 6)

Embedded in these three categories are subcategories of strategies that are designed to produce specific outcomes in students. Additionally, each of these ten subcategories has related questions teachers ask of themselves as they design instruction. The ten subcategories and their related design questions are presented in table A.1.

Table A.1: Ten Subcategories and Their Design Questions

	DESIGN AREAS	DESIGN QUESTIONS
Feedback	1. Providing and Communicating Clear Learning Goals	How will I communicate clear learning goals that help students understand the progression of knowledge they are expected to master and where they are along that progression?
	2. Using Assessments	How will I design and administer assessments that help students understand how their test scores and grades are related to their status on the progression of knowledge they are expected to master?

continued →

	DESIGN AREAS	DESIGN QUESTIONS
Content	3. Conducting Direct Instruction Lessons	When content is new, how will I design and deliver direct instruction lessons that help students understand which parts are important and how the parts fit together?
	4. Conducting Practicing and Deepening Lessons	After presenting content, how will I design and deliver lessons that help students deepen their understanding and develop fluency in skills and processes?
	5. Conducting Knowledge Application Lessons	After presenting content, how will I design and deliver lessons that help students generate and defend claims through knowledge application?
	6. Using Strategies That Appear in All Types of Lessons	Throughout all types of lessons, what strategies will I use to help students continually integrate new knowledge with old knowledge and revise their understanding accordingly?
Context	7. Using Engagement Strategies	What engagement strategies will I use to help students pay attention, be energized, be intrigued, and be inspired?
	8. Implementing Rules and Procedures	What strategies will I use to help students understand and follow rules and procedures?
	9. Building Relationships	What strategies will I use to help students feel welcome, accepted, and valued?
	10. Communicating High Expectations	What strategies will I use to help typically reluctant students feel valued and comfortable interacting with their peers and me?

Source: Marzano, 2017, pp. 6–7.

Finally, each of the ten design areas is further subdivided into elements that have specific functions instructionally. In all, there are forty-three elements. This is depicted in table A.2.

Table A.2: Elements Within the Ten Design Areas

FEEDBACK	CONTENT	CONTEXT
Providing and Communicating Clear Learning Goals	**Conducting Direct Instruction Lessons**	**Using Engagement Strategies**
Providing scales and rubrics	Chunking content	Noticing and reacting when students are not engaged
Tracking student progress	Processing content	Increasing response rates
Celebrating success	Recording and representing content	Using physical movement
Using Assessments	**Conducting Practicing and Deepening Lessons**	Maintaining a lively pace
Using informal assessments of the whole class	Using structured practice sessions	Demonstrating intensity and enthusiasm
Using formal assessments of individual students	Examining similarities and differences	Presenting unusual information
	Examining errors in reasoning	Using friendly controversy
		Using academic games
		Providing opportunities for students to talk about themselves
		Motivating and inspiring students

	Conducting Knowledge Application Lessons	**Implementing Rules and Procedures**
	Engaging students in cognitively complex tasks	Establishing rules and procedures
	Providing resources and guidance	Organizing the physical layout of the classroom
	Generating and defending claims	Demonstrating withitness
	Using Strategies That Appear in All Types of Lessons	Acknowledging adherence to rules and procedures
	Previewing strategies	Acknowledging lack of adherence to rules and procedures
	Highlighting critical information	
	Reviewing content	**Building Relationships**
	Revising knowledge	Using verbal and nonverbal behaviors that indicate affection for students
	Reflecting on learning	
	Assigning purposeful homework	Understanding students' backgrounds and interests
	Elaborating on information	
	Organizing students to interact	Displaying objectivity and control
		Communicating High Expectations
		Demonstrating value and respect for reluctant learners
		Asking in-depth questions of reluctant learners
		Probing incorrect answers with reluctant learners

Source: Marzano, 2017, pp. 7–8.

This appendix lists the specific strategies within each of the forty-three elements. For a detailed discussion of the strategies, consult *The New Art and Science of Teaching* (Marzano, 2017) and the Marzano Compendium of Instructional Strategies (MarzanoResources.com/online-compendium).

Feedback

The desired student outcomes for providing and communicating clear learning goals (table A.3, page 194) are that "students understand the progression of knowledge they are expected to master and where they are along that progression" (Marzano, 2017, p. 11).

Table A.3: Providing and Communicating Clear Learning Goals

Providing Scales and Rubrics	The teacher provides a clearly stated learning goal accompanied by a scale or rubric that describes performance levels relative to the learning goal. • Providing and communicating clear learning goals • Routines for using targets and scales • Teacher-created targets and scales • Student-friendly scales • Individual student learning goals
Tracking Student Progress	The teacher facilitates tracking of student progress on one or more learning goals using a formative approach to assessment. • Formative scores • Assessments that generate formative scores • Individual score-level assessments • Different types of assessments • Summative scores • Student progress chart • Class progress chart
Celebrating Success	The teacher provides students with recognition of their current status and their knowledge gain relative to the learning goal. • Final status celebration • Knowledge gain celebration • Verbal feedback

The desired student outcomes for using assessments (table A.4) are that "students understand how test scores and grades relate to their status on the progression of knowledge they are expected to master" (Marzano, 2017, p. 21).

Table A.4: Using Assessments

Conducing Informal Assessments of the Whole Class	The teacher uses informal assessments of the whole class to determine student proficiency with specific content. • Confidence-rating techniques • Voting techniques • Response boards • Unrecorded assessments
Conducting Formal Assessments of Individual Students	The teacher uses formal assessments of individual students to determine student proficiency with specific content. • Common assessments • Selected-response and short constructed-response items • Student demonstrations • Student interviews • Observations of students • Student-generated assessments • Response patterns

Content

The desired student outcome for conducting direct instruction lessons (table A.5) is that "when content is new, students understand which parts are important and how the parts fit together" (Marzano, 2017, p. 29).

Table A.5: Conducting Direct Instruction Lessons

Chunking Content	Based on student needs, the teacher breaks the content into small chunks (that is, digestible bites) of information that can be easily processed by students. The number and size of each chunk must be carefully planned for whole-class instruction. However, for small-group and individual instruction, the teacher can rely more heavily on cues provided by students in the moment. That is, the teacher can monitor students' levels of understanding to determine if it is the proper time to stop providing input (that is, to end the chunk). • Presenting content in small chunks • Using preassessment data to vary the size of each chunk • Chunk processing
Processing Content	During breaks in the presentation of content, the teacher engages students in actively processing new information. Processing activities typically involve small groups of students (for example, two to five). Therefore, these activities do not work well during individual instruction. • Perspective analysis (Marzano, 1992) • Thinking hats (de Bono, 1999) • Collaborative processing • Jigsaw cooperative learning • Reciprocal teaching • Concept attainment
Recording and Representing Content	The teacher engages students in activities that help them record their understanding of new content in linguistic ways or represent the content in nonlinguistic ways or both. These activities are equally useful in whole-group instruction, small-group instruction, and individual instruction. • Informal outlines • Combination notes, pictures, and summary • Graphic organizers • Free-flowing webs • Academic notebooks • Dramatic enactments • Rhyming pegwords • Link strategy

The desired student outcome for conducting practicing and deepening lessons (table A.6, page 196) is that "after teachers present new content, students deepen their understanding and develop fluency with skills and processes" (Marzano, 2017, p. 37).

Table A.6: Conducting Practicing and Deepening Lessons

Using Structured Practice Sessions	When the content involves a skill, strategy, or process, the teacher engages students in practice activities that help them develop fluency. Teachers can use these strategies in whole-group instruction, small-group instruction, and individual instruction. • Modeling • Guided practice • Close monitoring • Frequent structured practice • Varied practice • Fluency practice • Worked examples • Practice sessions prior to testing
Examining Similarities and Differences	When the content is informational, the teacher helps students deepen their knowledge by examining similarities and differences. Teachers can use these strategies in whole-group instruction, small-group instruction, and individual instruction. • Sentence stem comparisons • Venn diagrams • Double-bubble diagrams • Comparison matrices • Classification charts • Student-generated classification patterns • Similes • Metaphors • Sentence stem analogies • Visual analogies
Examining Errors in Reasoning	When content is informational, the teacher helps students deepen their knowledge by examining their own reasoning or the logic of the information as presented to them. Teachers can use these strategies in whole-group instruction, small-group instruction, and individual instruction. • Identifying errors of faulty logic • Identifying errors of attack • Identifying errors of weak reference • Identifying errors of misinformation • Practicing identifying errors in logic • Finding errors in the media • Examining support for claims • Recognizing statistical limitations

The desired student outcome for conducting knowledge application lessons (table A.7) is that "after the presentation of new content, students generate and defend claims through knowledge application tasks" (Marzano, 2017, p. 47).

Table A.7: Conducting Knowledge Application Lessons

Engaging Students in Cognitively Complex Tasks	The teacher engages students in complex tasks (for example, decision-making, problem-solving, experimental-inquiry, and investigation tasks) that require them to generate and test hypotheses. Teachers can use these strategies in whole-group instruction, small-group instruction, and individual instruction. • Experimental-inquiry tasks • Problem-solving tasks • Decision-making tasks • Investigation tasks
Providing Resources and Guidance	The teacher acts as resource provider and guide as students engage in cognitively complex tasks. Teachers can use these strategies in whole-group instruction, small-group instruction, and individual instruction. • Scoring scales • Interviews • Circulating around the room • Expressions and gestures • Collecting assessment information • Feedback
Generating and Defending Claims	The teacher helps students create claims or new ideas and defend them logically. Once students learn the process of generating and defending claims, they usually execute the process individually or with others in a small-group setting. • Generating claims • Providing support for claims • Providing grounds • Providing backing • Generating qualifiers

The desired student outcome for using strategies that appear in all types of lessons (table A.8, pages 198–199) is that "students continually integrate new knowledge with old knowledge and revise their understanding accordingly" (Marzano, 2017, p. 53).

Table A.8: Using Strategies That Appear in All Types of Lessons

Previewing Strategies	The teacher engages students in activities that help them link what they already know to the new content about to be addressed and facilitates these linkages. Teachers can use these strategies in whole-group instruction, small-group instruction, and individual instruction. • Hooks • Bell-ringers • What Do You Think You Know? • Overt linkages • Preview questions • Brief teacher summaries • Skimming • Teacher-prepared notes • K-W-L strategy (Ogle, 1986) • Advance organizers • Anticipation guides • Word splash activities • Preassessments
Highlighting Critical Information	The teacher identifies a lesson or part of a lesson as involving important information to which students should pay particular attention. Teachers can use these strategies in whole-group instruction, small-group instruction, and individual instruction. • Repetition of the most important content • Questions that focus on critical information • Visual activities • Narrative activities • Tone of voice, gestures, and body position • Pause time
Reviewing Content	The teacher engages students in a brief review of content that highlights the critical information. Teachers can use these strategies in whole-group instruction, small-group instruction, and individual instruction. • Cumulative review • Cloze activities • Summaries • Presented problems • Demonstrations • Brief practice tests or exercises • Questioning
Revising Knowledge	The teacher engages students in revision of previous knowledge about content addressed in previous lessons. Teachers can use these strategies in whole-group instruction, small-group instruction, and individual instruction. • Academic notebook entries • Academic notebook review • Peer feedback • Assignment revision

Reflecting on Learning	The teacher engages students in activities that help them reflect on their learning and the learning process. Teachers can use these strategies in whole-group instruction, small-group instruction, and individual instruction. • Reflective journals • Think logs • Exit slips • Knowledge comparison • Two-column note-taking
Assigning Purposeful Homework	When appropriate (as opposed to routinely), the teacher designs homework to deepen students' knowledge of informational content or practice a skill, strategy, or process. Teachers typically use these strategies in whole-group instruction. • Preview homework • Homework to deepen knowledge • Homework to practice a process or skill • Parent-assisted homework
Elaborating on Information	The teacher asks questions or engages students in activities that require elaborative inferences that go beyond what was explicitly taught. Teachers can use these strategies in whole-group instruction, small-group instruction, and individual instruction. • Questioning sequences • General inferential questions • Elaborative interrogation
Organizing Students to Interact	The teacher organizes students to interact in a thoughtful way that facilitates collaboration. Teachers typically use these strategies in whole- and small-group instruction. • Grouping for active processing • Group norms • Fishbowl demonstrations • Job cards • Predetermined buddies to help form ad hoc groups • Contingency plan for ungrouped students • Grouping students using preassessment information • Pair-check (Kagan & Kagan, 2009) • Think-pair-share and think-pair-square (Kagan & Kagan, 2009) • Student tournaments • Inside-outside circle (Kagan & Kagan, 2009) • Cooperative learning • Peer response groups • Peer tutoring

Context

The desired student outcome for using engagement strategies (table A.9, pages 200–201) is that "students are paying attention, energized, intrigued, and inspired" (Marzano, 2017, p. 65).

Table A.9: Using Engagement Strategies

Noticing and Reacting When Students Are Not Engaged	A teacher notes which students are not engaged and takes overt action to re-engage those students. Teachers can use these strategies in whole-group instruction, small-group instruction, and individual instruction. • Scanning the room • Monitoring attention levels • Measuring engagement
Increasing Response Rates	A teacher maintains student engagement by using response-rate techniques during questioning. These strategies are typically used during whole-group instruction. • Random names • Hand signals • Response cards • Response chaining • Paired response • Choral response • Wait time • Elaborative interrogation • Multiple question types
Using Physical Movement	A teacher uses physical movement to keep students engaged. Teachers typically use these strategies during whole-group instruction. • Stand up and Stretch • Give One, Get One • Vote With Your Feet • Corners activities • Stand and Be Counted • Body representations • Drama-related activities
Maintaining a Lively Pace	A teacher maintains student engagement by using pacing techniques. Teachers typically use these strategies during whole-group instruction. • Instructional segments • Pace modulation • The parking lot • Motivational hook or launching activity
Demonstrating Intensity and Enthusiasm	A teacher models intensity and enthusiasm for the content being taught. Teachers typically use these strategies during whole-group instruction. • Direct statements about the content's importance • Explicit connections • Nonlinguistic representations • Personal stories • Verbal and nonverbal signals • Humor • Quotations • Movie clips

Presenting Unusual Information	A teacher maintains student engagement by providing unusual or intriguing information about the content. Teachers can use these strategies in whole-group instruction, small-group instruction, and individual instruction. <ul><li>Teacher-presented information</li><li>WebQuests</li><li>One-minute headlines</li><li>Believe It or Not</li><li>History files</li><li>Guest speakers and firsthand consultants</li></ul>
Using Friendly Controversy	A teacher maintains student engagement through the use of friendly controversy techniques. Teachers typically use these strategies during whole-group instruction. <ul><li>Friendly controversy</li><li>Class votes</li><li>Seminars</li><li>Expert opinions</li><li>Opposite points of view</li><li>Diagramming perspectives</li><li>Debates</li><li>Town hall meeting (Hess, 2009)</li><li>Legal model (Hess, 2009)</li></ul>
Using Academic Games	A teacher uses inconsequential competition to maintain student engagement. Teachers typically use these strategies during whole-group instruction. <ul><li>What Is the Question?</li><li>Name That Category</li><li>Talk a Mile a Minute</li><li>Classroom Feud</li><li>Which One Doesn't Belong?</li><li>Academic games</li><li>Turning questions into games</li><li>Vocabulary review games</li></ul>
Providing Opportunities for Students to Talk About Themselves	A teacher provides students with opportunities to relate class content to their personal interests or lives. Teachers can use these strategies in whole-group instruction, small-group instruction, and individual instruction. <ul><li>Interest surveys</li><li>Student learning profiles</li><li>Life connections</li><li>Informal linkages during class discussion</li></ul>
Motivating and Inspiring Students	A teacher provides activities and resources that help students seek self-actualization and connection to causes that enhance the lives of others. Teachers can use these strategies in whole-group instruction, small-group instruction, and individual instruction. <ul><li>Possible selves activities</li><li>Personal projects</li><li>Inspirational stories</li><li>Gratitude journals</li><li>Altruism projects</li></ul>

The desired student outcome for implementing rules and procedures (table A.10) is that "students understand and follow rules and procedures" (Marzano, 2017, p. 79).

Table A.10: Implementing Rules and Procedures

Establishing Rules and Procedures	A teacher ensures effective execution of rules and procedures through a review process. Teachers can use these strategies in whole-group instruction, small-group instruction, and individual instruction. • Using a small set of rules and procedures • Explaining rules and procedures to students • Modifying rules and procedures with students • Generating rules and procedures with students • Using language of responsibility and statements of school beliefs • Posting rules around the room • Using class pledges or classroom constitutions • Displaying posters and graphics • Using gestures and symbols • Participating in vignettes and role playing • Conducting classroom meetings • Encouraging student self-assessments
Organizing the Physical Layout of the Classroom	A teacher arranges his or her classroom so that it facilitates movement and a focus on learning. Teachers can use these strategies in whole-group instruction, small-group instruction, and individual instruction. • Learning centers • Computers and technology equipment • Lab equipment and supplies • Bookshelves • Wall space • Student work • Classroom décor • Classroom materials • Teacher's desk • Students' desks • Areas for whole-group instruction • Areas for group work
Demonstrating Withitness	A teacher displays withitness (or classroom awareness) to maintain adherence to rules and procedures. Teachers can use these strategies in whole-group instruction, small-group instruction, and individual instruction. • Being proactive • Occupying the whole room physically and visually • Noticing potential problems • Using a series of graduated actions

Acknowledging Adherence to Rules and Procedures	A teacher consistently praises students or classes that follow the rules or procedures. Teachers can use these strategies in whole-group instruction, small-group instruction, and individual instruction. • Verbal affirmations • Nonverbal affirmations • Tangible recognition • Token economies • Daily recognition forms • Color-coded behavior • Certificates • Phone calls, emails, and notes
Acknowledging Lack of Adherence to Rules and Procedures	A teacher consistently applies consequences for students who fail to follow the rules or procedures. Teachers can use these strategies in whole-group instruction, small-group instruction, and individual instruction. • Verbal cues • Pregnant pauses • Nonverbal cues • Time-outs • Overcorrection • Interdependent group contingency • Home contingency • Planning for high-intensity situations • Overall disciplinary plan

The desired student outcome for building relationships (table A.11) is that "students feel welcome, accepted, and valued" (Marzano, 2017, p. 84).

Table A.11: Building Relationships

Using Verbal and Nonverbal Behaviors That Indicate Affection for Students	A teacher indicates affection for students through verbal and nonverbal cues. Teachers can use these strategies in whole-group instruction, small-group instruction, and individual instruction. • Greeting students at the classroom door • Conducting informal conferences • Attending after-school functions • Greeting students by name outside of school • Giving students special responsibilities or classroom leadership roles • Providing scheduled interactions • Displaying photo bulletin boards • Using physical behaviors • Using humor

continued →

Understanding Students' Backgrounds and Interests	A teacher produces a climate of acceptance and creates community by showing interest in students' interests and backgrounds. Teachers can use these strategies in whole-group instruction, small-group instruction, and individual instruction. • Student background surveys • Opinion questionnaires • Individual teacher-student conferences • Parent-teacher conferences • School newspapers, newsletters, or bulletins • Informal class interviews • Investigation of student culture • Autobiographical metaphors and analogies • Six-word biographies • Independent investigations • Quotes • Comments on student achievements or areas of importance • Lineups • Individual student learning goals
Displaying Objectivity and Control	A teacher maintains objectivity and control with students. Teachers can use these strategies in whole-group instruction, small-group instruction, and individual instruction. • Self-reflecting • Self-monitoring • Identifying emotional triggers • Self-caring • Using assertiveness • Maintaining a cool exterior • Active listening and speaking • Adjusting communication styles • Recognizing unique student needs

The desired student outcome for communicating high expectations (table A.12) is that "typically reluctant students feel valued and do not hesitate to interact with the teacher or their peers" (Marzano, 2017, p. 97).

Table A.12: Communicating High Expectations

Demonstrating Value and Respect for Reluctant Learners	A teacher actively demonstrates value and respect for reluctant learners. Teachers can use these strategies in whole-group instruction, small-group instruction, and individual instruction. • Identifying expectation levels for all students • Identifying differential treatment of reluctant learners • Using nonverbal and verbal indicators of respect and value

Asking In-Depth Questions of Reluctant Learners	A teacher actively engages reluctant learners in the classroom at the same rate as other students. Teachers can use these strategies in whole-group instruction, small-group instruction, and individual instruction.
	• Question levels
	• Response opportunities
	• Follow-up questioning
	• Evidence and support for student answers
	• Encouragement
	• Wait time
	• Tracking responses
	• Avoiding inappropriate reactions
Probing Incorrect Answers With Reluctant Learners	A teacher treats the questioning responses of reluctant learners in the same manner as he or she does with other students. Teachers can use these strategies in whole-group instruction, small-group instruction, and individual instruction.
	• Using an appropriate response process
	• Letting students off the hook temporarily
	• Answer revision
	• Think-pair-share (Lyman, 2006)

Appendix B

Resources for Creating a Shared Vision

This appendix contains resources to assist a school in facilitating the process of creating a shared vision. Specifically, it provides guidance regarding hosted conversations. *Hosted conversations* are discussions with specific stakeholder groups (for example, students, parents and guardians, teachers and other staff, administrators, business representatives, board of education members, and so on). Although separate meetings should be held for different stakeholder groups in order to tailor the questions and examples to their perspectives and needs, the meetings should be held within a short time frame to ensure all stakeholders have the opportunity to provide input without losing momentum for creating the shared vision. The following examples provide suggestions for working with different groups, including examples of scenarios and data that might work best with certain groups, essential questions, and activities.

We'll discuss (1) conversations with certified staff, (2) conversations with parents, (3) conversations with classified staff, and (4) conversations with students.

Conversations With Certified Staff

When facilitating conversations with teachers and other certified staff, we recommend several approaches.

- Examine trends in student data. Do the data demonstrate that students are prepared for college and careers?

- Push staff to describe in detail the ideal school day, the ideal roles and responsibilities of a student, and the ideal roles and responsibilities of a teacher.

- Push staff to challenge their assumptions about teaching and learning and the current system. (For example, Does the traditional grading system work well? Does a B in one teacher's class at this school mean the same thing as a B in another teacher's class?)

When shifting to a personalized competency-based system, teachers and other staff will need to rethink traditional approaches to curriculum, instruction, and assessment. Providing them with examples they can relate to may help them imagine new ways of teaching and learning. For example, a big issue for many teachers is the idea of allowing students multiple attempts at achieving proficiency on a measurement topic or allowing students to go back and raise a score on a measurement topic. To help teachers examine the rationale behind this concept, one could present different real-world examples of test taking. For example, when an accountant takes the Uniform CPA Examination to become a certified public accountant, does he or she only have one shot at passing? If you take your driver's license test and fail, can you never get a driver's license? How many states allow teachers multiple attempts to become licensed teachers? These examples provide good discussion points around the purpose of assessments, grades, and schooling—is the purpose to ensure we gain the knowledge and skills (to become certified, to get a driver's license, to master a measurement topic), or is the point to give everyone one chance?

Conversations With Parents

When facilitating hosted conversations with parents, a primary goal is to remove obstacles that might prevent them from attending a meeting (whether it be in person or online) or providing input. Depending on the size of the school, it may make sense to schedule multiple meeting times, hold some meetings via webinar or Twitter chats, or provide opportunities for input through online or paper surveys. Strategies for improving parent attendance and participation in events include the following.

- Sending a personal invitation to each student's parents or guardians
- Providing babysitting and student activities at in-person events
- Offering food and refreshments at in-person events
- Requesting an RSVP and sending reminders

For in-person events, pay attention to the environment. Arrange seats in small groups to encourage conversation, provide sticky notes, markers, and dots for voting, and offer beverages and snacks. Start with a presentation that outlines the objectives of the meeting and establishes the basic ground rules for participating. The remainder of the presentation should focus on setting the stage for change. Presenting school-, district-, and state-level data can be a powerful way to establish the need for change. Examples of data include grades, test scores, graduation rates, dropout rates, percentage of students accepted to postsecondary institutions, percentage of students in postsecondary institutions who must take remediation courses, and perception data from students, parents, and the community. Be sure to give participants time to react to key points in the presentation and provide essential questions for them to respond to, such as the following.

- Are students doing as well as we wish? Are they reaching their full potential?
- How are students doing after they graduate? Do they do well in college, or do they have to spend time taking classes to catch up? Do they get good jobs?

- Is the current way of educating students working? Are we preparing students for the future we want for them?

To encourage parents to envision the need for a new system that personalizes learning and measures and reports progress on identified knowledge and skills, provide scenarios to stimulate their thinking, such as the following.

- How does school currently prepare students for life as adults in college or in a job? For example, as an adult, how many decisions do you make a day? You may think about what to wear, what to eat, which route to take to work, whether to get up early to work out, how to prioritize projects at work, or when to schedule a vacation. Now, what does a typical day in a typical school look like for most students? They go from class to class focusing on one subject at a time. They have to get permission to speak or to go to the restroom. They have no choice over when to take a break and limited choice in what subjects they can study, how they can learn the knowledge and skills, and how they can demonstrate their learning. If we were to change this system, what might we do differently?

- Parents need to understand the benefits of a competency-based system for students. To help parents understand, take them back to their experiences in school. Questions might include: Did you ever sit in class bored, waiting for others to catch up so the entire class could move on? Were you ever the only one in the class who didn't understand the lesson but were afraid to raise your hand and ask for more help? Explain that the goals of a personalized system are to address these issues so that each student learns the content before moving on to the next topic or level. In small groups, facilitate discussions to help parents contribute to the shared vision for the school. Pose questions such as, What would an ideal school day look like for your child? What will our data look like if our school is doing its job? When your child graduates, what do you want him or her to know and be able to do?

Conversations With Classified Staff

Classified staff include those who are not certified, such as bus drivers, food service staff, office staff, and custodial staff. There are many important reasons to engage classified staff in the shared vision process. For one, engaging them in the process will make them feel valued and respected—an important feature of a system that seeks to value and respect the students it serves. For another, these staff members see students each day and play an important role in their lives, from preparing the food they eat to ensuring they get to and from school each day and providing an environment that is orderly and safe. And finally, participating in this process not only gives them a voice in the place they choose to work but also helps them understand that they play a role in educating students. Two important messages for classified staff are: (1) no matter what specific role you play, all adults who work in the school have a responsibility to encourage students to stay in school and learn as much as they can; and (2) as an employee of the district or school, you play an extremely important role and teachers cannot do their jobs effectively without your support. Other important aspects of the school's classified staff are location and credibility. More often than not, they live the closest to the school or district, and they are often considered by their friends and neighbors to know the real reasons for any changes occurring in the school or district. These staff members can be ambassadors for change.

When engaging staff in facilitated conversations related to the shared vision of the school, use questions and examples similar to those for parents. Ask them to envision the ideal school, the ideal student, the ideal graduate, and prompt their thinking by asking them to recall their own schooling, to reflect on what they see in schools today, and to imagine their role in a PCBE system.

Conversations With Students

Students are the school's customers, and hosting conversations with them will provide valuable insights into how best to meet their needs. Essential questions for students include the following.

- What works well at school for you? What does not work well for you?

- What is the purpose of school?

- If you could change one thing about the way school works right now, what would you change?

- What does a successful student look like?

- What do students need to learn to be successful in the future?

- How do you like to learn? How do you learn best?

- What does a perfect day at school look like?

One way to engage students in these conversations is to ask them to think of times when they were totally engaged in an activity. What type of activity was it, and why were they totally focused on it? For example, one question asked by an elementary student was, Why can't schools be more like video games? This analogy can be useful to help students examine key features of personalized competency-based systems. When playing a video game, gamers (learners) are:

- Highly engaged in the game (learning)

- Motivated to progress to the next level (master the expectation so they can move on)

- In charge of their own path through the game and not tied to the progress of others (ownership of learning)

- Following their own pace and making their own decisions (some students move faster or slower than others on particular targets)

- Learning from mistakes to get better (they must master the requirements before moving to the next level)

- Failing at times and trying again (multiple opportunities to master a skill)
- Earning badges or other indicators of accomplishment and skill, and tracking progress (self-assessing and reporting progress on knowledge and skills)

Helping to develop the shared vision of the school is one of the first empowering steps students can take in helping to design the system that supports them.

References

Alli, N., Rajan, R., & Ratliff, G. (2016, March/April). How personalized learning unlocks student success. *EDUCAUSE Review, 51*(2), 12–21.

American Educational Research Association, American Psychological Association, & National Council on Measurement in Education. (2014). *The standards for educational and psychological testing.* Washington, DC: Authors.

Arizona Department of Education. (n.d.). *Sample recommended instructional time.* Accessed at www .azed.gov/wp-content/uploads/WORD/SampleIstructionalTime.doc on February 15, 2017.

Black, P., & Wiliam, D. (1998). Inside the black box: Raising standards through classroom assessment. *Phi Delta Kappan, 80*(2), 139–148.

Capstone project. (2016, March 23). In S. Abbott (Ed.), *The glossary of education reform for journalists, parents, and community members.* Accessed at http://edglossary.org/capstone-project on August 9, 2016.

Carnegie Corporation of New York. (2013). *Shedding one-size-fits-all schools for mastery-based education models* [Press release]. Accessed at www.carnegie.org/news/articles/shedding-one-size-fits-all -schools-for-mastery-based-education-models/ on February 15, 2017.

Charleston County School District. (n.d.). *Personalized learning: The world in their hands.* Accessed at www.ccsdschools.com/Grants/RTT/index.php on August 9, 2016.

Christensen, C. M., Horn, M. B., & Johnson, C. W. (2011). *Disrupting class: How disruptive innovation will change the way the world learns.* New York: McGraw-Hill.

Common Core State Standards Initiative. (n.d.). *About the standards.* Accessed at www.corestandards .org/about-the-standards on August 10, 2016.

Competency-based education pilot program, HB 1365 (2016). Accessed at www.fldoe.org/core /fileparse.php/7513/urlt/1365-16.pdf on January 30, 2017.

Costa, A. L. (1991). *The school as a home for the mind.* Thousand Oaks, CA: Corwin Press.

Costa, A. L., & Kallick, B. (Eds.) (2009). *Habits of mind across the curriculum: Practical and creative strategies for teachers.* Alexandria, VA: Association for Supervision and Curriculum Development.

Council of Chief State School Officers. (2014). *Innovation lab network publishes roadmap to competency-based education* [Press release]. Accessed at www.ccsso.org/News_and_Events/Press _Releases/Innovation_Lab_Network_Publishes_Roadmap_to_Competency-Based_Education.html on February 15, 2017.

Damon, W., & Phelps, E. (1989). Critical distinctions among three approaches to peer education. *International Journal of Educational Research, 13*(1), 9–19.

de Bono, E. (1999). *Six thinking hats.* New York: Back Bay Books.

DeLorenzo, R. A., Battino, W. J., Schreiber, R. M., & Carrio, B. B. G. (2009). *Delivering on the promise: The education revolution.* Bloomington, IN: Solution Tree Press.

District Reform Support Network. (2016a). *Giving every child a fair shot: Progress under the Obama administration's education agenda.* Washington, DC: U.S. Department of Education. Accessed at https://rttd.grads360.org/#communities/pdc/documents/10562 on February 15, 2017.

District Reform Support Network. (2016b). *Transforming the culture of teaching and learning: Four Race to the Top–District grantees' implementation of personalized learning.* Washington, DC: U.S. Department of Education. Accessed at https://rttd.grads360.org/#communities/pdc /documents/12121 on February 15, 2017.

Education Week. (2016, October 27). Map: Tracking the Common Core State Standards. Accessed at www.edweek.org/ew/section/multimedia/map-states-academic-standards-common-core-or.html on February 15, 2017.

Ennis, R. H. (1985). Goals for a critical thinking curriculum. In A. Costa (Ed.), *Developing minds: A resource book for teaching thinking.* Alexandria, VA: Association for Supervision and Curriculum Development.

Ennis, R. H. (1987). A taxonomy of critical thinking dispositions and abilities. In J. Baron & R. Sternberg (Eds.), *Teaching thinking skills: Theory and practice.* New York: Freeman.

Ennis, R. H. (1989). Critical thinking and subject specificity: Clarification and needed research. *Educational Research, 18*(3), 4–10.

Every Student Succeeds Act of 2015, Pub. L. No. 114-95 § 114 Stat. 1177 (2015).

Ferguson, R. F. (with Phillips, S. F., Rowley, J. F. S., & Friedlander, J. W.). (2015, October). *The influence of teaching beyond standardized test scores: Engagement, mindsets, and agency—A study of 16,000 sixth through ninth grade classrooms.* Cambridge, MA: Achievement Gap Initiative at Harvard University. Accessed at www.agi.harvard.edu/projects/TeachingandAgency.pdf on August 10, 2016.

Ford, K. (2014). *Competency-based education: History, opportunities, and challenges.* Adelphi, MD: Center for Innovation in Learning and Student Success.

Foundation for Excellence in Education. (n.d.). *Competency-based education: Fundamental principles.* Tallahassee, FL: Author. Accessed at www.excelined.org/wp-content/uploads/CBE-2016 -Fundamental-Principles1.pdf on August 10, 2016.

Getting Smart Staff. (2015, August). *Getting smart on next-gen learning platforms.* Accessed at http:// gettingsmart.com/wp-content/uploads/2015/08/SBLP-Paper-26Aug2015.pdf on August 10, 2016.

Gewertz, C. (2015, September 28). The Common Core explained. *Education Week.* Accessed at www .edweek.org/ew/issues/common-core-state-standards/index.html on February 15, 2017.

Glowa, L., & Goodell, J. (2016, May). *Student-centered learning: Functional requirements for integrated systems to optimize learning.* Vienna, VA: International Association for K–12 Online Learning.

Hambleton, R. K. (1993). Principles and selected applications of item response theory. In R. L. Linn (Ed.), *Educational measurement* (3rd ed., pp. 147–200). Phoenix, AZ: Oryx Press.

Hattie, J. A. C. (2009). *Visible learning: A synthesis of over 800 meta-analyses relating to achievement.* New York: Routledge.

Hattie, J. A. C. (2012). *Visible learning for teachers: Maximizing impact on learning.* New York: Routledge.

Haystead, M. W. (2016). *An analysis of the relationship between English language arts and mathematics achievement and essential learning mastery in grades 3 and 4.* Centennial, CO: Marzano Resources.

Heflebower, T., Hoegh, J. K., & Warrick, P. (with Hoback, M., McInteer, M., & Clemens, B.). (2014). *A school leader's guide to standards-based grading.* Bloomington, IN: Marzano Resources.

Herman, J. L., & Choi, K. (2008, August). *Formative assessment and the improvement of middle school science learning: The role of teacher accuracy* (CRESST Report 740). Los Angeles: National Center for Research on Evaluation, Standards, and Student Testing.

Hess, D. E. (2009). *Controversy in the classroom: The democratic power of discussion.* New York: Routledge.

Idaho State Department of Education. (2017). *Mastery education.* Accessed at www.sde.idaho.gov /mastery-ed/ on February 15, 2017.

International Association for K–12 Online Learning. (2015). *Our work.* Accessed at www.inacol.org /our-work/ on February 15, 2017.

Kagan, S., & Kagan, M. (2009). *Kagan cooperative learning.* San Clemente, CA: Kagan.

Kane, T. J., Owens, A. M., Marinell, W. H., Thal, D. R. C., & Staiger, D. O. (2016). *Teaching higher: Educators' perspectives on Common Core implementation.* Accessed at http://cepr.harvard.edu/publications /teaching-higher-educators-perspectives-common-core-implementation on August 10, 2016.

Kelchen, R. (2015). *The landscape of competency-based education: Enrollments, demographics, and affordability.* Washington, DC: American Enterprise Institute. Accessed at www.aei.org/publication/landscape -competency-based-education-enrollments-demographics-affordability on February 15, 2017.

Kendall, J. S., & Marzano, R. J. (2000). *Content knowledge: A compendium of standards and benchmarks for K–12 education* (3rd ed.). Denver, CO: Mid-continent Regional Educational Laboratory.

KnowledgeWorks. (2016). *Recommendations for advancing personalized learning under the Every Student Succeeds Act (ESSA)*. Cincinnati, OH: Author. Accessed at www.knowledgeworks.org/sites/default /files/u1/personalized-learning-essa-recommendations.pdf on August 11, 2016.

Kolbe, K. (1990). *The conative connection*. Reading, MA: Addison-Wesley.

Langford, D. P. (2015). *Tool time for education handbook* (Version 15). Molt, MT: Langford International.

Le, C., Wolfe, R. E., & Steinberg, A. (2014). *The past and the promise: Today's competency education movement*. Boston: Jobs for the Future.

Lindsay Unified School District. (2017). *Beyond reform: Systemic shifts toward personalized learning*. Bloomington, IN: Marzano Resources.

Lord, F. M. (1953). The relation of test score to the trait underlying the test. *Educational and Psychological Measurement, 13*(4), 517–549.

Lord, F. M. (1959). Problems in mental test theory arising from errors of measurement. *Journal of the American Statistical Association, 54*(286), 472–479.

Lou, Y., Abrami, P. C., Spence, J. C., Paulsen, C., Chambers, B., & d'Apollonio, S. (1996). Within-class grouping: A meta-analysis. *Review of Educational Research, 66*(4), 423–458.

Lyman, F. (2006). *Think-pair-share SmartCard* [Reference card]. San Clemente, CA: Kagan.

Marzano, R. J. (1992). *A different kind of classroom: Teaching with dimensions of learning*. Alexandria, VA: Association for Supervision and Curriculum Development.

Marzano, R. J. (2000). *Transforming classroom grading*. Alexandria, VA: Association for Supervision and Curriculum Development.

Marzano, R. J. (2006). *Classroom assessment and grading that work*. Alexandria, VA: Association for Supervision and Curriculum Development.

Marzano, R. J. (2010). *Formative assessment and standards-based grading*. Bloomington, IN: Marzano Resources.

Marzano, R. J. (2017). *The new art and science of teaching*. Bloomington, IN: Solution Tree Press.

Marzano, R. J. (in press). *Making classroom assessments reliable and valid*. Bloomington, IN: Solution Tree Press.

Marzano, R. J., & Haystead, M. W. (2008). *Making standards useful in the classroom*. Alexandria, VA: Association for Supervision and Curriculum Development.

Marzano, R. J., Heflebower, T., Hoegh, J. K., Warrick, P., & Grift, G. (with Hecker, L., & Wills, J.). (2016). *Collaborative teams that transform schools: The next step in PLCs.* Bloomington, IN: Marzano Resources.

Marzano, R. J., & Kendall, J. S. (1996). *A comprehensive guide to designing standards-based districts, schools, and classrooms.* Alexandria, VA: Association for Supervision and Curriculum Development.

Marzano, R. J., & Marzano, J. S. (2015). *Managing the inner world of teaching: Emotions, interpretations, and actions.* Bloomington, IN: Marzano Resources.

Marzano, R. J., & Yanoski, D. C. (with Paynter, D. E.). (2016). *Proficiency scales for the new science standards: A framework for science instruction and assessment.* Bloomington, IN: Marzano Resources.

Marzano, R. J., Yanoski, D. C., Hoegh, J. K., & Simms, J. A. (with Heflebower, T., & Warrick, P.). (2013). *Using Common Core State Standards to enhance classroom instruction and assessment.* Bloomington, IN: Marzano Resources.

Mazur, E. (1997). *Peer instruction: A user's manual.* Upper Saddle River, NJ: Prentice Hall.

McCombs, B., & Whisler, J. (1989). The role of affective variables in autonomous learning. *Educational Psychologist, 24*(3), 277–306.

McREL International. (2014). *Content knowledge: Online edition.* Denver, CO: Author. Accessed at www2.mcrel.org/compendium on February 15, 2017.

Missouri School Improvement Program. (n.d.). *Recommended minutes of instruction for elementary schools.* Accessed at https://dese.mo.gov/sites/default/files/Recommended%20Minutes%20of%20 Instruction%20for%20Elementary%20Schools.pdf on February 15, 2017.

Morris, H. (2014). *Exploring the potential of competency-based education* [Blog post]. Accessed at http:// nextgenlearning.org/blog/exploring-potential-competency-based-education on February 15, 2017.

National Governors Association Center for Best Practices & Council of Chief State School Officers. (2010a). *Common Core State Standards for English language arts and literacy in history/social studies, science, and technical subjects.* Washington, DC: Authors.

National Governors Association Center for Best Practices & Council of Chief State School Officers. (2010b). *Common Core State Standards for English language arts & literacy in history/social studies, science, and technical subjects—Appendix A: Research supporting key elements of the standards and glossary of key terms.* Washington, DC: Authors.

National Governors Association Center for Best Practices & Council of Chief State School Officers. (2010c). *Common Core State Standards for English language arts & literacy in history/social studies, science, and technical subjects—Appendix B: Text exemplars and sample performance tasks.* Washington, DC: Authors.

National Governors Association Center for Best Practices & Council of Chief State School Officers. (2010d). *Common Core State Standards for mathematics*. Washington, DC: Authors.

National Governors Association Center for Best Practices & Council of Chief State School Officers. (2010e). *Reaching higher: The Common Core State Standards validation committee*. Washington, DC: Authors.

Nellie Mae Education Foundation. (2016). *The Nellie Mae Education Foundation*. Accessed at www.nmefoundation.org on February 15, 2017.

NGSS Lead States. (2013). *Next Generation Science Standards: For states, by states*. Washington, DC: National Academies Press.

No Child Left Behind (NCLB) Act of 2001, Pub. L. No. 107-110, § 115, Stat. 1425 (2002).

Nodine, T. R. (2016). How did we get here? A brief history of competency-based higher education in the United States. *Competency-Based Education, 1*(1), 5–11. doi:10.1002/cbe2.1004

Northern Arizona University. (n.d.). *Personalized learning*. Accessed at http://pl.nau.edu on August 9, 2016.

NYC Department of Education. (n.d.). *K–12 instructional time*. Accessed at http://schools.nycenet.edu/offices/teachlearn/Instructional_Time.pdf on February 15, 2017.

Ogle, D. M. (1986). K-W-L: A teaching model that develops active reading of expository text. *The Reading Teacher, 39*(6), 564–570.

Patrick, S., Kennedy, K., & Powell, A. (2013). *Mean what you say: Defining and integrating personalized, blended and competency education*. Vienna, VA: International Association for K–12 Online Learning. Accessed at www.inacol.org/wp-content/uploads/2015/02/mean-what-you-say.pdf on August 9, 2016.

Paul, R. (Ed.). (1990). *Critical thinking: What every person needs to survive in a rapidly changing world*. Rohnert Park, CA: Center for Critical Thinking and Moral Critique.

Pickering, D. (2010). Teaching the thinking skills that higher-order tasks demand. In R. J. Marzano (Ed.), *On excellence in teaching* (pp. 145–166). Bloomington, IN: Solution Tree Press.

RAND Corporation. (2014, November). *Early progress: Interim research on personalized learning*. Seattle, WA: Bill & Melinda Gates Foundation. Accessed at http://k12education.gatesfoundation.org/wp-content/uploads/2015/06/Early-Progress-on-Personalized-Learning-Full-Report.pdf on August 11, 2016.

Reigeluth, C. M., & Karnopp, J. R. (2013). *Reinventing schools: It's time to break the mold*. New York: Rowman & Littlefield Education.

Schneider, C., & Paul, J. (2015, September 16). Education chief Arne Duncan: U.S. is falling behind. *Indianapolis Star*. Accessed at www.indystar.com/story/news/politics/2015/09/16/education-chief -arne-duncan-us-falling-behind/32533827 on August 10, 2016.

Schunk, D. H., & Pajares, F. (2005). Competence perceptions and academic functioning. In A. J. Elliot & C. S. Dweck (Eds.), *Handbook of competence and motivation* (pp. 85–104). New York: Guilford Press.

Scott, D., & Marzano, R. J. (2014). *Awaken the learner: Finding the source of effective education.* Bloomington, IN: Marzano Resources.

Shepard, L. A. (2008). A brief history of accountability testing, 1965–2007. In K. E. Ryan & L. A. Shepard (Eds.), *The future of test-based educational accountability* (pp. 25–46). New York: Routledge.

Simms, J. A., (2016). *The critical concepts* (Final version: English language arts, mathematics, and science). Centennial, CO: Marzano Resources.

Snow, R. (1989). Toward assessment of cognitive and conative structures in learning. *Educational Researcher, 18*(9), 8–14.

Stevens, S. S. (1946, June 7). On the theory of scales of measurement. *Science, 103*(2684), 677–680.

Sturgis, C. (2015, June). *Implementing competency education in K–12 systems: Insights from local leaders* (CompetencyWorks Issue Brief). Vienna, VA: International Association for K–12 Online Learning. Accessed at www.competencyworks.org/wp-content/uploads/2015/06/iNCL_CWIssueBrief _Implementing_v5_web.pdf on August 9, 2016.

Sturgis, C. (2016a, February 15). *Lake County Schools: Designing a strategy to bring personalized learning to scale.* Accessed at www.competencyworks.org/case-study/lake-county-schools-designing-a -strategy-to-bring-personalized-learning-to-scale on August 10, 2016.

Sturgis, C. (2016b, March). *Chugach School District: A personalized, performance-based system.* Vienna, VA: International Association for K–12 Online Learning.

Tagami, T. (2016, January 17). Seeing momentum, teachers push to roll back testing. *The Atlanta Journal-Constitution*. Accessed at www.ajc.com/news/local-education/seeing-momentum-teachers -push-roll-back-testing/oYARWdXZG1JtnaGal3iH0N on August 9, 2016.

Tex. Educ. Code §110.16(b)(4) (2008). Accessed at http://ritter.tea.state.tx.us/rules/tac/chapter110 /ch110a.html on September 15, 2016.

Torlakson, T., & Kirst, M. W. (2016, January 13). *Every Student Succeeds Act* [Letter to U.S. Department of Education]. Sacramento: California Department of Education. Accessed at www .cde.ca.gov/nr/el/le/yr16ltr0113.asp on August 9, 2016.

U.S. Department of Education. (n.d.). *Competency-based learning or personalized learning.* Accessed at www.ed.gov/oii-news/competency-based-learning-or-personalized-learning on August 9, 2016.

U.S. Department of Education. (2014). *U.S. Department of Education expands innovation in higher education through the Experimental Sites Initiative.* Accessed at www.ed.gov/news/press-releases /us-department-education-expands-innovation-higher-education-through-experimental-sites -initiative on February 15, 2017.

U.S. Department of Education. (2015). Notice expanding an experiment under the Experimental Sites Initiative; Federal student financial assistance programs under Title IV of the Higher Education Act of 1965, as amended. *Federal Register, 80*(222), 72052–72055.

Westminster Public Schools. (2011). *Our competency based system (CBS).* Accessed at www.cbsadams50 .org on August 31, 2016.

Index

Professional Development
Designed for Success

Empower your staff to tap into their full potential as educators. As an all-inclusive research-into-practice resource center, we are committed to helping your school or district become highly effective at preparing every student for his or her future.

Choose from our wide range of customized professional development opportunities for teachers, administrators, and district leaders. Each session offers hands-on support, personalized answers, and accessible strategies that can be put into practice immediately.

Bring Marzano Resources experts to your school for results-oriented training on:

- ▶ Assessment & Grading
- ▶ Curriculum
- ▶ Instruction
- ▶ School Leadership

- ▶ Teacher Effectiveness
- ▶ Student Engagement
- ▶ Vocabulary
- ▶ Competency-Based Education